The Bedford/St. Martin's Textbook Reader

Second Edition

Ellen Kuhl Repetto

Bedford/St. Martin's   Boston ✦ New York

Manufactured in the United States of America.

7 6 5 4 3
f e d

For information, write: Bedford/St. Martin's, 75 Arlington Street, Boston, MA 02116   (617-399-4000)

ISBN: 978-0-312-44435-8

Acknowledgments

Bedford/St. Martin's gratefully acknowledges the following sources of the textbook chapters reprinted in this book: "Majors & Career Choices," Chapter 12 (pages 146–57) of *Step by Step to College and Career Success*, Fourth Edition, by John N. Gardner and Betsy O. Barefoot, Bedford/St. Martin's, 2011; "Document Design," Part X (pages 727–46) of *The Bedford Handbook*, Eighth Edition, by Diana Hacker and Nancy Sommers, Bedford/St. Martin's, 2010; "Public Relations and Framing the Message," Chapter 11 (pages 312–37) of *Media Essentials: A Brief Introduction*, by Richard Campbell, Christopher R. Martin, and Bettina Fabos, Bedford/St. Martin's, 2011; "The Growth of America's Cities, 1870–1900," Chapter 19 (pages 508–35) of *Understanding the American Promise: A Brief History*, by James L. Roark, Michael P. Johnson, Patricia Cline Cohen, Sarah Stage, Alan Lawson, and Susan M. Hartmann, Bedford/St. Martin's, 2011; "Stress, Health, and Coping," Chapter 13 (pages 538–69) of *Psychology*, Fifth Edition, by Don H. Hockenbury and Sandra E. Hockenbury, Worth Publishers, 2010; and "Land: Public and Private," Chapter 10 (pages 260–81) of *Environmental Science: Foundations and Applications*, by Andrew Friedland, Rick Relyea, and David Courard-Hauri, W. H. Freeman, 2012.

Preface for Instructors

It's no secret that reading is an essential skill. Reflective, thoughtful engagement with written texts is key not only to college success but also to just about everything we do outside the classroom. Basic skills courses—and the books designed for them—do much to familiarize students with the elements of active and critical reading, but knowing the skills is not enough. To become effective readers, students need practice. This is especially true with college textbooks because they're so different from what incoming students are accustomed to reading. Recognizing this, *The Bedford/St. Martin's Textbook Reader* encourages students to try out their newly acquired critical reading skills with just the kind of textbook materials they will encounter in their college courses.

Long overdue, this second edition builds on the successes of the first while responding to feedback from instructors and students. As was the case in the first edition, each of the units presents a textbook chapter drawn from a discipline students are likely to encounter in college, primarily in their first year. Of the disciplines represented here, three—college success, composition, and environmental science—are new. The units on mass communication and history are now drawn from brief versions of their textbooks to enhance readability and accessibility. Every unit, including psychology, reflects the most recent textbook editions available at the time of publication. As before, the chapters and the questions accompanying them progress from least to most challenging, allowing students to work their way up to a fairly demanding critical reading level. To help capture and maintain students' interest, a single theme—work, an inherently interesting topic relevant to all students—still connects the units. Rather than force students to read unrelated materials out of context, the chapters' varied perspectives on work—from the concerns of contemporary students considering career options to a historical interpretation of nineteenth-century workers' struggles for better job conditions—encourage students to make connections and provide them with information they can apply to their own lives.

The Bedford/St. Martin's Textbook Reader continues to provide extensive materials to aid students' understanding of and engagement with the textbook readings.

A new introduction, "How to Read College Textbooks," walks students through the process of active reading and explains how the various elements of college textbooks—such as chapter outlines, boxed features, and study tools—can help them become more successful readers and students.

Before the readings. Each unit begins with an introduction that provides an overview of the discipline it covers, discusses the textbook itself and the chapter's topic, and explains the key textbook features (such as headings, visuals, and summaries) that students need to understand in order to read the chapter successfully. Newly revised for ease of reading, each introduction ends with a quick overview of how the chapter fits into the work theme and draws connections to chapters in other units.

Following each introduction are three prereading questions ("Preparing to Read the Textbook Chapter"). The first question encourages students to think about how the chapter material applies to their own lives and experiences, the second helps them understand the function of a key tool the authors have provided to aid learning, and the third ties the chapter into the overall theme of work.

After the readings. Each chapter is followed by three sets of questions that get students comfortable with the kinds of questions most commonly found on college quizzes and tests:

- Ten "Practicing Your Textbook Reading Skills" questions test the discrete skills covered in most college reading courses and call students' attention to the textbook elements that aid reading. The reading skills addressed by these questions progress in difficulty from understanding vocabulary in the first chapter to interpreting arguments in the last.

- Twenty-five "Testing Your Understanding" questions (five true or false, ten multiple choice, five definition, and five short answer) ensure that students comprehend the textbook material.

- A "Making Thematic Connections" question encourages students to reflect more deeply on the chapter topic and to connect it with issues covered in other units of the reader. This question can be used for class discussion or for writing assignments.

Other assistance. *The Bedford/St. Martin's Textbook Reader* also provides a glossary that defines the key concepts used in each of the units. An answer key at the back of the book lets students check their work. The answer key includes the page numbers of the relevant chapter sections, so if students get an answer wrong they can review the material.

The Bedford/St. Martin's Textbook Reader will spark students' interest while helping them to become more critical and successful readers. We hope that it will be the start of a productive and rewarding engagement with reading in college and beyond.

You Get More Resources from Bedford/St. Martin's.

Online and in print, you'll find both free and affordable premium resources to help you teach and to help your students get even more out of your course. Students get a discount when they bundle our books and media and buy online. To order any of the products below, or to learn more about them, contact your Bedford/St. Martin's sales representative, e-mail sales support (sales_support@bfwpub.com), or visit **bedfordstmartins.com/english**.

The Bedford/St. Martin's Textbook Reader can be **packaged at a discount** with other Bedford/St. Martin's texts, including writing guides, readers, and handbooks. You may also be interested in exploring our **Trade Up** program — package any Macmillan trade title and save 50%. Visit **bedfordstmartins.com /tradeup** to learn more.

INSTRUCTOR RESOURCES

- *TeachingCentral* (bedfordstmartins.com/teachingcentral) offers the entire list of Bedford/St. Martin's print and online professional resources in one place. You'll find landmark reference works, sourcebooks on pedagogical issues, award-winning collections, and practical advice for the classroom — all free for instructors.

- *Testing Tool Kit* is a comprehensive and easy-to-use test bank CD-ROM that allows instructors to create secure, customized tests and quizzes to assess students' writing and grammar competency. ISBN: 978-0-312-43032-0

- *Teaching Developmental Reading: Historical, Theoretical, and Practical Background Readings*, edited by Norman H. Stahl and Hunter Boylan, offers 37 professional essays on topics that will engage teachers of basic reading, including strategic learning, the reading/writing connection, and teaching new-to-English learners. ISBN: 978-0-312-24774-4

- *Teaching Developmental Writing: Background Readings*, Third Edition, a professional resource edited by Susan Naomi Bernstein, offers a collection of essays on topics of interest to basic writing instructors, along with editorial apparatus pointing out practical applications for the classroom. The new edition includes revised chapters on technology and the writing process and focuses on topics relevant to instructors who work with multilingual students in the developmental writing course. ISBN: 978-0-312-43283-6

- *The Bedford Bibliography for Teachers of Basic Writing*, Third Edition, compiled by members of the Conference on Basic Writing under the general editorship of Gregory R. Glau and Chitralekha Duttagupta, is an annotated list of books, articles, and periodicals created specifically to help teachers of basic writing find valuable resources. (*The Bedford Bibliography* is also available online at www.bedfordstmartins.com/basicbib /content.asp.) ISBN: 978-0-312-58154-1

- **Free Coursepacks** for the most common course management systems — Blackboard, WebCT, Angel, and Desire2Learn — allow you to easily download Bedford/St. Martin's digital materials for your course. For more information about our course management offerings, visit **bedford stmartins.com/coursepacks**.

STUDENT RESOURCES

- *Re:Writing Basics* collects **free** diagnostic tests; thousands of free grammar exercises; and hundreds of model paragraphs and essays, tutorials, and podcasts for basic writers. And for Bedford, *free* means *quality*.

Recent updates include new videos, new visual exercises, and a student-friendly organization.

- *Exercise Central 3.0* (**bedfordstmartins.com/exercisecentral**) is a completely **free**, comprehensive resource for skill development as well as skill assessment. In addition to over 9,000 exercises offering immediate feedback and reporting to an instructor grade book, *Exercise Central 3.0* can help identify students' strengths and weaknesses, recommend personalized study plans, and provide tutorials for common problems.

- *WritingClass*, Bedford/St. Martin's completely customizable course space, makes it easier to show students what they've done and where they need to go next. Diagnostics, exercises, writing and commenting tools, and our new multimedia lessons give your students the help they need to improve their writing, grammar, punctuation, and editing skills. Visit **yourwritingclass.com** to learn more.

- *Re:Writing Plus*, now with *VideoCentral*, gathers all of our premium digital content for the writing class into one online collection. This impressive resource includes innovative and interactive help with writing a paragraph; tutorials and practices that show how writing works in students' real-world experiences; *VideoCentral*, with over 50 brief videos for the writing classroom; the first-ever peer review game, *Peer Factor*; *i-cite: visualizing sources*; plus hundreds of writing models and hundreds of readings. ISBN: 978-0-312-48849-9

- *Make-a-Paragraph Kit with Exercise Central to Go* is a fun, interactive CD-ROM that includes "Extreme Paragraph Makeover," a brief animation to teach students about paragraph development. It also contains exercises to help students build their own paragraphs, audiovisual tutorials on four of the most common errors for basic writers, and the content from *Exercise Central to Go: Writing and Grammar Practices for Basic Writers*. ISBN: 978-0-312-45332-9

- *The Bedford/St. Martin's ESL Workbook*, Second Edition, is a comprehensive collection of exercises that covers grammatical issues for multilingual students with varying English-language skills and from varying cultural backgrounds. Instructional introductions precede exercises in a broad range of topic areas. ISBN: 978-0-312-54034-0

- *The Bedford/St. Martin's Planner* includes everything that students need to plan and use their time effectively, with advice on preparing schedules and to-do lists plus blank schedules and calendars (monthly and weekly). The planner fits easily into a backpack or purse, so students can take it anywhere. ISBN: 978-0-312-57447-5

Acknowledgments

Putting together a reader like this would not have been possible without the substantial help of some of the very best people in college publishing. Thanks especially to Joan Feinberg, president of Bedford/St. Martin's; Denise Wydra, editorial director; Karen Henry, editor in chief; Erica Appel, director of development; and Alexis Walker, executive editor, for providing the opportunity to prepare this revision and for lending their faith, support, and ideas. Thanks also to production supervisor Sam Jones and managing editor Shuli Traub. Bill Davis sparked the idea for this reader and pushed for an update. Barbara Anne Seixas and Christine Buese at Worth Publishers, and Julia DeRosa and Karen Misler at W. H. Freeman, graciously helped locate essential production files and art research. Linda Winters juggled permissions across three publishing houses, and Susan Doheny tackled the onerous task of obtaining photo rights. Karrin Varucene proved to be a most invaluable new editor: She cheerfully tracked down materials, coordinated reviews, clarified the introductions and questions, and caught countless mistakes. Kellan Cummings managed to pull everything together and make it look good. A person couldn't ask for a better team.

The instructors who provided feedback on the first edition and answered questions about the second largely determined what this reader needed to be. A deep note of gratitude goes to Linda Gubbe of the University of Toledo; Tamara Kuzmenkov of Tacoma Community College; Tern Major of Olympic College; Linda Muñoz of the Texas Higher Education Coordinating Board; Angela Pettit of Tarrant County College; and Rhonda Pruitt of John Tyler Community College, who added to the original advice offered by Gertrude Coleman of Middlesex Community College; Jim Early of Doña Aña Branch Community College; and Mary Sulzer of Lorrain County Community College.

The heart of any reader, of course, is its readings. The chapters in this book were written by peerless groups of dedicated educators who always set high standards for themselves and others. Kudos to John N. Gardner and Betsy O. Barefoot; Diana Hacker and Nancy Sommers; Richard Campbell, Christopher R. Martin, and Bettina Fabos; James L. Roark, Michael P. Johnson, Patricia Cline Cohen, Sarah Stage, Alan Lawson, and Susan M. Hartmann; Don H. Hockenbury and Sandra E. Hockenbury; Andrew Friedland, Rick Relyea, and David Courard-Hauri; and all their editorial teams—for creating excellent textbooks. It's a pleasure to work with you.

Contents

PREFACE FOR INSTRUCTORS ■ iii

INTRODUCTION: HOW TO READ COLLEGE TEXTBOOKS ■ 1

1. COLLEGE SUCCESS ■ 7

Introduction 8

Preparing to Read the Textbook Chapter 9

***Step by Step to College and Career Success*, Chapter 12: "Majors & Career Choices" 10**

Practicing Your Textbook Reading Skills 22

Testing Your Understanding 23

Making Thematic Connections 27

2. COMPOSITION ■ 29

Introduction 30

Preparing to Read the Textbook Chapter 31

***The Bedford Handbook*, Part X: "Document Design" 33**

Practicing Your Textbook Reading Skills 53

Testing Your Understanding 54

Making Thematic Connections 58

3. MASS COMMUNICATION ■ 59

Introduction 60

Preparing to Read the Textbook Chapter 61

***Media Essentials*, Chapter 11: "Public Relations and Framing the Message" 62**

Practicing Your Textbook Reading Skills 89

Testing Your Understanding 91

Making Thematic Connections 95

4. HISTORY ■ 97

Introduction 98

Preparing to Read the Textbook Chapter 99

***Understanding the American Promise*, Chapter 19: "The Growth of America's Cities, 1870–1900" 100**

Practicing Your Textbook Reading Skills 128

Testing Your Understanding 130

Making Thematic Connections 134

5. PSYCHOLOGY ■ 135

Introduction 136

Preparing to Read the Textbook Chapter 137

***Psychology*, Chapter 13: "Stress, Health, and Coping" 138**

Practicing Your Textbook Reading Skills 177

Testing Your Understanding 178

Making Thematic Connections 182

6. ENVIRONMENTAL SCIENCE ■ 183

Introduction 184

Preparing to Read the Textbook Chapter 185

***Environmental Science*, Chapter 10: "Land: Public and Private" 186**

Practicing Your Textbook Reading Skills 208

Testing Your Understanding 210

Making Thematic Connections 214

Glossary of Terms ■ 215

Answer Key ■ 219

Acknowledgments ■ 227

Introduction

How to Read College Textbooks

By now you've probably noticed that college involves a lot of reading. Glance through your syllabi or browse the bookstore and you'll see all sorts of reading assignments: course packs, novels, nonfiction books, journal articles, newspapers and magazines, reference works, handouts—and textbooks.

College textbooks pose a special challenge to readers. By necessity, they cram a lot of information into a relatively small space. Textbook writers and publishers provide tools and features to help you understand and retain that information, but those features take some getting used to. It's common to become overwhelmed by the sheer volume of material in a textbook, and the tools meant to help with comprehension sometimes cause confusion themselves. Don't panic, though: with the help of this reader, you can learn your way around. You paid a lot of money for your books, and you'll spend a lot of time reading them—so make sure you get the most out of them.

Getting the most out of your textbooks is a simple matter of reading them **actively**. When you read for pleasure (if you read for pleasure), you might be content to let the words wash over you, taking in whatever interests or amuses you—but then moving on to something else. Active reading is different. It is a process of becoming thoroughly involved with what you read—paying close attention to, asking questions of, and interacting with a text. It is a practice you'll apply to many kinds of readings in college, especially textbooks.

The process of active reading breaks down into four basic steps: **previewing, close reading, note taking,** and **reviewing.** Most of your college textbooks are specifically designed to help you tackle each of these steps successfully. Let's say you've been instructed to read a chapter of one of your textbooks, maybe one of the chapters that appear later in this reader. What should you do?

Preview the Chapter

First, take a few minutes to familiarize yourself with the chapter before reading it. You want to get a general sense of what the chapter is about and what seems to be most important. That way, while you're reading you'll be able to follow the authors' line of thinking and make sense of what they're saying. If you read the chapter cold, on the other hand, you'll have to work much harder to understand individual points and see how they connect with each other.

This preliminary stage of active reading is called *previewing*. To do it, take note of the chapter's title (your first clue to its subject), then flip through the pages and skim the content without actually reading it. Most college textbooks include special elements and features that can help you quickly grasp the main ideas in any given chapter. Pay attention to the following elements as you preview, and you'll be well on your way to understanding.

- **Outlines** Check the beginning and end of the chapter for an overview of its main ideas. Usually presented in the form of a list of headings, key topics, learning objectives, or questions, these outlines tell you at a glance what the chapter will cover and what the major topics are.

- **Summaries** Skim the introductory and concluding paragraphs. Often (but not always) they summarize the main ideas of the chapter and explain not only what the most important points are but also how the other details support those points.

- **Headings** Graphically set apart from the text, headings and subheadings provide an ongoing outline of a chapter's major ideas and supporting points. Main headings usually appear on their own lines. Subheadings might also appear on their own lines, or they could be run into the text; in either case they'll be distinguishable from the main headings by a slightly different design, such as a smaller typeface or italics. Use the headings and subheadings to draw a mental map of a chapter's content, ensuring you don't get lost when you read it. (For a helpful overview of how headings work, see pages 731–32 of the composition chapter reprinted in Unit 2.)

- **Key terms** Notice any words or phrases printed in boldface, italics, all-capital letters, or color. These are almost always key terms: the concepts, definitions, or names most important to the discussion. In most cases, those terms are defined in the margins or in a glossary at the back of the book. The glossary for this book, for instance, appears on pages 195–98.

- **Illustrations** Definitely look at the pictures, especially if you're a visual learner. Textbooks use photographs, charts and tables, graphs, maps, and other images to illustrate and clarify the important points in a chapter. Usually these illustrations will include captions that describe them and explain their significance. Glancing through them will give you a good sense of what the authors want you to take away from a discussion.

- **Navigational aids** Finally, take a peek at the tops, bottoms, and edges of the pages. In addition to page numbers and chapter titles, these parts of a textbook typically offer very brief summaries of the main ideas in each section in the form of running heads. Sometimes, they'll include timelines, key terms, or special symbols to help you find information and follow the discussion.

As you preview a chapter, note any questions or concerns that occur to you. If you already know a little something about the subject, for example, consider what new information you might be about to learn and how it might change or add to your understanding. If you don't know anything, that's fine too. Try to find a way to connect what you've gathered from previewing the chapter to your experience and curiosity. What do you hope to learn? How will you benefit from reading the chapter?

Read Closely

Once you've completed a preview, you're ready to start reading in earnest. Remember, your goal is to read *actively*—to work with the text and against it, asking questions as you read and looking for the answers. Just plowing through the pages with one eye on the clock won't do. Give yourself ample time to read a chapter (how long that is varies, but a good rule of thumb is to allow at least two hours of reading time for each hour of class). Pay close attention as you read, looking for the main ideas and always thinking about how they relate to what you do and don't know, why they're relevant to your coursework, and what you can do with the information being presented.

MAIN IDEAS

Don't think you need to memorize every detail in a textbook. It won't *all* be on the test. Your reading will be more productive (and far more enjoyable) if you distinguish the main ideas from the supporting points.

If you've previewed a chapter, you should already have a working sense of its main ideas, or the most important general concepts. As you read, look for statements of those major points within the narrative text. Such statements usually appear in the first or second paragraph of a section, but are sometimes at the end. They might also be summarized in the chapter introduction or conclusion, or repeated in checklists and review sections. When you do find statements of main ideas in the discussion, make a note of them or highlight them in some way (see "Take Notes" on pages 4–5 of this introduction).

SUPPORTING POINTS

Most of what you read in a textbook chapter consists of supporting points: the examples, facts, opinions, and visuals the authors use to explain the main ideas.

Understand that not all supporting points are equally important. Some examples, for instance, are included to make a subject more interesting or to show how it relates to readers' own experiences; others are meant to flesh out an explanation. A string of relatively unimportant facts might be provided to prove a point or justify an opinion. Visuals, such as photographs and charts, are almost always there to reinforce or explain an important concept (this is not true of visuals that don't have captions or labels, however: free-floating images, such as those in the college success chapter in Unit 1 of this reader, are included to break up large chunks of text and to keep students interested in the discussion).

Part of your task as an active reader is to recognize which details are most significant and which are less so. The more attentively you read, the easier it will be to pick out the important points.

BOXED FEATURES

Many textbook chapters include brief sections set apart from the main text with boxes, lines, shading, or similar design elements. If the first few paragraphs are set in a different typeface than the rest of the chapter, for instance, they might be a chapter-opening story meant to give you a sense of the subject and its relevance, rather than a summary or straight introduction. You might find an extended example somewhere in the discussion, or a case study toward the end. In some textbooks, you'll see highlighted activities and exercises, tips, section reviews, and checklists; others might include boxed stories, debates, or analyses; still others discuss related materials, such as Web resources and digital tools.

Be aware that although boxed features often interrupt the text physically, you don't need to stop reading the main discussion to read a feature exactly where it appears. Finish the main discussion first, then go back to the feature to see how it relates—or read the boxed material first. With practice you'll find what works best for you.

REFERENCES

Boxed features aren't the only kind of textbook element that might interrupt the flow of a chapter's discussion. Most textbooks include references to related material that can be found in the book itself or elsewhere.

In disciplines that value research, for instance, a textbook chapter might include extensive source notes that cite authors, dates, and page numbers in parentheses within the text and list sources at the end (for an example, see the psychology chapter in Unit 5). Most textbooks have cross-references to related discussions that can be found on other pages of the book; these might appear in the margins or at the ends of sentences and paragraphs. Increasingly, textbooks also include Web links, references to additional resources provided online. These, too, might be part of the general discussion, or they might be called out in the margins.

Try not to be distracted by references when they appear within a discussion. Source notes can usually be ignored completely on a first reading, although you might want to use them to find additional information on a subject after you've read the chapter. Cross-references and Web links, too, can be skimmed over as you read. You don't have to jump to related material the moment it's mentioned: turn to it later, as necessary.

Take Notes

Put away your highlighters. Active reading demands that you mark up your reading materials with summaries, responses, and questions in your own words. To do that, you'll need a pen or pencil. If you don't want to or can't make marks in a book—because it doesn't belong to you, or you plan to sell it back at the end of the term, or you're reading it electronically—you can write your notes on separate sheets of paper, type them into an electronic file, or jot them on sticky notes attached to the book's pages. The most effective way to take notes, though, is to write in the margins while you're reading.

Taking notes while you read improves both your understanding and your memory of the material. That's because note-taking forces you to think while you're reading, engaging your mind with the content more actively than reading by itself can do. As you read, then, write. Some suggestions:

- **Mark the main ideas and important supporting points.** Some people double-underline the main ideas and single-underline the significant details; some put checkmarks, stars, exclamation points, and other symbols in the margins to highlight the important parts; some create a personal color-coding system, using different pens and pencils (even highlighters) to underline, circle, bracket, and mark different kinds of information. Experiment with these or other systems and find one that works for you. Just be careful not to overunderline or overhighlight. In most cases, about 10 percent or so of a chapter should be marked as important. If you highlight much more than that, you're creating extra work for yourself when the time comes to review.

- **Keep a running outline.** Summarize or paraphrase, in your own words, the main ideas and supporting points as you read them. This takes more time, it's true, but putting the information in your own words as you read will reinforce your understanding. Additionally, when you come back to the chapter to review the material for a quiz, a test, or a writing assignment, you'll have a quick overview ready.

- **Make connections.** If what you're reading reinforces or contradicts information and ideas you've read or heard somewhere else, comment on that in the margins. The same goes for points that remind you of something in your own experience, and for ideas that may have been discussed in class or in another course.

- **Ask questions.** Don't understand a word? Circle it and look it up later. Don't understand a point or see why it matters? Put a question mark in the margin and come back to it. You may find that after you've read the rest of the chapter, the point makes sense, or you may find that you need to ask your instructor or a classmate for help. Don't agree with something in the text? Say so, and say why.

Review What You've Read

The final step of actively reading a textbook chapter is to review the material and your notes to check your understanding while it's still fresh in your mind. The good news is that most textbooks go out of their way to help students with this stage. Several kinds of review tools and features are common.

CHECKLISTS

Appearing either at the end of a chapter or within major sections, highlighted lists of important concepts, events, learning objectives, major ideas, questions, goals, and the like summarize the most significant ideas in a chapter and make it possible to quiz yourself. Often they'll include page numbers to direct you to where those points are explained.

REVIEWS

Many textbooks provide a summary and overview of a chapter's main ideas at the end. These, too, are usually highlighted in some way, whether by shading, color, boxes, or typography. Read these reviews as closely as you read the rest of the chapter—more closely, even. They compress the most important ideas and concepts into a manageable size and make very clear what you will be expected to know as a result of reading the chapter.

ASSIGNMENTS

Textbooks routinely provide exercises, practice quizzes, review activities, and similar assignments to help students assess their understanding of the material. Look for them at the end of a chapter, although sometimes they appear at the ends of individual sections as well. Other times they might be collected in a separate workbook, on a CD-ROM, or on a Web site.

You may be asked to complete review assignments as homework. Even if you aren't, take the time to answer the questions—especially if the answers are provided at the back of the book (answers to the questions asked in this reader appear on pages 199–205). There's no better way to check that you've understood the material—and if you find that you haven't, you can re-read and re-review until you get it.

Learning to read textbooks actively and efficiently takes practice. That's what *this* textbook is for. In the following units, you'll develop and test your reading skills with a sampling of textbook chapters from a variety of college disciplines, all of them for courses you might expect to encounter in the first year of college. Although the chapters come from different fields and cover different topics, they all focus on the common theme of work, which should help you make connections among them. Each unit starts with an introduction to familiarize you with the general subject and the textbook itself, then reprints a complete chapter in its original format. Following the chapters are sets of questions to help you apply your growing textbook reading skills and to test your understanding of the material. Answers to those questions, and a glossary of terms, appear at the end of this book.

College Success

"Majors & Career Choices"

Introduction

The transition to college can be a challenging one. Whether students arrive straight out of high school or decide to enroll after years of working, they quickly discover that higher education involves more than taking higher-level classes. Surrounded by new people in a new environment, first-year students are adjusting to significant changes in routine and workload and are responsible for managing their time and limited resources on their own. Because of this, many schools offer seminars in college success, sometimes called "orientation" or "the first-year experience." The instructors who teach these classes are education professionals who have conducted and studied research on how people learn. These experts have developed techniques to help students overcome difficulties and make the most of the opportunities that college offers.

Step by Step to College and Career Success, by John N. Gardner and Betsy O. Barefoot, is a survival guide for new college students. The authors are award-winning teachers who designed the country's first, and most respected, first-year experience program. The chapter reprinted here, "Majors & Career Choices," looks at two elements of education that are crucial for any student's success: self-awareness and planning. You may (or may not) already have a major in mind, and you may (or may not) know exactly what career you want to pursue, but you probably aren't aware of just how many options there are. Learning about them—and about yourself—will help to ensure that your investment in a college education pays off.

As you read the chapter, you'll see that the authors have taken great care to help you understand it:

- The topics and questions listed at the beginning of the chapter help you assess your knowledge and find the information you need to achieve your goals.

- The book's magazine-style format makes the material easy and fun to read.

- A boxed personal narrative shares a real student's experience with career planning and course selection.

- Quick exercises throughout the chapter and at the end encourage you to apply the information to your own life.

- Review materials on the last two pages summarize what's important and offer tips on where and how to learn more.

Choosing the right major and knowing how to plan a career should improve your chances of being hired when you look for a job. Learning about the interconnected roles of education and work might even help you discover, and negotiate for, better opportunities. Many of the other textbook chapters in this reader will introduce you to unexpected major and career options, from public relations to environmental science. The chapter in the next unit will show you, among other things, how to prepare a winning résumé. Remember, too, that the working world changes constantly. The history chapter later in this book

---

This unit's textbook reading comes from *Step by Step to College and Career Success*, Fourth Edition, by John N. Gardner and Betsy O. Barefoot, Bedford/St. Martin's, 2011, Chapter 12, pages 146–57.

discusses what job conditions in America were like more than a hundred years ago. As you read this chapter, then, think about how things might have been different—and how they might continue to evolve.

Preparing to Read the Textbook Chapter

1. Why are you in college? Are you taking classes for the sake of education itself, or are you working toward a specific career? Maybe both? How do you expect your college experience will help you accomplish your goals?

2. The chapter you're about to read opens with a somewhat bleak overview of the global economy and recent changes in the workplace. Why do you think the authors start on such a sour note? What point might they be trying to get across to their readers?

3. Think about a recent job you have held, or a job you're hoping to have one day. What do you expect from a job besides money? What can you do to improve your job satisfaction, now and in the future?

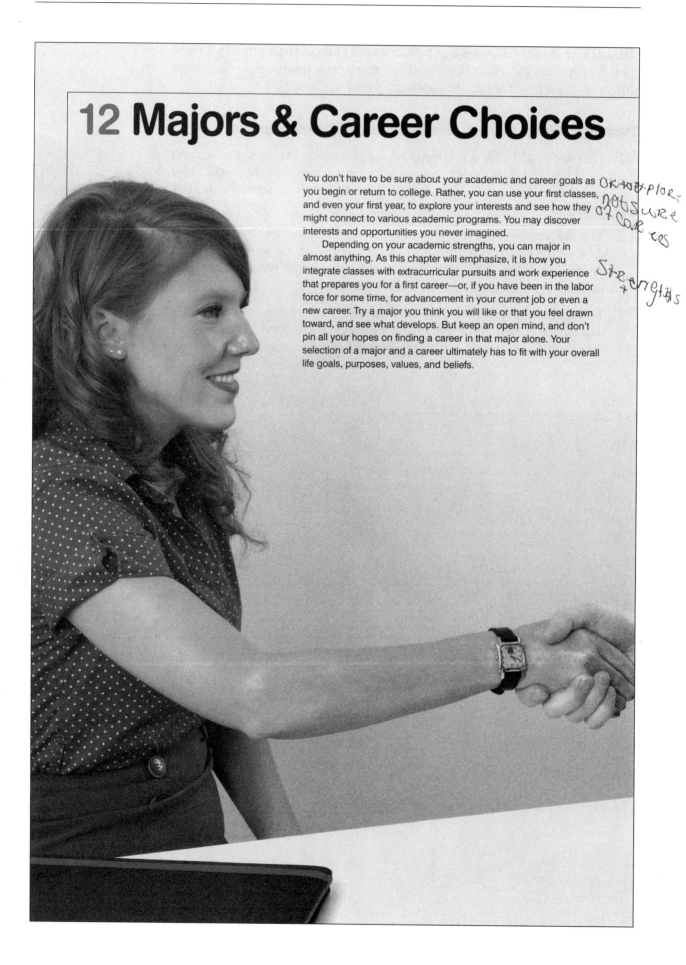

12 Majors & Career Choices

You don't have to be sure about your academic and career goals as you begin or return to college. Rather, you can use your first classes, and even your first year, to explore your interests and see how they might connect to various academic programs. You may discover interests and opportunities you never imagined.

Depending on your academic strengths, you can major in almost anything. As this chapter will emphasize, it is how you integrate classes with extracurricular pursuits and work experience that prepares you for a first career—or, if you have been in the labor force for some time, for advancement in your current job or even a new career. Try a major you think you will like or that you feel drawn toward, and see what develops. But keep an open mind, and don't pin all your hopes on finding a career in that major alone. Your selection of a major and a career ultimately has to fit with your overall life goals, purposes, values, and beliefs.

[Handwritten notes: "OK to explore, not sure of career" and "strengths"]

This chapter covers the following topics:

| Careers and the New Economy 148 | Aligning Your Sense of Purpose and Your Career 150 | Exploring Your Interests 152 | Working While in College 154 |

How Do You Measure Up?

1. I understand how the world economy is changing and how those changes might affect my job prospects.
   ○ Agree
   ○ Don't Know
   ○ Disagree

2. I have clear goals for attending college.
   ○ Agree
   ○ Don't Know
   ○ Disagree

3. I know my own strengths and how they might influence my career choice.
   ○ Agree
   ○ Don't Know
   ○ Disagree

4. I am aware of the advantages and disadvantages of working while I'm in college.
   ○ Agree
   ○ Don't Know
   ○ Disagree

Review the items you marked "don't know" or "disagree." Paying attention to all these aspects of your college experience can be important to your success. After reading this chapter, come back to this list and think about ways you can work on these areas.

Careers and the New Economy

Brett Kossick

First-year student near the end of his first term

"Well, I really admire your focus," said Dr. Woloshyn, my academic adviser, when I dropped by his office early to talk about my course schedule. Many people study a whole gamut of things until they settle on a major and don't specialize until graduate school. That's so not me.

"I've wanted to be an engineer for as long as I can remember," I said. "Which is why I'm here. I got your e-mail with the courses you suggested, and I'm confused. *Business Writing and Communication*? *Team Skills and Critical Thinking*? I plan to work in robotics," I said, "not marketing."

"Oh, really?" Dr. Woloshyn nodded. Then he leaned forward on his desk and made a tent with his hands. "Brett, didn't you tell me that you have an internship with a leading technology corporation this summer? Did anyone tell you what you would be doing there?"

"Not really," I said. "They just said I'd be helping out in different divisions of the company, depending on what they need."

"Right," said Dr. Woloshyn. "And is there a chance you might like to work there after you graduate?"

"Yes, are you kidding? That would be my dream job."

"Good. So, let's think about it: Some divisions of the company might be working on new business proposals and will value a gifted writer. Some might be working on projects involving media companies, investment bankers, schools, or even foreign governments. They will need someone who is great at teamwork. Some divisions might be working on new apps or software applications, which means—"

"Critical thinking," I cut in. We grinned at each other as I stood up. "Thanks, Professor. I guess I'll go register now."

What kinds of skills do you need to develop as a college student? How can an expertise in writing, critical thinking, and teamwork help you achieve your goals?

In your lifetime, companies have restructured to remain competitive. As a result, major changes have taken place in how we work, where we work, and the ways we prepare for work while in college. In many ways the following characteristics define today's economy:

Global Increasingly, industries have become multinational, not only moving into overseas markets but also seeking cheaper labor, capital, and resources abroad. Around the world, factories built to similar standards can turn out essentially the same products. Your career is bound to be affected by the global economy, even if you never leave the United States. For example, when you call an 800 number for customer service, the person who talks to you might be answering your call in Iowa, Ireland, or India. College graduates in the United States are now competing for jobs with others around the world who are often willing to work longer hours for less money than American workers.

Unstable In 2008 and 2009 the world economy suffered a series of events that led to downturns in stock markets, bankruptcies, foreclosures, failing businesses, and lost jobs. Scandals within the highest ranks of major companies and constant mergers and acquisitions of companies have destabilized the workforce. Depending on how long it takes to stabilize the economy in the United States and the rest of the world, your career goals might have to be refocused. Because the global economic situation is changing continuously, it's important to keep up-to-date on the economic situation as it relates to your prospective major and career.

Innovative The economy depends on creativity in new products and services to generate consumer interest around the world. Especially in times of economic instability, the flexibility and responsiveness of companies to the changing economic climate will affect their ability to survive.

Boundaryless Teams of workers within an organization need to understand the missions of other teams because they most likely will have to work together. You might be an accountant and find yourself working with the public relations division of your company, or you might be a human resources manager who does training for a number of different divisions in a number of different countries.

Customized   More and more, consumers are demanding products and services tailored to their specific needs. You have probably noticed the seemingly endless varieties of a single brand of shampoo or cereal crowding store shelves. Such market segmentation requires a constant adaptation of ideas to identify new products and services as new customer demands emerge.

Fast   When computers became popular, people rejoiced because they believed the new technology would reduce their workloads. Actually, the reverse happened. Whereas secretaries and other support workers once performed many tasks for executives, now executives design their own PowerPoint presentations and format their own documents. For better or worse, "We need it now" is the cry in the workplace, with product and service delivery time cut to a minimum (the "just-in-time" policy). Being fast requires constant thinking outside the lines to identify new approaches to designing and delivering products.

According to *Fast Company* magazine, the new economy has changed many of the rules about work. Leaders are now expected to teach and encourage others as well as to head up their divisions. Careers frequently zigzag into other areas. People who can anticipate the needs of the marketplace are in demand. Change has become the norm. Workers are being urged to continue their learning, and companies are volunteering to play a critical role in the welfare of all people through sponsorship of worthy causes. As the lines between work and the rest of life continue to blur, workers need to find a healthy balance in their lives. Bringing work home may be inevitable at times, but it shouldn't be the rule.

Essential Qualities and Skills for the New Economy

In addition to being well educated and savvy about the realities of the twenty-first-century economy, you'll also need a wide range of qualities and skills to succeed in your career, such as:

try it!

Thinking about a Career Choice

List your personal interests, preferences, characteristics, strengths, and skills. Match your list to what you believe to be the skills and interests of successful people in a field that interests you. Note other influences that may be drawing you to that career (such as your parents' preferences). Share the notes you have prepared with a career counselor, and get feedback on how you and your career interests mesh.

- Communication skills that demonstrate strong oral and listening abilities, in addition to a good foundation in the basic skill of writing

- Presentation skills, including the ability to justify and persuade as well as to respond to questions and serious critiques of your presentation material

- Leadership skills and the ability to take charge or relinquish control, according to the needs of the organization

- Team skills—the ability to work cooperatively and collaboratively with different people while maintaining autonomous control over some assignments

- Interpersonal abilities that allow you to relate to others, inspire others to participate, and resolve conflict between people

- Positive personal traits, including initiative and motivation, adaptability to change, a work ethic, reliability, honesty, and integrity

- Critical thinking and problem solving—the ability to identify problems and their solutions by integrating information from a variety of sources and effectively weighing alternatives

- A willingness to learn quickly and continuously from those with whom you work and others around the world

12

Aligning Your Sense of Purpose and Your Career

As you begin the process of choosing or confirming a major and career path, you will first want to consider why you decided to go to college and why you chose this particular institution. Ask yourself:

- Am I here to find out who I am and study a subject I'm truly passionate about, regardless of whether it leads to a career?

- Am I here to engage in an academic program that provides an array of possibilities when I graduate?

- Am I here to prepare myself for a graduate program or immediate employment?

- Am I here to obtain specific training in a field that I'm committed to?

- Am I here to gain specific skills for a job I already have?

Remember the following six simple, one-word questions. They can help you to prepare for a career and obtain that important first job:

- **Why?** Why do you want to be a _____? Knowing your goals and values will help you pursue your career with passion and an understanding of what motivates you.

- **Who?** Who at your college or university or in your community can help you make career decisions? Network with people who can help you find out what you want to do. Right now those people might be instructors in your major, an academic adviser, or someone at your campus career center. Later, network with others who can help you attain your goal.

- **How?** How will you develop the technical and communications skills required to work effectively? Don't be a technophobe. Learn how to do PowerPoint presentations, build Web pages, and create Excel spreadsheets. Take a speech course. Improve your writing skills. Even if you think your future job doesn't require these skills, you'll be more marketable with them.

- **What?** What opportunities are available in your preferred career fields? Be aware of the range of job options an employer presents, as well as such potential threats as outsourcing—a company's hiring of outside businesses to perform particular functions at a lower cost. Understand the employment requirements for the career field you have chosen. Know what

training you will need to remain and move up in your chosen profession.

- **Where?** Where will your career path take you? Will you be required to travel or live in a certain part of the country or the world? Or will job success require that you stay in one location? Although job requirements may change over the course of your lifetime, try to achieve a balance between your personal values and preferences and the predictable requirements of the field you are pursuing.

- **When?** When will you need to start looking for your first job? Certain professions, such as teaching, tend to hire employees at certain times of the year.

Connecting Your Major and Your Interests with Your Career

Some students are sure about their major when they enter college, but many others are at a loss. Either way, it's okay. At some point you might ask yourself: Why am I in college? Although it sounds like an easy question to answer, it's not. Many students would immediately respond, "So I can get a good job or an education for a specific career." Yet most majors do not lead to a specific career path or job. You actually can enter most career paths from any number of academic majors. Marketing, a common undergraduate business major, is a field that recruits from a wide variety of majors, including advertising, communications, and psychology. Sociology majors find jobs in law enforcement, teaching, and public service.

Today, English majors are designing Web pages, and history majors are sales representatives and business managers. You do not have to major in

try it!

Thinking about Your Major

Would you describe your major as something you're really passionate about? Why or why not? If your answer is no, why are you pursuing this particular major?

science to gain admittance to medical school. Of course, you do have to take the required science and math courses, but medical schools seek applicants with diverse backgrounds. Only a few technical or professional fields, such as accounting, nursing, and engineering, are tied to specific majors.

Exploring your interests is the best way to choose an academic major. If you're still not sure, take the advice of Patrick Coombs, author of *Major in Success,* who recommends that you major in a subject about which you are really passionate. Most advisers would agree.

You can major in almost anything. As this chapter emphasizes, it is how you integrate your classes with your extracurricular activities and work experience that prepares you for a successful transition to your career. Try a major you think you'll like, and see what develops. But keep an open mind, and don't pin all your hopes on finding a career in that major alone. Your major and your career ultimately have to fit your overall life goals, purposes, values, and beliefs.

Career Choice as a Process of Discovery

Students frequently encounter bumps along the road toward planning and achieving their career goals. Choosing a career is a process of discovery, involving a willingness to remain open to new ideas and experiences. Why should you begin thinking about your career early in your college experience? Because many of the decisions you make during your first year will have an impact on where you end up in the workplace.

As you think about your career, also consider that:

- **You are, more or less, solely responsible for your career.** At one time, organizations provided structured "ladders" that employees could climb to advance to higher professional levels. In most cases, such ladders have disappeared. Companies may assist you with assessments and information on available positions in the industry, but the ultimate task of engineering a career path is yours.

- **To advance your career, you must accept the risks that accompany employment and plan for the future.** Organizations continually restructure, merge, and either grow or downsize in response to economic conditions.

As a result, positions may be cut. Because you can be unexpectedly unemployed, keep other career options in mind as you take courses.

- **A college degree does not guarantee employment.** As a college graduate, you'll be able to pursue opportunities that are more rewarding, financially and otherwise, than if you did not have a degree. But simply wanting to work in a certain field or for a certain organization doesn't mean there will always be a job for you there. Be flexible when exploring your career options; you may have to begin your work life in a job that is not exactly in line with your major or career goals.

- **A commitment to lifelong learning will help keep you employable.** In your college courses you are learning a vital skill: how to learn. Actually, much of your learning will begin when you receive your diploma.

Now the good news: Thousands of graduates find jobs every year. Some may have to work longer to get where they want to be, but persistence pays off. If you start now, you'll have time to build a portfolio of academic and co-curricular experiences that will add substance to your career profile.

12

Exploring Your Interests

John Holland, a psychologist at Johns Hopkins University, developed a number of tools and concepts that can help you organize the various dimensions of yourself so that you can identify potential career choices and choose your major. Holland separates people into six general categories on the basis of differences in their interests, skills, values, and personality characteristics—in short, their preferred approaches to life.[1] Holland's system organizes career fields into the same six categories. Career fields are grouped according to what a particular career field requires of a person (skills and personality characteristics most commonly associated with success in those fields) and what rewards those fields provide (interests and values most commonly associated with satisfaction).

The Holland Model: Personality Characteristics

Realistic (R)   These people describe themselves as concrete, down-to-earth, and practical doers. They exhibit competitive and assertive behavior and show interest in activities that require motor coordination, skill, and physical strength. They tend to be interested in scientific or mechanical areas rather than the arts. Examples of career fields in this category include agricultural engineer, electrical contractor, industrial arts teacher, navy officer, fitness director, packaging engineer, electronics technician, and computer graphics technician.

Investigative (I)   These people describe themselves as analytical, rational, and logical problem solvers. They value intellectual stimulation and intellectual achievement and prefer to think rather than to act, to organize and understand rather than to persuade. They usually have a strong interest in physical, biological, or social sciences. They are less apt to be people oriented. Examples of career fields in this category include urban planner, chemical engineer, bacteriologist, flight engineer, genealogist, and college professor.

---

[1] Reproduced by special permission of the publisher, Psychological Assessment Resource, Inc., 16204 North Florida Ave., Lutz, FL 33549. Adapted from *The Self-Directed Search: Professional User's Guide*, by John L. Holland, Ph.D. Copyright © 1985, 1987, 1994, 1997. Further reproduction is prohibited without permission from PAR, Inc.

Artistic (A)   These people describe themselves as creative, innovative, and independent. They value self-expression and relating with others through artistic expression and are also emotionally expressive. Examples of career fields in this category include architect, film editor/director, actor, cartoonist, interior decorator, and reporter.

Social (S)   These people describe themselves as kind, caring, helpful, and understanding of others. They value helping and making a contribution. They satisfy their needs in one-on-one or small-group interaction using strong speaking skills to teach, counsel, or advise. Examples of career fields in this category include nurse, teacher, social worker, genetic counselor, marriage counselor, rehabilitation counselor, and convention planner.

Enterprising (E)   These people describe themselves as assertive, risk-taking, and persuasive. They value prestige, power, and status and are more inclined than other types to pursue it. Examples of career fields in this category include banker, city manager, FBI agent, health administrator, judge, labor arbitrator, salary and wage administrator, and marketing specialist.

Conventional (C)   These people describe themselves as neat, orderly, detail oriented, and persistent. They value order, structure, prestige, and status and possess a high degree of self-control. Examples of career fields in this category include accountant, statistician, database manager, and abstractor/indexer.

Your career choices ultimately will involve a complex assessment of the factors most important to you. To display the relationship between career fields and the potential conflicts people face as they consider them, Holland's model is commonly presented in a hexagonal shape (see Figure 12.1). The closer the types, the closer the relationships among the career fields; the farther apart the types, the more conflict between the career fields.

Holland's model can help you address the problem of career choice in two ways. First, you can begin to identify many career fields that are consistent with what you know about yourself. Once you've identified potential fields, you can use the career center at your college to get more information about those fields, such as daily activities for specific jobs, interests and abilities

12

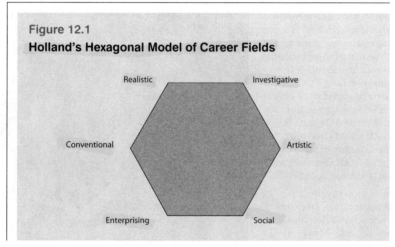

Figure 12.1
Holland's Hexagonal Model of Career Fields

Realistic · Investigative · Artistic · Social · Enterprising · Conventional

required, preparation required for entry, working conditions, salary and benefits, and employment outlook. Second, you can begin to identify the harmony or conflicts in your career choices.

Never feel you have to make a decision based on the results of only one assessment. Career choices are complex and involve many factors; furthermore, these decisions are reversible. Take time to talk your interests over with a career counselor. Another helpful approach is to shadow an individual in the occupation that interests you, to obtain a better understanding of what the occupation entails in terms of skills, commitment, and opportunity.

Factors That Affect Career Choices

Some people have a definite self-image when they enter college, but most of us are still in the process of defining (or redefining) ourselves throughout life. We can look at ourselves in several useful ways with respect to possible careers:

- **Values.** Today, more than ever, knowing your core values (your most important beliefs) will be important in shaping your career path. In a faltering and unpredictable economy, having a strong rudder will help you steer through the turbulent times.

- **Interests.** Your interests will develop from your experiences and beliefs and can continue to develop and change throughout life. You

may be interested in writing for the college newspaper because you wrote for your high school paper. It's not unusual to enter Psych 101 with a great interest in psychology and realize halfway through the course that psychology is not what you imagined.

- **Skills.** You may be aware of skills you currently have or skills you want to develop while you're in college. Almost always, the ability to do something well can be improved with practice.

- **Aptitudes.** Your inherent strengths, or aptitudes, are often part of your biological heritage or the result of early training. Each of us has aptitudes we can build on.

- **Personality.** Your personality makes you who you are and can't be ignored when you make career decisions. The quiet, orderly, calm, detail-oriented person probably will make a different work choice than the aggressive, outgoing, argumentative person will.

- **Life goals and work values.** Each of us defines success and satisfaction in our own way. The process is complex and very personal. Two factors influence our conclusions about success and happiness: knowing that we are achieving the life goals we've set for ourselves, and finding that we gain satisfaction from what we're receiving from our work. If your values conflict with the organizational values where you work, you might be in for trouble.

12

Working While in College

It's a fact that most students work, and there are pluses and minuses to working in college. Work can support you in attaining your college goals, provide you with the financial means to complete college, and help you structure your time so that you are a much better time manager. It can help you meet people who will later serve as important references for graduate school and/or employment. However, working too much can interfere with your college success, your ability to attend class, your homework, and your participation in many other valuable parts of college life, such as group study, foreign study and travel, and group activities.

If you have to work in order to pay for your tuition and/or your living expenses, take some time to determine how much you need to work, and stay within reasonable limits. Many college students work too many hours just to support a lifestyle and acquire things they want. It's important to keep a reasonable balance between work and study. Don't fall into the trap of thinking "I can do it all." Too many college students have found that "doing it all" means they don't do anything very well.

On-Campus Jobs

If you want or need to work, explore on-campus opportunities as soon as (or even before) you arrive. Even if a campus job pays less than you could earn off campus, there are real advantages to on-campus employment. Generally, on-campus supervisors will be much more flexible than off-campus employers in helping you balance your study demands and your work schedule. And the relationships you'll develop with influential people who really care about your success in college and who will write those all-important reference letters will make the smaller paycheck well worth it.

Your career center can tell you how to access your college's employment system. You may have to register in person or online, but the process is easy, especially if you have a résumé or a draft of one. College employment systems generally channel all jobs collected through faculty, advisers, and career counselors into one database, so it is convenient for you to identify jobs you are looking for.

Many campuses offer an on-campus job fair early in the fall term. Even if you might not be interested at the time, a visit to the job fair will give

you a great idea of the range and types of jobs available on campus. You might be pleasantly surprised to learn that there are more opportunities than washing dishes in the cafeteria. Job fairs usually include off-campus community employers, in part because your institution must spend some of the federal college work-study funds it receives supporting off-campus work by students.

It is a good idea to pursue job opportunities that are related to your major or your career. For example, if you are a pre-med major, you might be able to find on-campus work in a biology or chemistry lab. That work would help you to gain knowledge and experience and to make connections with faculty experts in these fields. In fact, getting an on-campus job is one of the best ways to develop relationships with instructors and administrators on your campus.

Off-Campus Jobs

The best places to start looking for off-campus jobs are your campus career center and financial aid office. They might well have listings or Web sites with off-campus employment opportunities. Don't hesitate to speak to a career counselor for suggestions. You can also use the following job search strategies:

- Learn the names of the major employers in your college's geographic area: manufacturers, service industries, resorts, and so on. Once you

12

know who the major employers are, check them out, visit their Web sites, and learn the details.

- Check out the Web site for the agency in your state that collects and disseminates information about available employment opportunities. Find out whether this agency has an office in the community where you are attending college.

- Visit employment agencies, particularly those that seek part-time temporary workers. This is a convenient, low-risk (for both you and the employer) way to "shop" for a job and to obtain flexible, short-term, low-commitment employment.

- Visit online job boards, and look at the classified ads in the local newspaper, in print or online. Don't forget the classifieds in the national press. Some national firms will have jobs that can be done part-time in your area or even from your own living space.

- Check your campus student newspaper. Employers who favor hiring college students often advertise there.

- Be aware that many jobs are never posted. Employers find it easier to hire people recommended to them by current employees, friends, or the person vacating the position. Faculty members often hire students for their research labs on the basis of performance in the classroom.

- Realize that who you know is important. Your friends who already work on campus or who have had an internship can be the best people to help you when you are ready to search for your job. In fact, nearly 50 percent of all student jobs are found through family and friends.

Internships

Your academic department or the campus career center can provide information on off-campus internships that may be available. Internships offer valuable hands-on experience in a career you may want to pursue. Through an internship, you'll learn not only about the nature of the industry and the daily work routine but also about employment in an organization. You'll work with people who can be instrumental in helping you find a job when your studies are done. And adding the experience of having been an intern to your résumé will make it all the stronger when the time comes for a job search.

try it!

College Jobs and Your Career

At this point in your college experience, you probably have at least tentative plans about the major and/or the career you will pursue. If you must take a job while going to school, think about what jobs may be available on campus and in the outside community that might provide valuable experience with respect to your goals. Make two lists—one for on-campus jobs and the other for off-campus jobs—that identify jobs related to your career interests, and look into the availability of such work.

Co-op Programs

Some colleges and universities have "co-op programs," in which you spend some terms in class and other terms in temporary job settings in your field. Although they usually prolong your education somewhat, co-op programs have many advantages. They offer an excellent preview of what work in your chosen field is like and give you valuable experience and contacts that you can tap into to get a job when you finish college; in fact, many firms offer successful co-op students permanent jobs when they graduate. Alternating work and school terms may be a more agreeable schedule for you than eight or ten straight terms of classes would be, and the work/academics balance may help you keep your ultimate goal in mind. Co-op programs can help you pay for college, too; during their co-op terms, some co-op students, especially in technical fields, make almost as much as their professors do!

The bottom line is to try to limit the number of hours you work while you're in college. Research finds that full-time students who work more than fifteen or twenty hours a week have a lower chance of finishing college. And students who work off campus, as opposed to on campus, are also less likely to be successful in college unless their work is directly connected with their major.

12

12 Chapter Review

One-minute paper . . .

Making the right choices when it comes to picking a major and a career can be intimidating. What did you learn in this chapter that will help you prepare for declaring a major? Of the topics covered in this chapter, which would you like to learn more about?

Applying what you've learned . . .

Now that you have read and discussed this chapter, consider how you can apply what you have learned to your academic and personal life. The following prompts will help you reflect on chapter material and its relevance to you both now and in the future.

1. Sometimes the best way to learn about a career is to talk to someone who is working or teaching in that field. Set up an appointment to talk with a professor who teaches in the area in which you are interested. Find out as much as possible about the education required for a specific career in the field.

2. Choosing a major is a big decision and should include consideration of your personal learning style, your personality, and your goals and values. Review what you learned in Chapter 3 about your emotional intelligence and preferred ways of learning. How will those insights guide your exploration of majors and careers?

Building your portfolio . . .
Investigating occupations

How can you select a major if you are not sure what you want to do when you graduate? College classes, out-of-class activities, and part-time jobs will help you narrow your choices and make decisions about a major and a potential career.

1. Create a Word document and list at least two majors that you are considering right now or that you would like to know more about. Why do you find these majors interesting?

2. Name two or more careers you think you might be interested in after you graduate. Explain your choice.

3. The U.S. Bureau of Labor Statistics publishes the online *Occupational Outlook Handbook,* which provides details about hundreds of jobs. You can find in-depth information on any job in which you might have an interest.

   a. Visit the *Occupational Outlook Handbook* online at **http://www.bls.gov/oco/**; in the search field, enter one or two of the careers you listed above.

   b. Create a chart like the one below. Note the training or degree required, describe the job outlook, and list the median earnings for each career. Look through the other descriptions to learn more about the careers.

	Example	Career 1	Career 2
Career	Computer software engineer		
Training Required	Bachelor's degree, computer science/ software engineering		
Job Outlook	One of the fastest-growing occupations from 2004 to 2014		
Median Annual Earnings	About $74,980		

4. Save your findings in your portfolio on your personal computer or flash drive. Even in your first college year it is important that you begin to think about what you are going to do after graduation. The more you investigate different types of careers, the easier it will be for you to identify a major or decide what kind of internship, part-time job, or service learning opportunity you want to experience while you are still in college.

Where to go for help . . .

On Campus

Your college Web site: Search your campus career resources. Larger campuses might have specialized career service centers for specific professional schools and clusters of majors. Often student professional organizations, academic advisers, and departments will provide relevant career information on their Web sites.

Career center: Almost every college campus has a career center where you can obtain free counseling and information on careers. A career professional will work with you to help you define your interests, interpret the results of any assessment you complete, coach you on interview techniques, and critique your résumé. It's important to schedule an appointment. By the end of your first year you should be familiar with the career center, where it is located, and the counselor who is responsible for your academic major or interests. You might also find opportunities for internships and interview practice there.

Academic advising: More and more advisers have been trained in what is known as "developmental advising," or helping you see beyond individual classes and working to help you initiate a career search. Talking to your adviser is often the best place to start. If you have not declared a major—which is true of many first-year students—your adviser might be able to help you with that decision as well.

Faculty: On many campuses, faculty members take an active role in helping students connect academic interests to careers. A faculty member can recommend specific courses that relate to a particular career. Faculty members in professional curricula, such as business and other applied fields, often have direct contact with companies and serve as contacts for internships. If you have an interest in attending graduate school, faculty sponsorship is critical to admission. Developing a relationship with a faculty mentor can open a number of important doors.

Library: Some campuses have a separate library in the career center staffed by librarians whose job is to help you locate career-related information resources. Of course, all campuses have a main library that contains a wealth of information on careers. The reference librarian at the main desk will be glad to help you. If you are a student on a large university campus, you might find additional libraries that are specific to certain professional schools and colleges within the university,

such as business, education, law, medicine, music, and engineering; these are also excellent sources for career information.

Upperclass students: Ask whether more experienced students can help you navigate courses and find important resources. Upperclass students might also have practical experience gained from internships and volunteering. Since they have tested the waters, they can alert you to potential pitfalls or inform you of opportunities.

Student organizations: Professional student organizations that focus on specific career interests meet regularly throughout the year. Join them now. Not only will they put you in contact with upperclass students, but also their programs often include employer representatives, helpful discussions on searching for internships or jobs, and exposure to current conditions in the workplace.

Online

Career center: Go to your campus career center's home page, and check its resources, such as links to useful pages.

Occupational Information Network: http://www .online.onetcenter.org. This federal government site has information on occupations, skill sets, and links to professional sites for selected occupations. This is a great place to get started thinking about your interests.

Mapping Your Future: http://www.mappingyour future.org. This comprehensive site provides support for those who are just starting to explore careers.

The Riley Guide: http://www.rileyguide.com. One of the best sites for interviewing, job search strategies, and other critical career tips.

My Institution's Resources

_____

_____

_____

_____

_____

_____

_____

Practicing Your Textbook Reading Skills

1. Where in the chapter can you find information to help you balance school and job demands?

   a. under "Careers and the New Economy" beginning on page 148

   b. under "Aligning Your Sense of Purpose and Your Career" beginning on page 150

   c. under "Exploring Your Interests" beginning on page 152

   d. under "Working While in College" beginning on page 154

2. Evaluate the chapter's headings to identify which of the following is a subtopic of "Exploring Your Interests."

   a. Holland's Hexagonal Model of Career Fields

   b. Realistic (R)

   c. Factors That Affect Career Choices

   d. Life goals and work values

3. According to the Holland Model, as illustrated in Figure 12.1, which of the following two career fields are most closely related?

   a. conventional and artistic

   b. realistic and investigative

   c. artistic and enterprising

   d. social and conventional

4. What is the specialized meaning of "ladders" as it is used in the section titled "Career Choice as a Process of Discovery"?

   a. household tools

   b. structured steps for career advancement

   c. a group of employers

   d. a ranking of competitors

5. Brett Kossick, featured on page 148, is a

   a. career counselor.

   b. textbook author.

   c. college student.

   d. college professor.

6. What is the focus of the "try it!" activity on page 155?

   a. finding a part-time job

   b. picking a career

c. choosing a major

d. enrolling in a co-op program

7. The list of questions labeled "How Do You Measure Up?" on page 147 is a

   a. practice quiz.

   b. table of contents.

   c. study aid.

   d. self-assessment tool.

8. What topic does the photograph on page 154 relate to?

   a. on-campus jobs

   b. off-campus jobs

   c. internships

   d. co-op programs

9. The purpose of the "Building your portfolio" activity on page 156 is to

   a. test your understanding of the chapter content.

   b. apply what you've learned.

   c. explore careers that interest you.

   d. none of the above

10. The "Where to go for help" section at the end of the chapter lists which of the following resources for researching jobs?

    a. career center

    b. upperclass students

    c. Occupational Information Network

    d. all of the above

Testing Your Understanding

Identify the following statements as *true* or *false*.

1. A person's college major determines his or her career options.

   T _____   F _____

2. All job openings can be found through Web sites, advertisements, employment agencies, online job boards, or college recruitment fairs.

   T _____   F _____

3. Most careers will be affected in some way by the global economy.

   T _____ F _____

4. Full-time students who work more than twenty hours a week are less likely to finish college than those who work fewer hours.

   T _____ F _____

5. Having a college degree guarantees a good job.

   T _____ F _____

Select the best answer to each of the following questions.

6. Which of the following statements describes working in today's economy?

   a. Workers need to be flexible because their jobs can change quickly.

   b. Most available workers are unskilled.

   c. Many more women work from home.

   d. A global recession has made it impossible to find work.

7. According to the author of *Major in Success*, students should major in

   a. business and technology.

   b. the liberal arts.

   c. something they're passionate about.

   d. whatever is most popular at their school.

8. Ideally, a job applicant should have

   a. good writing and presentation skills.

   b. the ability to collaborate with different kinds of people.

   c. positive personality traits.

   d. all of the above

9. The *Occupational Outlook Handbook*

   a. requires employers to verify that employees can legally work in the United States.

   b. provides detailed information about career fields and job options.

   c. offers legal advice for workers who have been wrongfully terminated.

   d. explains workplace benefits such as disability insurance and retirement plans.

10. Career fields appropriate for social personality types include

    a. agricultural engineer, electrical contractor, navy officer, and computer graphics technician.

b. urban planner, bacteriologist, flight engineer, and genealogist.

c. nurse, teacher, marriage counselor, and convention planner.

d. banker, city manager, FBI agent, and marketing specialist.

11. Which of the following sources can provide leads for off-campus jobs?

    a. friends

    b. on-campus job databases

    c. work-study programs

    d. none of the above

12. When choosing a career path, a person should consider

    a. potential wages.

    b. paid holidays, vacation, and sick days.

    c. values, interests, skills, aptitudes, personality, and life goals.

    d. which college major would provide the best preparation.

13. One benefit of working in an on-campus job is

    a. higher pay.

    b. guaranteed employment.

    c. easier tasks.

    d. flexibility to study.

14. Why do students attend college?

    a. to learn about themselves or something they care about

    b. to prepare for a graduate program or a particular career field

    c. to gain specific skills for a job they already have

    d. for any of the above reasons

15. Who is responsible for planning and structuring a person's career?

    a. that individual person

    b. the campus career center

    c. faculty members

    d. employers

Using your own words, define the following terms as they are used in the chapter.

16. *global economy*

_____

_____

17. *just-in-time*

_____

_____

18. *team skills*

_____

_____

19. *co-op programs*

_____

_____

20. *developmental advising*

_____

_____

Answer each of the following questions using the space provided.

21. Identify and briefly explain the personality characteristics used in the Holland model of career fields.

_____

_____

_____

_____

_____

22. What are some of the risks of employment?

_____

_____

_____

_____

_____

_____

23. What six questions should people ask themselves to prepare for a career and find a job?

_____

_____

_____

_____

_____

24. Briefly describe the benefits of taking an internship while in college.

_____

_____

_____

_____

25. List at least three services offered by campus career centers.

_____

_____

_____

_____

Making Thematic Connections

Juggling school and work is a primary source of stress for some students, while others might not be bothered by competing demands at all. The chapter in Unit 5, "Stress, Health, and Coping," from *Psychology*, Fifth Edition, examines what causes stress, how people respond to it, and what coping strategies can help people deal with it effectively. The authors, Don H. Hockenbury and Sandra E. Hockenbury, define *stress* as "a negative emotional state occurring in response to events that are perceived as taxing or exceeding a person's resources or ability to cope." (Read or re-read pages 561–65 of the psychology chapter for more information.) They also explain that stress can make a person ill, resulting in sick days or poor performance. As a college student, what can you do to reduce your stress levels without lightening your workload? What on-campus resources are available to help you manage your workload? Explain your answer.

Composition

"Document Design"

Introduction

Almost every college student is required to take at least one course in composition, or writing. The ability to communicate ideas clearly in writing is a crucial skill for success in college, in the workplace, and in life. And yet writing is difficult, even for people who do it for a living. Learning how to write well takes practice, so composition instructors focus on teaching their students how to master the process, one step at a time. In your writing classes you'll learn how to come up with ideas, how to put your thoughts in order, and how to express them so that others will understand you. You'll also learn how to rethink what you've written and revise it, making it the best it can possibly be. Few of your courses will be as immediately practical or as rewarding.

In your composition course, you will probably be required to purchase a handbook. Unlike the other college textbooks included in this reader, handbooks are references. They are meant to help you find answers to questions—about grammar, punctuation, mechanics, and similar details—as you plan, write, revise, and edit your work. You won't normally sit down and read a whole handbook chapter at a time. Instead, you'll look up information when you need it. Keep in mind, too, that although much of that information takes the form of rules, much of it is practical advice for making your ideas clear to yourself and to others. The rules themselves evolved to help readers understand you, not to make writing more difficult.

The Bedford Handbook, Eighth Edition, by Diana Hacker and Nancy Sommers, is a fairly typical composition handbook. It is also one of the most popular textbooks in the United States, used by over a million writers. Part of its success is due to the many reference aids the authors provide, including these:

- Two topic menus, a detailed table of contents, and a plain-language index (not included here), offer multiple points of access.

- Chapters and their subsections are numbered and lettered, making it easy to locate cross-referenced sections elsewhere in the book.

- The running heads at the top of each page include chapter and section numbers, abbreviated topic tabs, main topic descriptions, and key terms to help you skim for information.

- The clean, simple page design pinpoints what's important.

- Most headings are written in the form of direct advice to make the material easier to follow.

- Plentiful examples show you how to apply the advice to your own writing.

- Shaded boxes in the margins, called "Making the most of your handbook," tell you where in the book to find related information.

The section that follows covers an increasingly important aspect of writing: document design. As computers have become more capable and more common,

This unit's textbook reading comes from *The Bedford Handbook*, Eighth Edition, by Diana Hacker and Nancy Sommers, Bedford/St. Martin's, 2010, Part X, pages 727–46.

readers have become more visually oriented, and they now expect a polished appearance in written documents. Accordingly, the three brief chapters in this part of the handbook emphasize and outline the visual conventions for different kinds of documents, from college papers to résumés to memos to e-mails. As you skim through these chapters, think about how you can apply these conventions and suggestions to your own writing, both for school and for work.

Preparing to Read the Textbook Chapter

1. What have you written so far today? Some text messages, an online status update, an e-mail, maybe a homework assignment or a report? Did *what* you were writing affect *how* you wrote it? In what ways?

2. Flip through the chapter without reading it. Which topic do you think would be most helpful to you the next time you have to write an essay for a class? Why?

3. To apply for most kinds of postcollege jobs, you will need a résumé. Have you written one yet? What do you think your résumé will have to do to make potential employers interested in hiring you?

Part X
Document Design

58 Become familiar with the principles of document design. 728
59 Use standard academic formatting. 738
60 Use standard business formatting. 738

The term *document* is broad enough to describe anything you might write in a college class, in the business world, and in everyday life. How you design a document (format it for the printed page or for a computer screen) will affect how readers respond to it.

58   Become familiar with the principles of document design.

Good document design promotes readability, but what *readability* means depends on your purpose and audience and perhaps on other elements of your writing situation, such as your subject, length restrictions, or any other specific requirements (see the checklist on p. 9). All of your design choices—formatting options, headings, and lists—should be made with your writing situation in mind. Likewise, different types of visuals—tables, charts, and images—can support your writing if they are used appropriately.

58a Select appropriate format options.

Similar types of documents share similar design features. Taken together, these features—layout, margins and line spacing, alignment, fonts, and font styles—form an appearance that helps to guide readers.

Layout

Most readers have set ideas about how different kinds of documents should look. Advertisements, for example, have a distinctive appearance, as do newsletters and brochures. Instructors have expectations about how a college paper should look (see 59). Employers too expect documents such as letters, résumés, memos, and e-mail messages to be presented in standard ways (see 60).

Unless you have a compelling reason to stray from convention, it's best to choose a document layout that conforms to your readers' expectations. If you're not sure what readers expect, look at examples of the kind of document you are producing.

format • readability • layout •
page setup • margins • line spacing   **dd 58a**   729

Margins, line spacing, and alignment   need Room   double space   bus/tech single

(handwritten margin note: Elements ⒶAppropformat ⒷOption (readability) ⒷHeading Ⓒlists Ⓓvisuals)

Margins help control the look of a page. For most academic and business documents, leave a margin of one to one and a half inches on all sides. These margins create a visual frame for the text and provide room for annotations, such as an instructor's comments or an editor's suggestions. Tight margins generally make a page crowded and difficult to read.

Most manuscripts in progress are double-spaced to allow room for editing. Final copy is often double-spaced as well, since single-spaced text is less inviting to read. If you are unsure about margin and spacing requirements for your document, check with your instructor or consult documents similar to the one you are writing.

At times, the advantages of wide margins and double-spaced lines are offset by other considerations. For example, most business and technical documents are single-spaced, with double-spacing between paragraphs, to save paper and promote quick scanning. Keep your purpose and audience in mind as you determine appropriate margins and line spacing for your document.

SINGLE-SPACED, UNFORMATTED

Obesity in Children   1

Can Medication Cure Obesity in Children?
A Review of the Literature
In March 2004, U.S. Surgeon General Richard Carmona called attention to a health problem in the United States that, until recently, has been overlooked: childhood obesity. Carmona said that the "astounding" 15% child obesity rate constitutes an "epidemic." Since the early 1980s, that rate has "doubled in children and tripled in adolescents." Now more than 9 million children are classified as obese (paras. 3, 5). While the traditional response to a medical epidemic is to hunt for a vaccine or a cure-all pill, childhood obesity has proven more elusive. The lack of success of recent initiatives suggests that medication might not be the answer for the escalating problem. This literature review considers whether the use of medication is a promising approach for solving the childhood obesity problem by responding to the following questions: What are the implications of childhood obesity? Is medication effective at treating childhood obesity? Is medication safe for children? Is medication the best solution? Understanding the limitations of medical treatments for children highlights the complexity of the childhood obesity problem in the United States and underscores the need for physicians, advocacy groups, and policymakers to search for other solutions.
Obesity can be a devastating problem from both an individual and a societal perspective. Obesity puts children at risk for a number of medical complications, including type 2 diabetes, hypertension, sleep apnea, and orthopedic problems (Henry J. Kaiser Family Foundation, 2004, p. 1). Researchers Hoppin and Taveras (2004) have noted that obesity is often associated with psychological issues such as depression, anxiety, and binge eating (Table 4).
Obesity also poses serious problems for a society struggling to cope with rising health care costs. The cost of treating obesity currently totals $117 billion per year—a price, according to the surgeon general, "second only to the cost of [treating] tobacco use" (Carmona, 2004, para. 9). And as the number of children who suffer from obesity grows, long-term costs will only increase.
The widening scope of the obesity problem has prompted medical professionals to rethink old conceptions of the disorder and its causes. As researchers Yanovski and Yanovski (2002) have explained, obesity

DOUBLE-SPACED, FORMATTED

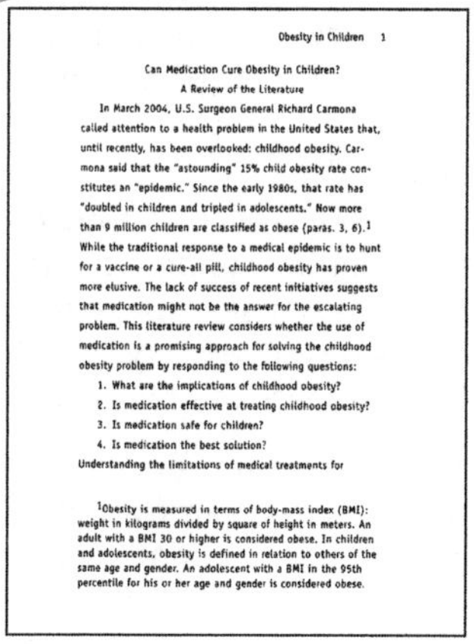

Obesity in Children   1

Can Medication Cure Obesity in Children?
A Review of the Literature
In March 2004, U.S. Surgeon General Richard Carmona called attention to a health problem in the United States that, until recently, has been overlooked: childhood obesity. Carmona said that the "astounding" 15% child obesity rate constitutes an "epidemic." Since the early 1980s, that rate has "doubled in children and tripled in adolescents." Now more than 9 million children are classified as obese (paras. 3, 6).[1] While the traditional response to a medical epidemic is to hunt for a vaccine or a cure-all pill, childhood obesity has proven more elusive. The lack of success of recent initiatives suggests that medication might not be the answer for the escalating problem. This literature review considers whether the use of medication is a promising approach for solving the childhood obesity problem by responding to the following questions:
1. What are the implications of childhood obesity?
2. Is medication effective at treating childhood obesity?
3. Is medication safe for children?
4. Is medication the best solution?
Understanding the limitations of medical treatments for

[1] Obesity is measured in terms of body-mass index (BMI): weight in kilograms divided by square of height in meters. An adult with a BMI 30 or higher is considered obese. In children and adolescents, obesity is defined in relation to others of the same age and gender. An adolescent with a BMI in the 95th percentile for his or her age and gender is considered obese.

Word processing programs allow you to align text and visuals on a page in four ways:

LEFT-ALIGNED   **RIGHT-ALIGNED**   **CENTERED**   **JUSTIFIED**

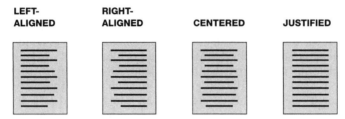

Most academic and business documents are left-aligned for easy reading.

Fonts

If you have a choice, select a font that fits your writing situation in an easy-to-read size (usually 10 to 12 points). Although off-beat fonts may seem attractive, they slow readers down and can distract them from your ideas. For example, using Comic Sans, a font with a handwritten, childish feel, can make an essay seem too informal or unpolished, regardless of how well it's written. Fonts that are easy to read and appropriate for college and work-place documents include the following: Arial, Courier, Georgia, Times New Roman, and Verdana. Check with your instructor; he or she may expect or prefer a particular font.

Font styles

Font styles—such as **boldface**, *italics*, and underlining—can be useful for calling attention to parts of a document. On the whole, it is best to use restraint when selecting styles. Applying too many different styles within a document can result in busy-looking pages and may confuse readers.

TIP: Never write a document in all capital or all lowercase letters. Doing so can frustrate or annoy readers. Although some readers have become accustomed to instant messages and e-mails that omit capital letters entirely, their absence makes a piece of writing difficult to read.

58b Use headings to guide readers.

You will have little need for headings in short essays, especially if you use paragraphing and clear topic sentences to guide readers. In more complex documents, however, such as longer essays, research papers, business reports, and Web sites, headings can be a useful visual cue for readers.

Headings help readers see at a glance the organization of a document. If more than one level of heading is used, the headings also indicate the hierarchy of ideas—as they do throughout this book.

Headings serve a number of functions, depending on the needs of different readers. When readers are simply looking up information, headings will help them find it quickly. When readers are scanning, hoping to pick up a document's meaning or message, headings will guide them. Even when readers are committed enough to read every word, headings can help them preview a document before they begin reading.

TIP: While headings can be useful, they cannot substitute for transitions between paragraphs (see 3d). Keep this in mind as you write college essays.

Phrasing headings

Headings should be as brief and as informative as possible. Certain styles of headings—the most common being *-ing* phrases, noun phrases, questions, and imperative sentences—work better for some purposes, audiences, and subjects than others.

Whatever style you choose, use it consistently. Headings on the same level of organization should be written in parallel structure (see 9), as in the following examples from a report, a history textbook, a financial brochure, and a nursing manual, respectively.

-ING PHRASES AS HEADINGS

Safeguarding the earth's atmosphere

Charting the path to sustainable energy

Conserving global forests

NOUN PHRASES AS HEADINGS

The antiwar movement

The civil rights movement

The feminist movement

QUESTIONS AS HEADINGS

How do I buy shares?

How do I redeem shares?

How has the fund performed in the past three years?

IMPERATIVE SENTENCES AS HEADINGS

Ask the patient to describe current symptoms.

Take a detailed medical history.

Record the patient's vital signs.

Placing and formatting headings

Headings on the same level of organization should be placed and formatted in a consistent way. If you have more than one level of heading, you might center your first-level headings and make them boldface; then you might make the second-level headings left-aligned and italicized, like this:

First-level heading

Second-level heading

A college paper with headings typically has only one level, and the headings are often centered, as in the sample paper on pages 674–83. Business memos often include headings. Important headings can be highlighted by using white space around them. Less important headings can be downplayed by using less white space or by running them into the text.

58c Use lists to guide readers.

Lists are easy to read or scan when they are displayed, item by item, rather than run into your text. You might choose to display the following kinds of lists:

- steps in a process
- advice or recommendations
- items to be discussed
- criteria for evaluation (as in checklists)
- parts of an object

Lists are usually introduced with an independent clause followed by a colon (*All mammals share the following five characteristics:*). Periods are not used after items in a list unless the items are complete sentences. Lists are most readable when they are presented in parallel grammatical form (see 9).

If you are describing a sequence or a set of steps, number your list with arabic numerals (1, 2, 3) followed by periods. If the order of items is not important, you can use bullets (circles or squares) or dashes to draw readers' eyes to a list.

Although lists can be useful visual cues, don't overdo them. Too many will clutter a document.

58d Add visuals to support your purpose.

Visuals can convey information concisely and powerfully. Charts, graphs, and tables, for example, can simplify complex numerical information. Images—including photographs and diagrams—often express an idea more vividly than words can. With access to the Internet, digital photography, and word processing or desktop publishing software, you can download or create your own visuals to enhance your document. Keep in mind that if you download a visual—or use published information to create your own visual—you must credit your source (see 48).

Choosing appropriate visuals

Use visuals to supplement your writing, not to substitute for it. Always consider how a visual supports your purpose and how your audience might respond to it. A student writing about electronic surveillance in the workplace, for example, used a cartoon to illustrate her point about employees' personal use of the Internet at work (see 54c). Another student, writing about treatments for childhood obesity, created a table to display data she had found in two different sources and discussed in her paper (see 56f).

As you draft and revise a document, choose carefully the visuals that support your main point, and avoid overloading your text with too many images. The chart on pages 736–37 describes eight types of visuals and their purposes.

Placing and labeling visuals

A visual may be placed in the text of a document, near a discussion to which it relates, or it can be put in an appendix, labeled, and referred to in the text.

Placing visuals in the text of a document can be tricky. Usually you will want the visual to appear close to the sentences that relate to it, but page breaks won't always allow this placement. At times you may need to insert the visual at a later point and tell readers where it can be found; sometimes you can make the text flow, or wrap, around the visual. No matter where you place a visual, refer to it in your text. Don't expect visuals to speak for themselves.

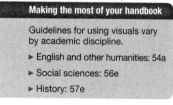

Making the most of your handbook

Guidelines for using visuals vary by academic discipline.

▶ English and other humanities: 54a

▶ Social sciences: 56e

▶ History: 57e

Most of the visuals you include in a document will require some sort of label. A label, which is typically placed above or below the visual, should be brief but descriptive. Most commonly, a visual is labeled with the word "Figure" or the abbreviation "Fig.," followed by a number: *Fig. 4*. Sometimes a title might be included to explain how the visual relates to the text: *Fig. 4. Voter turnout by age.*

Using visuals responsibly

Most word processing and spreadsheet software will allow you to produce your own visuals. If you create a chart, a table, or a graph using information from your research, you must cite the source of the information even though the visual is your own. The visual on page 735 credits the source of its data.

visuals (diagrams, charts, photos) •
labeling visuals • citing visuals   dd **58d**   **735**

Percent of American Adults Who Have Had Sleep Problems Prior to and Following September 11

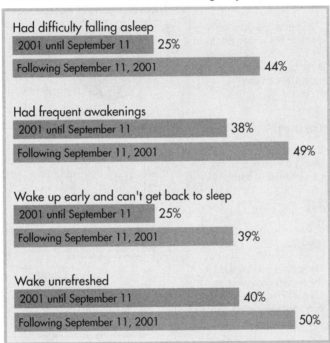

Source: Data from National Sleep Foundation, 2002 "Sleep in America" poll, March 2002.

If you download a photograph from the Web or scan an image from a magazine or book, you must credit the person or organization that created it, just as you would cite any other source you use in a college paper (see 48). Make sure any cropping or other changes you make to the visual do not distort the meaning of the original. If your document is written for publication outside the classroom, you will need to request permission to use any visual you borrow.

Choosing visuals to suit your purpose

Pie chart

Pie charts compare a part or parts to the whole. Segments of the pie represent percentages of the whole (and always total 100 percent).

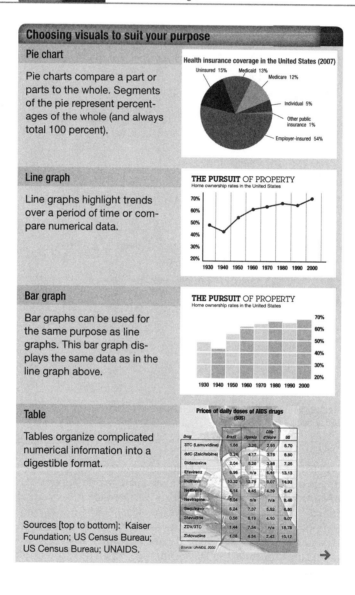

Health insurance coverage in the United States (2007)

Uninsured 15% Medicaid 13% Medicare 12% Individual 5% Other public insurance 1% Employer-insured 54%

Line graph

Line graphs highlight trends over a period of time or compare numerical data.

THE PURSUIT OF PROPERTY
Home ownership rates in the United States

Bar graph

Bar graphs can be used for the same purpose as line graphs. This bar graph displays the same data as in the line graph above.

THE PURSUIT OF PROPERTY
Home ownership rates in the United States

Table

Tables organize complicated numerical information into a digestible format.

Prices of daily doses of AIDS drugs ($US)

Drug	Brazil	Uganda	Côte d'Ivoire	US
3TC (Lamivudine)	1.56	3.28	2.95	8.70
ddC (Zalcitabine)	0.24	4.17	3.75	8.80
Didanosine	2.04	5.26	3.88	7.25
Efavirenz	6.96	n/a	6.41	13.13
Indinavir	10.32	12.79	9.07	14.93
Nelfinavir	4.14	4.45	4.39	6.47
Nevirapine	5.04	n/a	n/a	8.40
Saquinavir	6.24	7.37	5.52	8.50
Stavudine	0.56	6.19	4.10	9.07
ZDV/3TC	1.44	7.34	n/a	18.78
Zidovudine	1.08	4.34	2.43	10.12

Source: UNAIDS, 2000

Sources [top to bottom]: Kaiser Foundation; US Census Bureau; US Census Bureau; UNAIDS.

Photograph

Photographs vividly depict people, scenes, or objects discussed in a text.

Diagram

Diagrams, useful in scientific and technical writing, concisely illustrate processes, structures, or interactions.

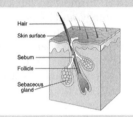

Flowchart

Flowcharts show structures or steps in a process. (See also p. 227 for another example of a flowchart.)

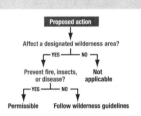

Map

Maps indicate distances, historical information, or demographics.

Sources [top to bottom]: Fred Zwicky; NIAMS; Arizona Board of Regents; Lynn Hunt et al.

59 Use standard academic formatting.

Instructors have certain expectations about how a college paper should look. If your instructor provides guidelines for formatting an essay, a report, a research paper, or another document, you should follow them. Otherwise, use the manuscript format that is recommended for your academic discipline.

In most English and other humanities classes, you will be asked to use the MLA (Modern Language Association) format (see 54a). In most social science classes, such as psychology and sociology, and in most business and health-related classes, you will be asked to use APA (American Psychological Association) format (see 56e). In history and some other humanities classes, you will be asked to use *Chicago* format (see 57e).

Most composition instructors require MLA format, which is illustrated in the sample on pages 739–40. For more detailed MLA manuscript guidelines and a sample MLA-style research paper, see 54.

60 Use standard business formatting.

This section provides guidelines for preparing business letters, résumés, and memos.

60a Use established conventions for business letters.

In writing a business letter, be direct, clear, and courteous, but do not hesitate to be firm if necessary. State your purpose or request at the beginning of the letter and include only relevant information in the body. By being as direct and concise as possible, you show that you value your reader's time.

For the format of the letter, use established business conventions. The sample business letter on page 741 is typed in what is known as *full block* style. Paragraphs are not indented and are typed single-spaced, with double-spacing between them.

format • college writing •
MLA paper format • business letters   dd **60a**   739

MLA ESSAY FORMAT

½″
1″   Orlov 1

Anna Orlov

1″   Professor Willis

English 101

17 March 2009

Online Monitoring: Title is centered.

A Threat to Employee Privacy in the Wired Workplace

½″   As the Internet has become an integral tool of businesses,

company policies on Internet usage have become as common as

policies regarding vacation days or sexual harassment. A 2005 study by

the American Management Association and ePolicy Institute found that

76% of companies monitor employees' use of the Web, and the number   1″

of companies that block employees' access to certain Web sites has

increased 27% since 2001 (1). Unlike other company rules, however,   Double-spacing is
used throughout.

Internet usage policies often include language authorizing companies

to secretly monitor their employees, a practice that raises questions

about rights in the workplace. Although companies often have

legitimate concerns that lead them to monitor employees' Internet

usage—from expensive security breaches to reduced productivity—the

benefits of electronic surveillance are outweighed by its costs to

employees' privacy and autonomy.

While surveillance of employees is not a new phenomenon,

electronic surveillance allows employers to monitor workers with

unprecedented efficiency. In his book *The Naked Employee*, Frederick

Lane describes offline ways in which employers have been permitted

to intrude on employees' privacy for decades, such as drug testing,

background checks, psychological exams, lie detector tests, and in-store

video surveillance. The difference, Lane argues, between these old

methods of data gathering and electronic surveillance involves quantity:

1″

740   **60a**   dd   Academic and business formatting

MLA ESSAY FORMAT (*continued*)

½″
Orlov 6

1″

Heading is centered.   Works Cited

Adams, Scott. *Dilbert and the Way of the Weasel*. New York: Harper,
2002. Print.

American Management Association and ePolicy Institute. "2005
½″ Electronic Monitoring and Surveillance Survey." *American
Management Association*. Amer. Management Assn., 2005. Web.
1″ 15 Feb. 2009.

"Automatically Record Everything They Do Online! Spector Pro 5.0
FAQ's." *Netbus.org*. Netbus.Org, n.d. Web. 17 Feb. 2009.

Flynn, Nancy. "Internet Policies." *ePolicy Institute*. ePolicy Inst., n.d.
Web. 15 Feb. 2009.   1″

Frauenheim, Ed. "Stop Reading This Headline and Get Back to Work."
CNET News.com. CNET Networks, 11 July 2005. Web. 17 Feb.
2009.

Gonsalves, Chris. "Wasting Away on the Web." *eWeek.com*. Ziff Davis
Enterprise Holdings, 8 Aug. 2005. Web. 16 Feb. 2009.

Kesan, Jay P. "Cyber-Working or Cyber-Shirking? A First Principles
Examination of Electronic Privacy in the Workplace." *Florida Law
Review* 54.2 (2002): 289-332. Print.

Double-spacing is   Lane, Frederick S., III. *The Naked Employee: How Technology Is
used throughout; no   Compromising Workplace Privacy*. New York: Amer. Management
extra space between   Assn., 2003. Print.
entries.

Tam, Pui-Wing, et al. "Snooping E-mail by Software Is Now a
Workplace Norm." *Wall Street Journal* 9 Mar. 2005: B1+. Print.

Tynan, Daniel. "Your Boss Is Watching." *PC World*. PC World
Communications, 6 Oct. 2004. Web. 17 Feb. 2009.

Verespej, Michael A. "Inappropriate Internet Surfing." *Industry Week*.
Penton Media, 7 Feb. 2000. Web. 16 Feb. 2009.

This style is usually preferred when the letter is typed on letterhead stationery, as in the example.

Below the signature, aligned at the left, you may include the abbreviation *Enc.* to indicate that something is enclosed with the letter or the abbreviation *cc* followed by a colon and the name of someone who is receiving a copy of the letter.

BUSINESS LETTER IN FULL BLOCK STYLE

LatinoVoice

March 16, 2009 ⟶ Date

Jonathan Ross
Managing Editor
Latino World Today
2971 East Oak Avenue
Baltimore, MD 21201 ⟶ Inside address

Dear Mr. Ross: ⟶ Salutation

Body —

Thank you very much for taking the time yesterday to speak to the University of Maryland's Latino Club. A number of students have told me that they enjoyed your presentation and found your job search suggestions to be extremely helpful.

As I mentioned to you when we first scheduled your appearance, the club publishes a monthly newsletter, *Latino Voice*. Our purpose is to share up-to-date information and expert advice with members of the university's Latino population. Considering how much students benefited from your talk, I would like to publish excerpts from it in our newsletter.

I have taken the liberty of transcribing parts of your presentation and organizing them into a question-and-answer format for our readers. When you have a moment, would you mind looking through the enclosed article and letting me know if I may have your permission to print it? I would be happy, of course, to make any changes or corrections that you request. I'm hoping to include this article in our next newsletter, so I would need your response by April 4.

Once again, Mr. Ross, thank you for sharing your experiences with us. You gave an informative and entertaining speech, and I would love to be able to share it with the students who couldn't hear it in person.

Sincerely, ⟶ Close

Jeffrey Richardson   ⟶ Signature

Jeffrey Richardson
Associate Editor

Enc.

210 Student Center University of Maryland College Park MD 20742

60b Write effective résumés and cover letters.

An effective résumé gives relevant information in a clear and concise form. You may be asked to produce a traditional résumé, a scannable résumé, or a Web résumé. The cover letter gives a prospective employer a reason to look at your résumé. The trick is to present yourself in a favorable light without including unnecessary details.

Cover letters   Always include a cover letter to introduce yourself, state the position you seek, and tell where you learned about it. The letter should also highlight past experiences that qualify you for the position and emphasize what you can do for the employer (not what the job will do for you). End the letter with a suggestion for a meeting, and tell your prospective employer when you will be available.

Traditional résumés   Traditional résumés are produced on paper, and they are screened by people, not by computers. Because screeners often face stacks of applications, they may spend very little time looking at each résumé. Therefore, you will need to make your résumé as reader-friendly as possible. Here are a few guidelines:

- Limit your résumé to one page if possible, two pages at the most. (If your résumé is longer than a page, repeat your name at the top of the second page.)
- Organize your information into clear categories—Education, Experience, and so on.
- Present the information in each category in reverse chronological order to highlight your most recent accomplishments.
- Use bulleted lists or some other simple, clear visual device to organize information.
- Use strong, active verbs to state your accomplishments. Use present-tense verbs (*manage*) for current activities and past-tense verbs (*managed*) for past activities.

TRADITIONAL RÉSUMÉ

Jeffrey Richardson

121 Knox Road, #6
College Park, MD 20740
301–555–2651
jrichardson@jrichardson.localhost

OBJECTIVE	To obtain an editorial internship with a magazine
EDUCATION	
Fall 2006–present	University of Maryland
	• BA expected in June 2010
	• Double major: English and Latin American studies
	• GPA: 3.7 (on a 4-point scale)
EXPERIENCE	
Fall 2008–present	Associate editor, *Latino Voice*, newsletter of Latino Club
	• Assign and edit feature articles
	• Coordinate community outreach
Fall 2007–present	Photo editor, *The Diamondback*, college paper
	• Shoot and organize photos for print and online publication
	• Oversee photo staff assignments; evaluate photos
Summer 2008	Intern, *The Globe,* Fairfax, Virginia
	• Wrote stories about local issues and personalities
	• Interviewed political candidates
	• Edited and proofread copy
	• Coedited "The Landscapes of Northern Virginia: A Photoessay"
Summers 2007, 2008	Tutor, Fairfax County ESL Program
	• Tutored Latino students in English as a Second Language
	• Trained new tutors
ACTIVITIES	Photographers' Workshop, Latino Club
PORTFOLIO	Available at http://jrichardson.localhost/jrportfolio.htm
REFERENCES	Available on request

Scannable résumés Scannable résumés might be submitted on paper, by e-mail, or through an online employment service. The résumés are scanned and searched electronically, and a database matches keywords in the job description with keywords in the résumés. A human screener reads the résumés selected by the database.

In general, follow these guidelines when preparing a scannable résumé:

- Include a Keywords section that lists words likely to be searched by a scanner. Use nouns (*manager*), not verbs (*manage* or *managed*).
- Use standard résumé headings (for example, Education, Experience, References).
- Avoid special characters, graphics, or font styles.
- Avoid formatting such as tabs, indents, columns, or tables.

Web résumés Posting your résumé on a Web site is an easy way to provide recent information about your goals and accomplishments. Most guidelines for traditional résumés apply to Web résumés; keep the following guidelines in mind as well.

- Make the opening screen of your Web site simple and concise. Provide links to your résumé and to any other relevant pages, such as an electronic portfolio.
- Consider providing your résumé in HTML format and as a PDF file.
- Include your name, address, phone number, and e-mail address at the top of your résumé page.
- Always list the date that you last updated the résumé.

60c Write clear and concise memos.

Usually brief and to the point, a memo reports information, makes a request, or recommends an action. The format of a memo, which varies from company to company, is designed for easy distribution, quick reading, and efficient filing.

BUSINESS MEMO

COMMONWEALTH PRESS

MEMORANDUM

February 26, 2009

To: Editorial assistants, Advertising Department
cc: Stephen Chapman
From: Helen Brown
Subject: New database software

The new database software will be installed on your computers next week. I have scheduled a training program to help you become familiar with the software and with our new procedures for data entry and retrieval.

Training program
A member of our IT staff will teach in-house workshops on how to use the new software. If you try the software before the workshop, please be prepared to discuss any problems you encounter.

We will keep the training groups small to encourage hands-on participation and to provide individual attention. The workshops will take place in the training room on the third floor from 10:00 a.m. to 2:00 p.m.

Lunch will be provided in the cafeteria.

Sign-up
Please sign up by March 1 for one of the following dates by adding your name in the department's online calendar:

- Wednesday, March 4
- Friday, March 6
- Monday, March 9

If you will not be in the office on any of those dates, please let me know by March 1.

Most memos display the date, the name of the recipient, the name of the sender, and the subject on separate lines at the top. Many companies have preprinted forms for memos, and most word processing programs have memo templates. Memos are often distributed via e-mail.

The subject line of a memo, on paper or in e-mail, should describe the topic as clearly and concisely as possible, and the introductory paragraph should get right to the point. In addition, the body of the memo should be well organized and easy to skim. To promote skimming, use headings where possible and set off any items that deserve special attention (in a list, for example, or in boldface). A sample memo appears on page 745.

60d Write effective e-mail messages.

In business and academic contexts, you will want to show readers that you value their time. Your e-mail message may be just one of many that your readers have to wade through. Here are some strategies for writing effective e-mails:

- Use a meaningful, concise subject line to help readers sort through messages and set priorities.
- Put the most important part of your message at the beginning so it will be seen without scrolling.
- For long, detailed messages, provide a summary at the beginning.
- Write concisely, and keep paragraphs fairly short.
- Avoid writing in all capital letters or all lowercase letters.
- Use an appropriate tone.
- Before forwarding an e-mail message, check that the original sender has no objections.
- Be sparing with boldface, italics, and special characters; not all e-mail systems handle such elements consistently.
- Proofread for typos and obvious errors that are likely to slow down readers.

Practicing Your Textbook Reading Skills

1. Which of the following is *not* a chapter in Part X: Document Design?

    a. 58 Become familiar with the principles of document design.

    b. 58a Select appropriate format options.

    c. 59 Use standard academic formatting.

    d. 60 Use standard business formatting.

2. Of the following statements, which offers the authors' definition of *document*?

    a. "The term *document* is broad enough to describe anything you might write in a college class, in the business world, and in every-day life."

    b. "How you design a document (format it for the printed page or for a computer screen) will affect how readers respond to it."

    c. "Become familiar with the principles of document design."

    d. "Good document design promotes readability, but what *readability* means depends on your purpose and audience."

3. Notice the shaded tabs at the top of each page in these chapters. What does the "dd" stand for?

    a. document design

    b. dramatic dialogue

    c. designing diagrams

    d. don't digress

4. Based on the running head at the top of page 733, what are the key topics covered in sections 58c and 58d?

    a. format, alignment, and fonts

    b. MLA paper format and business letters

    c. academic and business formatting

    d. headings, lists, and visuals (diagrams, charts, photos)

5. According to the example on page 739, how should the title of an MLA-style essay be formatted?

    a. It should appear on a separate page.

    b. It should be italicized.

    c. It should be centered.

    d. It should be in boldface.

6. Examine the headings and subheadings to determine which of the following is a subtopic of "Select appropriate format options."

   a. Use headings to guide readers.

   b. Left-aligned

   c. Become familiar with the principles of document design.

   d. Font styles

7. The image on page 735 illustrates

   a. job options for college graduates.

   b. crediting the source of a visual.

   c. placing and labeling visuals.

   d. downloading a document.

8. Examine the table on pages 736–37 to determine which of the following kinds of visuals would be appropriate to explain a process.

   a. pie chart

   b. bar graph

   c. flowchart

   d. map

9. According to the "Making the most of your handbook" box on page 734, where in *The Bedford Handbook* can you find guidelines for using visuals in a history paper?

   a. section 54a

   b. section 56e

   c. section 57e

   d. section 58d

10. The sample memo on page 745 is provided to

    a. illustrate how business documents are formatted.

    b. show that publishing employees don't know how to use computers.

    c. invite readers to attend software training.

    d. teach readers how to write a memo.

Testing Your Understanding

Identify the following statements as *true* or *false*.

1. Most college papers should have half-inch margins.

   T _____ F _____

2. Writing in ALL-CAPITAL letters tends to annoy readers.

   T _____   F _____

3. It is not necessary to document material found on the Internet.

   T _____   F _____

4. Visuals speak for themselves.

   T _____   F _____

5. A résumé should always be accompanied by a cover letter.

   T _____   F _____

Select the best answer to each of the following questions.

6. Of the following options, how should most business documents be aligned?

   a. left

   b. right

   c. centered

   d. justified

7. Why is it a bad idea to use decorative fonts like Comic Sans?

   a. They look weird.

   b. They distract readers.

   c. Not all computers can display them.

   d. It's not a bad idea.

8. How do headings function in a document?

   a. They clarify the organization.

   b. They show how ideas relate to each other.

   c. They help readers find information.

   d. all of the above

9. When should you use periods after items in a list?

   a. always

   b. never

   c. when they are complete sentences

   d. when they are words or phrases

10. Ideally, where in a document should a visual be placed?

    a. at the end

    b. as close as possible to the sentences that relate to it

    c. at the bottom of the page

    d. before it is mentioned

11. If you create your own table or chart from published data, do you have to cite the sources?

    a. yes

    b. no

    c. sometimes

    d. only if you copy the original

12. Which formatting style is usually used for psychology papers?

    a. MLA

    b. *Chicago*

    c. APA

    d. IEEE

13. In a business letter, what does the abbreviation *Enc.* mean?

    a. encyclopedia

    b. everybody not counted

    c. encrypted

    d. something is enclosed with the letter

14. What kind of résumé has a Keywords section?

    a. traditional

    b. scannable

    c. Web

    d. portfolio

15. E-mail messages should

    a. have an informative subject line.

    b. start with the most important point.

    c. be brief.

    d. all of the above

Using your own words, define the following terms as they are used in the chapter.

16. *design*

_____

_____

17. *pie chart*

_____

_____

18. *scannable résumé*

_____

_____

19. *memo*

_____

_____

20. *full block style*

_____

_____

Answer each of the following questions using the space provided.

21. What is the purpose of document design?

_____

_____

_____

_____

22. Summarize the basic formatting guidelines for a college essay.

_____

_____

_____

_____

23. Identify at least three categories of information typically provided in a résumé.

_____

_____

_____

_____

24. Why are most drafts and some final documents double-spaced with wide margins, and when is single-spacing appropriate?

_____

_____

_____

_____

_____

25. The authors explain that business correspondence (letters, memos, and e-mails) should brief and to the point. Why?

_____

_____

_____

_____

Making Thematic Connections

In the next unit, you'll learn about how people working in the field of public relations use writing, visuals, and other communication tools to influence public opinion about businesses and governments. Glance through the text-book chapter and look closely at the different kinds of documents pictured in it. Look, also, at how the textbook chapter itself is designed. How does the appearance of each document reflect its purpose? How have the documents' creators applied the principles of document design described in this unit?

Mass Communication

"Public Relations and Framing the Message"

Introduction

Mass communication is the study of how individuals and groups spread information, ideas, and entertainment to a wide audience. Newspapers and magazines, television and radio, movies, the Internet, and advertising and public relations are all part of the media examined by mass communication scholars. As an academic discipline, mass communication seeks not only to understand the various channels of communication available to those who want to spread a message or entertainment but also to train students in how to work in one of the mass media industries.

Media Essentials: A Brief Introduction, by Richard Campbell, Christopher R. Martin, and Bettina Fabos, is a popular introductory textbook used by thousands of college students across the United States. Because the media pervade almost every aspect of our lives and because they change at such a rapid pace, the book aims to help its readers "focus on the fundamentals of media studies so that no matter how the media evolve in the future, students can understand what's *really* going on."

Like any good introductory textbook, *Media Essentials* is carefully designed and written to teach the content it covers. It includes a number of features and tools to help you read it successfully:

- Bold-faced paragraphs at the beginning of each major section preview the material about to be discussed by highlighting the main points and key ideas.

- The chapter's opening story, images with captions, and a "Media Literacy Case Study" show examples of public relations work in action and help to keep the material interesting.

- Different levels of headings help you determine how the information is connected and what is most important.

- Tables and figures provide data and facts to back up or explain elements of the chapter's main discussion.

- Bold-faced terms identify important concepts, which are defined in the glossary.

- A bulleted list of learning objectives at the beginning of the chapter, and sections at the end called "Review," "Study Questions," and "Media Literacy Practice," help you review what you have learned, think critically about it, and (if you were taking a course in mass communication) study for a quiz or a test.

How does this mass communication chapter fit into this reader's overall theme of work? First, it explores a field that may interest you as a potential career. As you're about to learn, public relations is a growing business with many job opportunities, ranging from researching to writing to making television appearances. At the same time, the chapter looks closely at how others have worked in this field, and it examines some of the ethical and practical

---

This unit's textbook reading comes from *Media Essentials: A Brief Introduction* by Richard Campbell, Christopher R. Martin, and Bettina Fabos, Bedford/St. Martin's, 2011, Chapter 11, pages 312–37.

public issues that public relations workers face. The history of public relations that begins on page 315 of this chapter covers much of the same period (the late 1800s) that is discussed in the history chapter reprinted in Unit 4. Consider also that people who work in public relations often communicate their messages in writing, the subject of the composition chapter in Unit 2 of this book.

Preparing to Read the Textbook Chapter

1. Has your opinion of a company, a politician, or a product ever been influenced by a public relations campaign? How do you know?

2. Take a moment to scan through the chapter. Are any of the images familiar? Which ones capture your interest? Why?

3. Imagine that you work for a major clothing company. Its most recent line of children's play wear was defective—the seams fell apart on the first washing—and a competitor has been quick to emphasize the durability of its children's clothes in a recent round of ads. What would you recommend your employer do to regain your customers' confidence and their business?

Marlon Brando in *The Wild One* (1953) symbolized the delinquent in jeans.

Media Framing Industries

Public Relations and Framing the Message

315
Early History of
Public Relations

320
The Evolution of
Public Relations

329
Tensions between
Public Relations and
the Press

332
Public Relations in a
Democratic Society

In the mid-1950s, the blue jeans industry was fading. After peaking in 1953, jeans sales began shrinking. The one-hundred-year-old product had become associated with rock and roll and teenage troublemakers. In 1957, the public school system in Buffalo, New York, even banned jeans from high schools.

In response to the crisis, the denim industry waged a public relations (PR) campaign to rejuvenate denim's image. In 1956, the nation's top blue jeans manufacturers formed the Denim Council "to put schoolchildren back in blue jeans through a concerted national public relations, advertising, and promotional effort."[1] The companies soon realized that the problem lay with parents, administrators, teachers, and school boards—not teens. It was adults who felt threatened by a fashion trend that seemed to promote disrespect through casualness. In response, the council hired a PR firm to transform the image of blue jeans in adults' minds, especially in the minds of mothers.

To change negative perceptions of denim among women, the PR team encouraged fashion designers to produce new women's sportswear styles made from the fabric. Media outlets and fashion editors were soon inundated with news releases about the "new look" of durable denim. The team next enlisted sportswear designers to provide innovative designs for men's and women's work and utility clothes, long the backbone of denim sales. It also planned retail store promotions nationwide (including "jean queen" beauty contests) and published positive stories about denim in men's periodicals.

The team achieved its greatest PR coup, however, in 1961, when it associated denim with the newly formed national Peace Corps. That year, the Denim Council agreed to outfit the first group of two hundred corps volunteers in denim. Thanks to the PR push, manufacturers were flooded with orders by 1963, and sales of jeans and other denim goods took off. The delinquency connotation disappeared, and people gradually began associating jeans simply with casualness.

AS THE BLUE JEANS STORY REVEALS, an effective public relations effort involves numerous activities, including shaping the public image of a product (or a person or an organization), establishing or restoring communication between consumers and companies, and promoting particular individuals or organizations. Broadly defined, **public relations** refers to the total communication strategy conducted by a person, a government, or an organization attempting to reach an audience and persuade it to adopt a point of view.[2] Or, in the brief definition offered by the Public Relations Society of America (PRSA), "Public relations helps an organization and its publics adapt mutually to each other."

While public relations may sound very similar to advertising, which also seeks to persuade audiences, it differs in important respects. Advertising uses simple and fixed messages ("Our appliance is the most efficient and affordable") transmitted directly to the public through the purchase of ads for specific products or services. Whereas advertising focuses mainly on sales, public relations develops a marketable image for a person, an organization, a product, a service, or an issue. In doing so, public relations creates more complex messages that may evolve over time (for example, a political campaign, or a long-term strategy to dispel unfavorable reports about "fatty processed foods"). PR may be transmitted to the public indirectly, often through articles and reports in the news media. Finally, public relations messages often reflect larger trends and ideas that are percolating through society—such as the notion that it is good to recycle, or that smoking is bad for you. PR thus shapes and is shaped by what is going on in society at large.

Since its inception, PR has exerted a huge influence on American society and culture. For example, after the Industrial Revolution, when people began purchasing (rather than making) many goods they needed, manufacturers used PR to emphasize how various industries benefited consumers. By helping to drive economic activity, the public relations profession thus contributed to an improvement in standards of living in the United States. PR also set the tone for the corporate image-building that characterized the twentieth century—and for the debates over today's environmental, energy, and labor issues. However, PR's most significant impact is probably on the political process: Politicians and organizations hire PR professionals to shape their image in the media, which influences how people vote.

Today, there are more than twenty-nine hundred PR firms worldwide, including nineteen hundred in the United States. Many organizations also have in-house departments devoted to PR. Moreover, since the 1980s, the formal study of public relations has grown significantly at colleges and universities. By 2009, the Public Relations Student Society of America (PRSSA) boasted nearly ten thousand members and 284 chapters in colleges and universities.

In this chapter, we examine the workings and the impact of public relations in more detail through the following approaches:

- looking at the early days of public relations, including the emergence of press agents and the birth of modern PR

- considering how the PR profession has evolved in terms of how public relations firms are structured and what functions PR practitioners perform (such as formulating messages about their clients and conveying those messages to the public)

- exploring the tensions that have arisen between public relations professionals and the press, and the causes behind those tensions

- considering the role PR plays in our democratic society, by focusing on the impact of public relations on the political process in particular

Early History of Public Relations

Public relations traveled an interesting path in its journey toward becoming a profession. The first PR practitioners were **press agents**, people who conveyed favorable messages to the public about their clients, often by staging stunts that reporters described in newspapers. As the United States became industrialized and people began purchasing more goods and services, larger companies—impressed by press agents' power to shape public opinion—began hiring them to further their interests. Some

316   Media Framing Industries

PR tactics proved deceitful, but when journalists and citizens complained, PR agencies began policing themselves to foster more ethical practices in the profession.

Age of the Press Agent: P. T. Barnum and Buffalo Bill

The earliest press agents excelled at **publicity**—a type of PR communication that uses various media messages to spread information and interest (or "buzz") about a person, a corporation, an issue, or a policy. The most effective publicity efforts not only excited people's imagination but also helped establish enduring national values.

"Buffalo Bill's Wild West and Congress of Rough Riders of the World" show, depicted here, was internationally popular as a touring show for more than thirty years.

In the 1800s, some publicity tactics could also border on outrageous. Consider press agent Phineas Taylor (P. T.) Barnum, who used gross exaggeration, fraudulent stories, and staged events to secure newspaper coverage for his clients, for his American Museum, and (later) for his circus, which he dubbed "The Greatest Show on Earth."

William F. Cody was another notorious publicity hound. From 1883 to 1916, Cody, who once killed buffalo for the railroads, used press agents to promote himself and his traveling show: "Buffalo Bill's Wild West and Congress of Rough Riders of the World." The show employed sharpshooter Annie Oakley and Lakota holy man Sitting Bull, whose legends were partially shaped by Cody's press agents. These agents were led by John Burke, one of the first to use an array of media channels to generate publicity. Burke promoted Cody's show through a heady mix of newspaper

CHAPTER 11 // TIMELINE

1840–1880 Early Promotions through Media
Theatrical agent P. T. Barnum employs early PR tactics to promote his many acts.

1880 The Railroads
The PR practice of bribing reporters for positive news stories and deadheading reaches its height.

1914 "Poison Ivy" Lee
After opening one of the first PR firms in New York in the early 1900s, "Poison Ivy" Lee works for the wealthy Rockefeller family.

1923 Edward Bernays
Bernays teaches the first public relations course at New York University and writes the first PR textbook.

1948 PRSA
To better its standing among the public and the news media, the PR industry forms the Public Relations Society of America (PRSA) to function as an international watchdog.

stories, magazine articles and ads, dime novels, theater marquees, poster art, and early films. Burke and Buffalo Bill fired up Americans' love of rugged individualism and frontier expansion—a national mythology that later showed up in books, radio programs, and Hollywood films about the American West.

Business Adopts Press Agent Methods

The successes enjoyed by P. T. Barnum, Buffalo Bill, John Burke, and others demonstrated that publicity not only could stimulate business, it also could help any individual or organization (such as not-for-profit groups and government agencies) spread the word about its value and fulfill its mission. For businesses, press agentry became an important mechanism for generating the profits and (in some cases) bringing in the government funding needed to achieve their mission. However, in these early days of press agents, some tactics used were especially deceptive.

Around 1850, for example, the railroads began hiring press agents to help them obtain federal funds—which hinged on positive public perceptions of the railroads' value. These agents' tactics included bribing journalists to write favorable news stories about rail travel. Agents also engaged in **deadheading**—giving reporters free rail passes with the tacit understanding that they would write glowing reports about traveling by rail. Finally, larger railroads used **lobbyists**—professionals who seek to influence lawmakers' votes—to gain federal subsidies and establish policies (such as rate reductions) that made it harder for smaller regional lines to compete. Thanks to such efforts, a few large rail companies gained dominance over the industry.

Utility companies such as Chicago Edison and AT&T also used press agent strategies in the late 1800s for similar ends. Again, some of their tactics were deceptive. For instance, they, too, bought votes of key lawmakers, and they

1982 Tylenol Scare
After a criminal laces Tylenol capsules with cyanide, Johnson & Johnson responds with rapid and ethical PR crisis management, saving the Tylenol brand.

1989 *Exxon Valdez* Disaster
Exxon's initial denials of responsibility and slow response to the *Exxon Valdez* oil spill severely damage its reputation.

1996 Wal-Mart and Sweatshop Labor
Human-rights groups bring attention to sweatshop labor when they expose the production conditions of Wal-Mart's Kathie Lee Gifford clothing line.

2005 Video News Releases (VNRs)
Responding to citizen pressure, the FCC mandates that the source of a video news release (VNR) must be clearly disclosed when broadcast.

■ **318** Media Framing Industries

hired third-party editorial services to produce written pieces in their favor. For example, these services sent articles touting the utilities to newspapers, produced ghostwritten articles lauding the utilities' value, and influenced textbook authors to write historical accounts that put the utilities in a positive light.[3]

Professional Public Relations Emerges

By the early 1900s, some journalists began investigating and reporting on the questionable promotional practices businesses were using. Their efforts helped increase awareness of these tactics among the public. Facing a more informed citizenry, businesses found it harder to buy favorable press and use it to mislead people. Two PR pioneers—Ivy Ledbetter Lee and Edward Bernays—realized that public relations needed to be more professional. They ushered in new approaches that emphasized honesty, directness, and an understanding of psychology and sociology.

Ivy Ledbetter Lee: Two Sides to Every Story

Press agent Ivy Ledbetter Lee counseled his corporate clients that honesty and directness were better PR devices than the deceptive practices of the 1800s, which had given big business a bad name. Lee opened one of the first PR firms in the early 1900s with George Parker. A few years later, Lee quit the firm to work for the Pennsylvania Railroad. Following a rail accident, Penn Railroad had hired him to help downplay the resulting unfavorable publicity. Lee advised Penn Railroad to admit its mistake, vow to do better, and let newspapers in on the story—rather than trying to cover up the accident or deny responsibility.

Ivy Lee, a founding father of public relations, did innovative crisis work with John D. Rockefeller Jr., staging photo opportunities at the Ludlow mines.

Edward Bernays and his business partner and wife, Doris Fleischman, creatively influenced public opinion. Bernays worked on behalf of a client, the American Tobacco Company (who owned Lucky Strike and other brands), to make smoking socially acceptable for women.

In 1914, Lee went to work for John D. Rockefeller Jr., who by the 1880s controlled 90 percent of the nation's oil industry. Rockefeller and his Standard Oil company had image problems, especially after journalists published a powerful muckraking series about his business tactics and after his company's strikebreakers and members of the state militia battled striking coal miners trying to win recognition for their union. Fifty-three workers and their family members were killed in Ludlow, Colorado. The oil magnate hired Lee to contain the damaging publicity fallout. Lee immediately distributed a series of "fact sheets" to the press, telling the company's side of the story and discrediting the tactics of the United Mine Workers, who had organized the strike. Lee clearly recognized that there are several sides to every story, and that decisions about which facts to present to the public, and which to leave out, could strongly shape public perceptions. Lee also brought in the press and staged photo opportunities at Rockefeller's company, which helped rehabilitate the Rockefeller family's image.

Edward Bernays: Public Relations Counselor

Edward Bernays opened his own PR office in 1919. He was the first person to apply the findings of psychology and sociology to the public relations profession. Bernays described the shaping of public opinion through PR as the "engineering of consent." That is, he believed that skilled experts, leaders, and PR professionals could shape messages and ideas in ways people could rally behind.[4]

Indeed, Bernays referred to himself as a "public relations counselor" rather than a "publicity agent." Over the years, his client list included such big-name companies as the American Tobacco Company (now R. J. Reynolds Tobacco), General Electric, and General Motors. Bernays also worked for the Committee on Public Information (CPI) during World War I. In that role, he developed propaganda that supported the U.S. entry into the war and promoted the image of President Woodrow Wilson as a peacemaker.

Bernays also demonstrated that women could work in the PR profession. His business partner and later his wife, Doris Fleischman, collaborated with him on many of his campaigns as a researcher and coauthor. PR later became one of the few professions accessible to women who chose to work outside the home. Today, women outnumber men by more than three to one in the profession.

The Evolution of Public Relations

As the PR profession evolved, two major types of public relations organizations took shape: PR agencies and in-house PR services. Practitioners in this field began excelling at specific functions, such as researching target audiences and formulating messages conveyed to them.

PR Agencies and In-House PR Services

Almost two thousand U.S. companies identify themselves as public relations agencies today. Many large ones are owned by, or are affiliated with, multinational communications holding companies like WPP, Omnicom, and Interpublic. (See Figure 11.1.) Two of the largest PR agencies—Burson-Marsteller and Hill & Knowlton—generated part of the $13.59 billion in PR revenue for their parent corporation, the WPP Group, in 2009. Other PR firms are independent. These companies tend to be smaller than the conglomerate-owned ones and have just local or regional operations. New York–based Edelman, the largest independent PR agency, is an exception, boasting global operations and clients from around the world.

Many corporations, professional organizations, and nonprofit entities retain PR agencies to provide a range of services. Large organizations of all types— particularly in the manufacturing and service industries—often have their own in-house PR staffs as well. These departments handle numerous tasks, such as

FIGURE 11.1 // THE TOP SIX HOLDING FIRMS, WITH PUBLIC RELATIONS SUBSIDIARIES, 2009 (BY WORLDWIDE REVENUE IN U.S. DOLLARS)

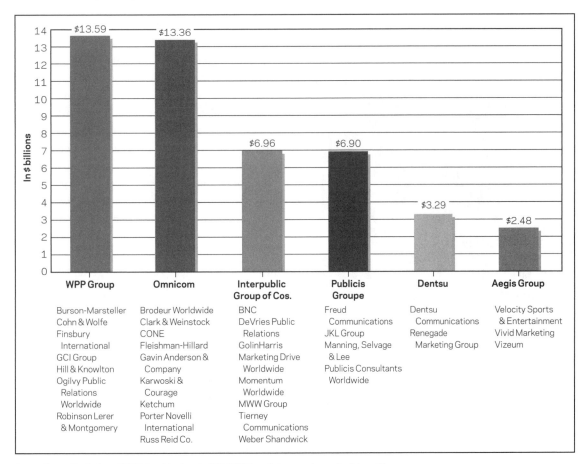

WPP Group	Omnicom	Interpublic Group of Cos.	Publicis Groupe	Dentsu	Aegis Group
Burson-Marsteller	Brodeur Worldwide	BNC	Freud Communications	Dentsu Communications	Velocity Sports & Entertainment
Cohn & Wolfe	Clark & Weinstock	DeVries Public Relations	JKL Group	Renegade Marketing Group	Vivid Marketing
Finsbury International	CONE	GolinHarris	Manning, Selvage & Lee		Vizeum
GCI Group	Fleishman-Hillard	Marketing Drive Worldwide	Publicis Consultants Worldwide		
Hill & Knowlton	Gavin Anderson & Company	Momentum Worldwide			
Ogilvy Public Relations Worldwide	Karwoski & Courage	MWW Group			
Robinson Lerer & Montgomery	Ketchum	Tierney Communications			
	Porter Novelli International	Weber Shandwick			
	Russ Reid Co.				

Source: "Agency Family Trees 2009," Advertising Age, April 27, 2009, http://adage.com/agencyfamilytrees09.
Note: Revenue represents total company income including PR agencies.

writing press releases, managing journalists' requests for interviews with company personnel, and staging special events.

A Closer Look at Public Relations Functions

Regardless of whether they work at a PR agency or on staff at an organization's in-house PR department, public relations professionals pay careful attention to the needs of their clients and to the perspectives of their targeted audiences.

322 Media Framing Industries

World War II was a time when the U.S. government used propaganda, such as Uncle Sam, and other PR strategies to drum up support for the war.

They provide a multitude of services, including developing publicity campaigns and formulating messages about what their clients are doing in areas such as government relations, community outreach, industry relations, diversity initiatives, and product or service development. Some PR professionals also craft **propaganda.** This is communication that is presented as advertising or publicity and that is intended to gain public support for a special issue, program, or policy—such as a nation's war effort. In addition, PR practitioners might produce employee newsletters, manage client trade shows and conferences, conduct historical tours, appear on news programs, organize damage control after negative publicity, or analyze complex issues and trends affecting a client's future.

Research: Formulating the Message

Like advertising, PR makes use of mail, telephone, Internet surveys, and focus groups to get a fix on an audience's perceptions of an issue, a policy, a program, or a client's image. This research also helps PR firms focus their campaign messages. For example, the Liz Claiborne Foundation has tried to combat domestic violence (specifically, teen dating abuse) by using survey results from 683 teens to develop its "Love Is Not Abuse" campaign.

Communication: Conveying the Message

Once a PR group has formulated a message, it conveys the message through a variety of channels. **Press releases**, or news releases, are announcements written in the style of news reports that provide new information about an individual, a company, or an organization. In issuing press releases, PR agents hope that journalists will pick up the information and transform it into news reports about the agents' clients.

Since the introduction of portable video equipment in the 1970s, PR agencies and departments have also been issuing **video news releases (VNRs)**—thirty- to ninety-second visual press releases designed to mimic the style of a broadcast news report. Although networks and large TV news stations do not usually broadcast VNRs, news stations in small TV markets regularly use material from these releases. As with press releases, VNRs give PR firms some control over what constitutes "news" and a chance to influence the public's opinions about an issue, a program, or a policy, although the FCC requires that the source of a VNR be disclosed if video from the VNR is broadcast in a news program.

PR firms can also bring attention to nonprofits by creating **public service announcements (PSAs)**: usually fifteen- to sixty-second audio or video reports that promote government programs, educational projects, volunteer agencies, or social reform.

The Internet has also become an essential avenue for transmitting PR messages. Public relations practitioners use the Internet to send electronic press releases and VNRs, make press kits available for downloading, post YouTube videos, and host PR-based Web sites (for instance, the official Web sites of political candidates).

Managing Media Relations

Some PR practitioners specialize in media relations. They promote a client or an organization by securing publicity or favorable coverage in the various news media. In an in-house PR department, media-relations specialists will speak on behalf of their organization or direct reporters to experts inside and outside the company who can provide information about whatever topic the reporter is writing about.

Media-relations specialists may also recommend advertising to their clients when it seems that ads would help focus a complex issue or enhance a client's image. In addition, they cultivate connections with editors, reporters, freelance writers, and broadcast news directors to ensure that their press releases or VNRs are favorably received. (See "Media Literacy Case Study: Improving the Credibility Gap" on page 324.)

Public service announcements also include print and Web components (not just TV or radio ads). The National Youth Anti-Drug Media Campaign created the Above the Influence brand to help teens resist pressure to use drugs.

MEDIA LITERACY
Case Study

Improving the Credibility Gap

In the 1990s, a growing tide of Americans focused on the problems of outsourcing: using the production, manufacturing, and labor resources of foreign companies to produce American brand-name products, sometimes under deplorable working conditions. Outsourcing was pushed into the public eye in 1996 after major media attention focused on morning talk-show host Kathie Lee Gifford when investigations by the National Labor Committee revealed that part of her clothing line, made and distributed by Wal-Mart, came from sweatshops in New York and Honduras. The sweatshops paid less than minimum wages, and some employed child laborers. Human-rights activists claimed that in overseas sweatshops in particular, children were being exploited in violation of international child-labor laws.

Many leading clothing labels and retailers continue to ignore pressure from consumer and labor groups, and still tolerate sweatshop conditions in which workers take home minimal pay. Gap Inc.—one of the world's largest clothing retailers with more than thirty-one hundred Gap, Banana Republic, Old Navy, and Forth & Towne stores (and an online shoe store)—made a huge statement in the industry by publicizing its efforts to watch over labor conditions at its overseas factories. The move was an enormous policy shift from the company's past defensiveness against allegations of worker exploitation. Gap issued its first Social Responsibility Report in 2004—the first time any company has ever publicly detailed the production and labor information of the factories with which it contracts.

The report is Gap's effort for improved transparency and better communication with its employees,

shareholders, and those concerned about garment industry operations. The company now employs a team of more than ninety people to inspect and improve working conditions in its approximately three thousand contracted garment factories in fifty countries, and continues to issue progress reports. In most cases, Gap is able to improve labor conditions, but it also cancels contracts when needed. Gap terminated seventy factory contracts in 2004, and another sixty-two in 2005. Typical violations include lack of compliance with child-labor laws, pay below minimum wage, work weeks in excess of sixty hours, psychological coercion and verbal abuse, locked or inaccessible exits, and lack of access to potable water.

Gap's social responsibility efforts also involve co-sponsorship of the global (PRODUCT) RED campaign, founded in part by rock singer Bono to raise awareness of and money for HIV/AIDS in Africa.

Gap's role includes spending millions in advertising dollars to sell (PRODUCT) RED clothing to support HIV/AIDS relief, and helping to develop a sustainable garment industry in Lesotho. The campaign also includes other consumer products manufacturers, such as Converse, Giorgio Armani, American Express, Motorola, and Apple. Social responsibility has sprung up in entire new clothing lines as well.

Edun, for example, is a collection established by Bono; his wife, Ali Hewson; and designer Rogan Gregory to create fair, sustainable microindustries in developing countries, particularly in Africa. As Hewson says, "People are reading the labels on their clothes. They're asking themselves if they want to wear something that was made out of someone else's despair."[1]

APPLYING THE CRITICAL PROCESS

DESCRIPTION Select three clothing retailers—for example, chains like Target, Macy's, Dillard's, JCPenney, J. Crew, Ann Taylor, Limited Brands, or Abercrombie & Fitch.

ANALYSIS Go to each retailer's corporate Web site, and (often under investor relations) find its social responsibility statement or guidelines. (If there is not a category like this, look for its code of ethics or business practices.) Look for the patterns—similarities and differences—among the three. Do their ethics apply to only the corporate environment of the company, or do they also consider the environmental impact and labor conditions of their suppliers in the United States and developing countries?

INTERPRETATION How comprehensive and transparent should a corporation's ethical and social responsibility guidelines be? (In other words, how broadly should a corporation define its "publics"—its employees, its customers, the local communities, the entire world—and what should the corporation promise to do?)

EVALUATION Which of the three companies has the most comprehensive and transparent corporate social/ethical policy? What made it the best of the three?

ENGAGEMENT Engage directly with the business by writing or e-mailing the one(s) you were most impressed with, and telling it why. Contact the one(s) with deficient policies, and tell it how it could improve. You can also connect with a number of other groups, such as the National Labor Committee, to learn more about corporate labor records.

Hurricane Katrina slammed into the Gulf Coast on August 29, 2005, creating the worst natural disaster in the nation's history and an unimaginable opportunity for crisis communications.

If a client company has had some negative publicity (for example, one of its products has been shown to be defective or dangerous, or a viral video on the Internet quickly spreads disinformation about the company), media-relations specialists also perform damage control or crisis management. In fact, during a crisis, these specialists might be the sole source of information about the situation for the public. How PR professionals perform this part of their job can make or break an organization. The handling of the *Exxon Valdez* oil spill and Tylenol tampering deaths in the 1980s offer two contrasting examples.

In 1989, the *Exxon Valdez* oil tanker spilled eleven million gallons of crude oil into Prince William Sound. The accident contaminated fifteen hundred miles of Alaskan coastline and killed countless birds, otters, seals, and fish. In one of the biggest PR blunders of that century, Exxon reacted to the crisis grudgingly and accepted responsibility slowly. Although the company's PR advisers had advised a quick response, Exxon failed to send any of its chief officers immediately to the site—a major gaffe. Many critics believed that Exxon was trying to duck responsibility by laying the burden of the crisis on the shoulders of the tanker's captain. Even though the company changed the name of the tanker to *Mediterranean* and implemented other strategies intended to salvage the company's image, the public continued to view Exxon in a negative light.

A decidedly different approach was taken in the 1982 tragedy involving Tylenol pain-relief capsules. Seven people in the Chicago area died after consuming capsules that someone had laced with poison. The parent company, Johnson & Johnson, and its PR representatives discussed whether to pull all Tylenol capsules from store shelves. Some participants in these discussions worried that this move might send the message that corporations could be intimidated by a single deranged person. Nevertheless, Johnson & Johnson's chairman and the company's PR agency, Burson-Marsteller, opted to fully disclose the tragedy to the media and to immediately recall all Tylenol capsules across the nation. The recall cost the company an estimated $100 million and cut its market share in half.

Burson-Marsteller tracked public opinion about the crisis and about its client nightly through telephone surveys. It also organized satellite press conferences to debrief the news media. In addition, it set up emergency phone lines to take calls from consumers and health-care providers who had questions about the crisis.

When the company reintroduced Tylenol three months later, it did so with tamper-resistant bottles that almost every major drug manufacturer soon copied. According to Burson-Marsteller, which received PRSA awards for its handling of the crisis, the public thought Johnson & Johnson had responded admirably to the situation and did not hold Tylenol responsible for the deaths. In fewer than three years, Tylenol recaptured its dominant share of the market.

Coordinating Special and Pseudo Events

Another public relations practice involves coordinating *special events* to raise the profile of corporate, organizational, or government clients. Through such events, a corporate sponsor aligns itself with a cause or an organization that has positive stature among the public. For example, John Hancock Financial has been the primary sponsor of the Boston Marathon since 1986 and provides the race's prize money.

In contrast to a special event, a **pseudo event** is any circumstance created for the sole purpose of gaining coverage in the media. Pseudo events may take the form of press conferences, TV and radio talk-show appearances, or any other staged activity aimed at drawing public attention and media coverage. Clients and sometimes paid performers participate in these events, and their success is strongly determined by how much media attention the event attracts. For example, during the 1960s, antiwar and Civil Rights activists staged protest events only if news media were assembled. Today, politicians running for national office use this strategy by scheduling press conferences and interviews around 5:00 or 6:00 P.M.—when local TV news is live. This timing enables them to take advantage of TV stations' appetite for live remote feeds and breaking news.

The intense media coverage at sports press conferences, often conducted when a team drafts a new player or signs a free agent, drums up revenue for teams as fans buy merchandise for the new player (such as the Detroit Lions' # 1 draft pick in 2009, Matthew Stafford). Can we consider this a pseudo event?

Fostering Positive Community and Consumer Relations

Another responsibility of PR practitioners is to sustain goodwill between their clients and the public. Many public relations professionals define "the public" as consisting of two distinct audiences: communities and consumers. Thus they carefully manage relations with both groups.

PR specialists let the public know that their clients or companies are valuable members of the communities in which they operate. They design

Public relations also works for nonprofits such as the Rainforest Action Network, which has worked to protect millions of acres of forests in North and South America, and has convinced companies like Home Depot and Boise Cascade to change their practices.

opportunities for their clients to demonstrate that they are good citizens. For example, they arrange for client firms to participate in community activities such as hosting plant tours and open houses, making donations to national and local charities, participating in town events like parades and festivals, and allowing employees to take part in local fund-raising drives for good causes.

PR strategists also strive to show that their clients care about their customers. For example, a PR campaign might send the message that the business has established product-safety guarantees, or that the company will answer all calls and mail from customers promptly. These efforts result in satisfied customers, which translates into repeat business and new business, as customers spread the word about their positive experiences with the organization.

Cultivating Government Relations

PR groups working for or in corporations also cultivate connections with the government agencies that have some say in how companies operate in a particular community, state, or nation. Through such connections, these groups can monitor the regulatory environment and determine new laws' potential implications for the organization's they represent. For example, a new regulation might require companies to provide more comprehensive reporting on their environmental-safety practices, which would represent an added responsibility.

Government PR specialists monitor new and existing legislation, look for opportunities to generate favorable publicity, and write press releases and direct-mail letters to inform the public about the pros and cons of new regulations. In many industries, government relations has developed into **lobbying**: the process of trying to influence lawmakers to support legislation that would serve an organization's or industry's best interests. In seeking favorable legislation, some lobbyists contact government officials on a daily basis. In Washington, D.C., alone, there are more than thirty-four thousand registered lobbyists—up from only eleven thousand lobbyists in 1995.[5]

The millions of dollars that lobbyists inject into the political process—treating lawmakers to special events and campaign contributions in return for legislation that accommodates their clients' interests—is viewed by many as unethical. Another unethical practice is **astroturf lobbying**, which consists of phony grassroots public-affairs campaigns engineered by unscrupulous public relations firms. Through this type of lobbying, PR firms deploy massive phone banks and computerized mailing lists to drum up support and create the impression that millions of citizens back their client's side of an issue—even if the number is much lower.

Just as corporations use PR to manage government relations, some governments have used PR to manage their image in the public's mind. For example, following the September 11, 2001, terrorist attacks on the United States, the Saudi Arabian government hired the PR firm Qorvis Communications to help repair its image with American citizens after it was revealed that many of the 9/11 terrorists were from Saudi Arabia.[6]

Tensions between Public Relations and the Press

The relationship between PR and the press has long been antagonistic. This tension has several sources, including the complex interdependence of the two professions as well as the press's skepticism about PR practices. Some of the press's complaints about PR have led public relations practitioners to take steps to enhance their profession's image.

Elements of Interdependence

Journalists have historically viewed themselves as independent professionals providing a public service: gathering and delivering the facts about current events to the public. Some have accused PR professionals of distorting the facts to serve their clients' interests. Yet journalists rely heavily on public relations practitioners to provide the information used in creating news reports. Many editors, for instance, admit that more than half of their story ideas each day originate from PR work such as press releases. In the face of newspaper staff cutbacks and television's growing need to cover local news events, professionals in the news media need PR story ideas more than ever. This doesn't sit comfortably with some journalists.

As another example of the two professions' interdependence, PR firms often raid news media's workforces for new talent. Because most press releases are written in the style of news reports, the PR profession has always sought skilled writers who are well connected to sources and knowledgeable about the news business. But although many reporters move into the PR profession, few public relations practitioners—especially those who started their careers as journalists—move into journalism. Why? The news media are reluctant to take them back once they have left the fold.

PR practitioners, for their part, maintain that they make reporters' jobs easier—supplying the kinds of information reporters used to gather themselves. Some members of the news media criticize their own ranks for being lazy. Others, grateful for the help, have hesitated to criticize a particular PR firm's clients— which brings up questions of journalistic ethics.

Journalists' Skepticism about PR Practices

In addition to the uncomfortable interdependence characterizing the journalism and PR professions, several specific complaints about PR from journalists have heightened the tension between the two groups. Specifically, some journalists maintain that PR professionals undermine the facts and block reporters' access to information. Others dislike the PR field's tendency to present publicity as news.

The manipulation of scientific facts by "experts" trying to promote a specific agenda is addressed in a series of books by John Stauber and Sheldon Rampton.

HOW INDUSTRY MANIPULATES SCIENCE AND GAMBLES WITH YOUR FUTURE

TRUST US, WE'RE EXPERTS!

SHELDON RAMPTON AND JOHN STAUBER

AUTHORS OF TOXIC SLUDGE IS GOOD FOR YOU!

"If you want to know how the world wags, and who's wagging it, here's your answer."—Bill Moyers

Undermining Facts and Blocking Access

Journalism's most prevalent criticism of public relations is that it counters the truths reporters seek to bring to the public by selectively choosing which facts to communicate or by delivering deceptive information. To be sure, outright deception is unethical, and the PR profession has worked to eradicate it in its own ranks. But deciding which facts to present is something that journalists do, too. After all, a reporter cannot say everything about a particular event, so he or she must choose which information to include and which to leave out. Still, some journalists believe that PR professionals—by emphasizing some facts while downplaying others—make it hard for reporters to gather accurate information to use in their own work.

Journalists have also objected that PR professionals block the press's access to business leaders, political figures, and other newsworthy people. This blocking, reporters explain, disrupts a longheld tradition in which reporters would vie for interviews with top government and business leaders. Journalists further claim that PR agents manipulate reporters in two ways: (1) by giving exclusives to reporters most likely to cast a story in a favorable light; and (2) by cutting off a reporter's access to a newsworthy figure if the reporter has written unfavorably about the PR agency's client.

Presenting Publicity as News

According to one industry observer, PR agents help companies "promote as news what otherwise would have been purchased in advertising".[7] Journalists critical of the PR profession claim that PR thus takes media space and time away from organizations and individuals who do not have the money or sophistication required to attract the public eye. These critics also complain that by presenting client information in a journalistic context, PR gains credibility for its clients that the purchase of advertising does not offer.

Some reporters have also pointed out that PR firms with the biggest, richest clients get the lion's share of media coverage for those clients. For example, a business reporter at a large metro daily sometimes receives as many as a hundred press releases a day containing information about large companies and the executives and managers who lead them. This far outnumbers the fraction of releases generated by less affluent and smaller entities, such as organized labor or grassroots organizations, and their leaders. To be sure, most newspapers have business sections, but few also have sections covering labor, worker, or employee concerns.[8]

Shaping PR's Image

Questionable PR moves in the past and journalism's hostility toward PR prompted some public relations practitioners to direct their skills toward improving their profession's image. In 1948, the PR industry formed its own professional organization, the PRSA (Public Relations Society of America). The PRSA functions as an internal watchdog group that accredits PR agents and firms, maintains a code of ethics, and probes its own practices, especially those pertaining to its influence on the news media. In addition to the PRSA, independent organizations devoted to uncovering shady or unethical public relations activities publish their findings in periodicals like *PR Week* and *PR Watch*. In particular, the Center for Media and Democracy, publisher of *PR Watch*, seeks to serve the public by discussing and investigating PR practices. Indeed, ethical issues have become a major focus of the PR profession (see Table 11.1 on page 332).

PR practitioners have also begun using different language—such as *institutional relations*, *corporate communications*, and *news and information services*—to describe what they do. Their hope is that the new language will signal a more ethically responsible industry. Public relations' best strategy, however, may be to point out the shortcomings of the journalism profession itself. Journalism organizations only occasionally examine their own practices, and journalists have their own vulnerability to manipulation by public relations. Thus, by not publicly revealing PR's strategies to influence their news stories, many journalists have allowed PR professionals to interpret "facts" to their clients' advantage.

■ **332** Media Framing Industries

TABLE 11.1 // PUBLIC RELATIONS SOCIETY OF AMERICA ETHICS CODE

In 2000, the PRSA approved a completely revised Code of Ethics, which included core principles, guidelines, and examples of improper conduct. Here is one section of the code.

PRSA Member Statement of Professional Values

This statement presents the core values of PRSA members and, more broadly, of the public relations profession. These values provide the foundation for the Member Code of Ethics and set the industry standard for the professional practice of public relations. These values are the fundamental beliefs that guide our behaviors and decision making process. We believe our professional values are vital to the integrity of the profession as a whole.

Advocacy

We serve the public interest by acting as responsible advocates for those we represent. We provide a voice in the marketplace of ideas, facts, and viewpoints to aid informed public debate.

Honesty

We adhere to the highest standards of accuracy and truth in advancing the interests of those we represent and in communicating with the public.

Expertise

We acquire and responsibly use specialized knowledge and experience. We advance the profession through continued professional development, research, and education. We build mutual understanding, credibility, and relationships among a wide array of institutions and audiences.

Independence

We provide objective counsel to those we represent. We are accountable for our actions.

Loyalty

We are faithful to those we represent, while honoring our obligation to serve the public interest.

Fairness

We deal fairly with clients, employers, competitors, peers, vendors, the media and the general public. We respect all opinions and support the right of free expression.

Source: The full text of the PRSA Code of Ethics is available at http://www.prsa.org.

Public Relations in a Democratic Society

PR's most significant impact on our democracy may be its involvement in the political process, especially when organizations hire public relations specialists to favorably shape or reshape a candidate's image. Consider PR's role in national election campaigns. During these immense efforts, all candidates have an extensive PR and strategy staff. Sometimes things go well; other times, they don't. For example, in the 2008 presidential contest, Democratic nominee Barack Obama's team was headed by David Axelrod, founder of Chicago-based political and media consulting firm AKPD Message and Media, who smoothly guided Obama to the White House. By contrast, Republican nominee John McCain and his running mate Sarah Palin went through numerous campaign and PR strategists in their more tumultuous bid for the Oval Office.

David Axelrod was the chief strategist for Obama's 2008 campaign and was later appointed the president's senior adviser.

The year 2008 presented additional evidence that mixing PR and politics can result in ethical conflicts. To illustrate, Mark Penn, the chief strategist of Hillary Clinton's campaign to be the Democratic nominee, became a news story himself when he resigned from her campaign over a conflict of interest. (Penn worked for Clinton while maintaining his position as chief executive of PR agency Burson-Marsteller, where he lobbied on behalf of Colombia for a trade treaty that Clinton opposed.) In addition, Scott McClellan, President George W. Bush's press secretary from 2003 to 2006, disclosed in his 2008 book that the White House had a "carefully orchestrated campaign to shape and manipulate sources of public approval" and decided to "turn away from honesty and candor" before and during the Iraq War.[9]

Despite some of PR's ethical missteps, PR professionals have begun policing their own ranks, looking to identify and root out unethical or irresponsible practices. But the news media can play a part as well—by monitoring the public relations industry just as they do other government and business activities. The journalism profession itself must also institute changes to become less dependent on PR for news content and more conscious of how its own practices play into the hands of PR strategists. As a positive example of change on this front, many major newspapers and TV networks now offer regular assessments of the facts and falsehoods contained in political advertising.

Finally, the fact that the most affluent people and corporations can afford the most media exposure through PR raises questions about whether this restricts the expression of ideas from other less-affluent sources. If so, our democracy is being harmed—because in a true democracy, everyone should have a voice. One question we must ask is: How can we ensure that other voices—those less well financed and less commercial—also receive an adequate hearing in our society? Only by hearing all voices (not just those of the powerful and wealthy) can Americans make informed decisions about whom to vote for, which laws to support, and other choices that affect the quality of our lives. To that end, journalists need to become less willing conduits in the distribution of publicity. And PR agencies, for their part, must help their clients see that participating as responsible citizens in the democratic process can serve their clients' interests in the short term and enhance their clients' image in the public's mind for years to come.

CHAPTER ESSENTIALS

Now that you have finished reading this chapter, you can use the following tools:

REVIEW

Understand the Early History of Public Relations

- **Public relations** refers to the total communication strategy conducted by a person, a government, or an organization attempting to reach and persuade its audience to adopt a point of view. The first PR practitioners in the 1800s were **press agents**, such as P . T. Barnum and John Burke, who conveyed favorable messages to the public about their clients, often by staging stunts that reporters described in newspapers. These agents focused on **publicity**, using various media messages to spread information and interest about a person, a corporation, an issue, or a policy (pp. 315–317).

- As the United States became more industrialized and moved toward a consumer society, larger companies, such as railroads and utility organizations like AT&T, began hiring press agents to generate profits and spread the word on whatever they were promoting.

However, in these early days of press agents, some tactics used were deceptive. Agents bribed journalists to write favorable stories and engaged in **deadheading**, or giving reporters free rail passes. Larger railroads and utility companies used **lobbyists**, professionals who seek to influence lawmakers' votes, to gain federal subsidies and establish policies (pp. 317–318).

- By the early 1900s journalists began investigating some of the questionable PR practices being used, precipitating the professionalization of public relations. This professionalization effort was spearheaded by two pioneers of PR, Ivy Ledbetter Lee and Edward Bernays. Lee counseled his clients that honesty and directness were better PR devices and later worked with John D. Rockefeller. Bernays was the first to apply the findings of psychology and sociology to the PR profession (pp. 318–320).

Track the Evolution of Public Relations

- As the PR profession grew, two major types of public relations organizations took shape:

PR agencies and in-house PR services (pp. 320–321).

- Many large PR agencies are owned or affiliated with multinational holding companies like WPP, Omnicom, and Interpublic. Other firms are independent and have local or regional operations, such as Edelman (pp. 320–321).

- Both PR agencies and in-house services have many functions. They sometimes craft **propaganda**, or communication that is presented as advertising or publicity intended to gain public support (p. 322).

- In addition, PR professionals research or formulate the message for a given product, policy, program, or issue. They are responsible for conveying the message, often via **press releases** (news releases), **video news releases (VNRs)**, or **public service announcements (PSAs)**, which are press releases for nonprofits (pp. 322–323).

- Some PR practitioners manage media relations. This includes responding to negative images or crisis situations (pp. 323, 326–327).

- PR agents may also coordinate special and **pseudo events** (staged activities aimed at drawing public attention and media coverage) in an effort to raise the profile of a corporate, organizational, or business client (p. 327).

- PR practitioners foster positive community and consumer relations and cultivate government relations, which is sometimes accomplished via **lobbying** (the process of trying to influence lawmakers to support legislation that would serve an organization or industry's best interest). **Astroturf lobbying** is a kind of lobbying that consists of phony grassroots public-affairs campaigns engineered by unscrupulous PR firms (pp. 327–329).

Discuss the Tensions between Public Relations and the Press

- The tense relationship between PR and the press consists of a complex interdependence of the two professions as well as journalists' skepticism about some PR practices (pp. 329–331).

- PR practitioners maintain they make journalists' jobs easier by supplying information, while journalists argue that PR agents selectively choose which facts to bring forward (pp. 329–331).

- Some of the complaints from the press about PR have led some public relations practitioners to take steps to improve the profession's image. The industry formed its own professional organization (the Public Relations Society of America) in 1948, which functions as a watchdog group. PR practitioners have also begun using different language to describe what they do (pp. 331–332).

335

Explain the Role of Public Relations in Our Democratic Society

---

- PR's impact on the political process is significant as many organizations hire public relations specialists to shape or reshape a candidate's image (pp. 332–333).

- The fact that most affluent people and corporations can afford the most media exposure through PR raises questions about whether this restricts the expression of ideas from other, less-affluent sources (p. 333).

STUDY QUESTIONS

1. Who were the individuals who conducted the earliest type of public relations in the nineteenth century? How did they contribute to the development of modern public relations in the twentieth century?
2. What are the two organizational structures for a PR firm? What are some of the ways these structures conduct business for their clients?
3. Explain the antagonism between journalism and public relations. Can and should the often hostile relationship between the two be mended? Why or why not?
4. In what ways does the profession of public relations serve the process of election campaigns? In what ways can it impede election campaigns?

MEDIA LITERACY PRACTICE

As noted earlier, public relations and journalism are extremely interdependent. To investigate this relationship, examine the public relations practices of an organization that interests you.

DESCRIBE the list of the most recent ten or twelve press releases from a local/regional business or organization large enough to have its own PR department (your own college or university might be a worthy subject).

ANALYZE the resulting patterns: How many of the releases resulted in stories in the local city or university newspaper? (Alternatively, you could use another local news organization.) Were the releases published in the newspaper verbatim, or were the stories just loosely based on the press releases?

INTERPRET what these patterns mean. For example, do press releases from this organization make an impact in the local news? Do you think the size of the newspaper and its staff makes a difference in how press releases are handled?

EVALUATE the relationship between public relations and journalism in your community. Based on this case study, is the level of the newspaper's reliance on public relations a good thing or bad thing for the people in your community? Are the press releases promoting a healthy dialogue in the community or trying to publicize something not worthy of the news?

ENGAGE with the community by writing to the newspaper's editor and letting her or him know about your case study and conclusions.

For review quizzes, links to media-related Web sites, and more, go to **bedfordstmartins.com/mediaessentials**.

Notes

11 Public Relations and Framing the Message

1. Matthew J. Culligan and Dolph Greene, *Getting Back to the Basics of Public Relations and Publicity* (New York: Crown Publishers, 1982), 90.
2. Ibid., 100.
3. Marvin N. Olasky, "The Development of Corporate Public Relations, 1850–1930," *Journalism Monographs*, no. 102 (April 1987): 15.
4. Michael Schudson, *Discovering the News: A Social History of American Newspapers* (New York: Basic Books, 1978), 136.
5. Fareed Zakaria, ABC News, *This Week*, November 19, 2006.
6. Philip Shenon, "3 Partners Quit Firm Handling Saudis' P.R.," *The New York Times*, December 6, 2002, http://www.nytimes.com/2002/12/06/international/middleeast/06S AUD.html?ex=1040199544&ei=1&en=c061b2d98376e7ba.
7. Schudson, *Discovering the News*, 136.
8. See Jonathan Tasini, "Lost in the Margins: Labor and the Media," *Extra!* (Summer 1992): 2–11.
9. Elisabeth Bumiller, "In Ex-Spokesman's Book, Harsh Words for Bush," *The New York Times*, May 28, 2008, http://www.nytimes.com/2008/05/28/washington/28mcclellan.html.

MEDIA LITERACY CASE STUDY: Improving the Credibility Gap, p. 324
1. Nia Elizabeth Shepherd et al., "Who's Who: The Eco-Guide," *Time*, April 20, 2006, http://www.time.com/time/magazine/article/0,9171,1185518,00.html.

Practicing Your Textbook Reading Skills

1. According to the chapter-opening story, popular attitudes toward denim changed in the 1950s and 1960s because of

   a. popular movies.

   b. public schools.

   c. the Peace Corps.

   d. a public relations campaign.

2. Notice the timeline that runs across the bottom of pages 316 and 317. How does this figure relate to the text?

   a. It provides new information not included in the chapter discussion.

   b. It highlights the most important point of the text.

   c. It summarizes the major events discussed in the text and puts them in chronological order.

   d. There is no relationship between the timeline and the text.

3. The advertisement and caption on page 319 are provided to

   a. illustrate how public relations campaigns fail.

   b. show an example of the work of Edward Bernays.

   c. prove that Edward Bernays was an unprincipled hypocrite.

   d. demonstrate how easily fooled consumers are.

4. Which sentence in the following paragraph (from pages 317–18) expresses the paragraph's main point?

   (1) Utility companies such as Chicago Edison and AT&T also used press agent strategies in the late 1800s for similar ends. (2) Again, some of their tactics were deceptive. (3) For instance, they, too, bought votes of key lawmakers, and they hired third-party editorial services to produce written pieces in their favor. (4) For example, these services sent articles touting the utilities to the newspapers, produced ghostwritten articles lauding the utilities' value, and influenced textbook authors to write historical accounts that put the utilities in a positive light.

   a. Sentence 1

   b. Sentence 2

   c. Sentence 3

   d. Sentence 4

5. What is the relationship between the following two sentences from page 329? "Some [journalists] have accused PR professionals of distorting the facts to serve their clients' interests. Yet journalists rely heavily on public relations practitioners to provide the information used in creating news reports."

a. The second sentence shows a contrast to the idea of the first sentence.

b. The second sentence provides an example of the point made in the first sentence.

c. The first sentence introduces the second sentence.

d. The first sentence clarifies the second sentence.

6. According to Table 11.1, on page 321, approximately how much money did the world's biggest PR firm make in 2009?

a. $13.59

b. $13.5 million

c. $13.5 billion

d. none of the above

7. The purpose of the "Case Study" on pages 324–25 is to

a. make Gap Inc. look good.

b. criticize the practice of outsourcing.

c. explain the concept of *social responsibility* in public relations.

d. provide a reading break.

8. The photograph on page 327 provides a real-world illustration of the ideas in which titled section of the chapter?

a. Managing Media Relations

b. Coordinating Special and Pseudo Events

c. Fostering Positive Community and Consumer Relations

d. Tensions Between Public Relations and the Press

9. Which of the shaded sections in the chapter would best help you prepare for a quiz or an exam on the subject of public relations?

a. Review

b. Timeline

c. Media Literacy Case Study

d. Media Literacy Practice

10. Where can you take practice quizzes to test your understanding of the chapter?

a. page 336

b. in the back of the book

c. bedfordstmartins.com/mediaessentials

d. no such quizzes exist

Testing Your Understanding

Identify the following statements as *true* or *false*.

1. Public relations has little social or cultural impact in the United States.

    T _____ F _____

2. Buffalo Bill hired press agents to help shape the legends of Annie Oakley and Sitting Bull.

    T _____ F _____

3. More women work in public relations than men do.

    T _____ F _____

4. Video press releases are sometimes aired as television news.

    T _____ F _____

5. Public relations experts influence the results of presidential elections.

    T _____ F _____

Select the best answer to each of the following questions.

6. Which of the following statements applies to public relations?

    a. It is controlled publicity that a company or an individual buys.

    b. It attempts to secure favorable media publicity to promote a company or client.

    c. Clients buy space or time for their products or services.

    d. Consumers know who paid for the messages.

7. Who among the following was *not* an early influence on the practice of public relations?

    a. P. T. Barnum

    b. Buffalo Bill

    c. John Burke

    d. Marlon Brando

8. What behavior did PR agent "Poison Ivy" Lee recommend to the Pennsylvania Railroad after a rail accident?

    a. Downplay the story and try to cover it up.

    b. Avoid talking to the press.

    c. Admit its mistake to reporters.

    d. Deny responsibility.

9. Which of the following definitions of *public relations* was written by the Public Relations Society of America?

   a. "Broadly defined, public relations refers to the entire range of efforts by an individual, an agency, or any organization attempting to reach or persuade audiences."

   b. "Public relations is the attempt, by information, persuasion, and adjustment, to engineer public support for an activity, cause, movement, or institution."

   c. "Public relations helps an organization and its publics adapt mutually to each other."

   d. "Public relations expands the public discourse, helps provide a wide assortment of news, and is essential in explaining the pluralism of our total communication system."

10. Which of the following offers an example of an unsuccessful public relations effort?

   a. the *Exxon Valdez* oil tanker spill

   b. the Tylenol recall

   c. (PRODUCT) RED

   d. blue jeans sales

11. All except which of the following jobs are available to public relations personnel?

   a. conducting historical tours

   b. purchasing advertising space and time

   c. appearing on news programs

   d. coordinating special events

12. Of the following types of communication issued by public relations professionals, which might result in news coverage?

   a. press releases

   b. video news releases

   c. YouTube videos

   d. all of the above

13. Which of the following practices is unethical?

   a. astroturf lobbying

   b. distributing propaganda

   c. writing press releases

   d. coordinating special events

14. For companies, what is one of the benefits of community and consumer relations?

    a. It provides a source of potential new employees.

    b. It provides a source of potential new customers.

    c. It helps companies get around federal safety regulations.

    d. It offers inexpensive employee training.

15. The first American company to disclose information about its labor and manufacturing practices overseas was

    a. Standard Oil.

    b. Gap Inc.

    c. Burson-Marsteller.

    d. Wal-Mart.

Using your own words, define the following terms as they are used in the chapter.

16. *publicity*

    _____

    _____

17. *pseudo event*

    _____

    _____

18. *propaganda*

    _____

    _____

19. *lobbying*

    _____

    _____

20. *astroturf lobbying*

    _____

    _____

Answer each of the following questions using the space provided.

21. Explain how the major American railroads convinced the U.S. government to subsidize their business in the nineteenth century.

_____

_____

_____

_____

_____

_____

_____

_____

_____

_____

22. List three PR practices of late-nineteenth-century utilities that contributed to the bad reputation of public relations as a profession.

_____

_____

_____

_____

23. According to the text, why do politicians tend to schedule press conferences and interviews between five and six o'clock in the evening?

_____

_____

_____

_____

24. Identify and describe the two primary sources of public relations jobs.

_____

_____

_____

_____

25. Why is there tension between public relations and journalism?

_____

_____

_____

_____

_____

_____

_____

_____

Making Thematic Connections

As environmental concerns mount, many companies are hiring public relations firms to "green" their image—that is, to reassure policy makers and consumers that their corporate practices help, rather than hurt, the planet. In this chapter you read about the failed public relations response to an environmental disaster: the *Exxon Valdez* oil spill of 1989. In the final unit of this book, you'll learn how environmental groups have pressured some companies and city governments to change their practices for the good of the environment (see pages 261–62 and 278 of *Environmental Science* in Unit 6). How do examples like these help to explain why businesses and organizations want to appear environmentally friendly? Do you think it's ethical for them to use public relations to achieve that goal? Why or why not?

History

"The Growth of America's Cities, 1870–1900"

Introduction

History is more than a collection of facts about the past. Although names and dates are important, the historian's primary job is to make connections among events and interpret what happened. In many ways, the study of history is detective work. And because interpretation and analysis are central to the field, historians often disagree. New pieces of information—even new questions—lead scholars to revise their ideas. As a result, reading history demands critical and active reading. Historians report their findings and express their opinions; as with any opinion, what they write is open to debate. Both historians and the people who read their work, then, must observe details, make connections and inferences, and draw conclusions.

Understanding the American Promise: A Brief History, by James L. Roark, Michael P. Johnson, Patricia Cline Cohen, Sarah Stage, Alan Lawson, and Susan M. Hartmann, is a survey of United States history. It outlines for students the major events and actors of America's past. At the same time, it devotes a lot of attention to the lives of everyday people to show "what's exciting and even fun about history." As you read the following chapter about the rise of city living at the end of the nineteenth century, be aware that the stories of individual people are provided as examples: Nobody expects you to memorize the name of every person mentioned in the chapter.

The authors all teach introductory history courses, so they were careful to provide features and tools to help new students like you understand the subject:

- To help you focus on what's important, they provide a list of historical questions at the front of the chapter. Those same questions appear in the "Chapter Locator" that runs across the bottom of each page to remind you where in the chapter's discussion you are.

- Chronologies and definitions in the margins call out key dates and terms to help you better understand the major points of the chapter.

- Images, tables, and maps are accompanied by captions designed to help you interpret visual information.

- Review questions that close out each major section encourage you to make sense of what you've just read before you move to the next topic.

- A three-step "Study Guide" at the end of the chapter shows you how to review key terms, think critically about history, and understand the big picture.

The chapter you're about to read, "The Growth of America's Cities, 1870–1900," puts today's work issues into historical perspective. The business developments discussed under "White-Collar Workers: Managers, 'Typewriters,' and Salesclerks" apply directly to the history of public relations you read about in Unit 3. Many of those workers had to write for their jobs, a topic covered in the handbook excerpted in Unit 2. Think, also, about the

This unit's textbook reading comes from *Understanding the American Promise: A Brief History*, by James L. Roark, Michael P. Johnson, Patricia Cline Cohen, Sarah Stage, Alan Lawson, and Susan M. Hartmann, Bedford/St. Martin's, 2011, Chapter 19, pages 508–35.

psychological concerns regarding stress and how changes in the American workforce more than a century ago illustrate the coping mechanisms discussed in Unit 5.

Preparing to Read the Textbook Chapter

1. Are working conditions today better or worse than they were a century ago? Explain your answer.

2. Throughout the chapter, you'll find photographs and illustrations of everyday objects, such as baseball gloves, and everyday people, such as visitors to Coney Island. How do these images confirm or contradict your ideas about history as an academic subject?

3. In recent years, resident assistants and teaching assistants on many college campuses have joined unions to protect themselves from what they argue are unfair employment practices. Are their complaints legitimate? Can organizing help them improve their working conditions?

19
THE GROWTH OF AMERICA'S CITIES

1870–1900

> This chapter explores the rise of urban, industrial America. It examines urban growth and its consequences, focusing on the nature of industrial labor, tensions between workers and employers, the impact of urbanization on daily life, and the cities' efforts to respond to the demands of their fast-growing populations.

> Why did American cities grow so fast in the late nineteenth century?

> What kinds of work did people do in industrial America?

> What steps did workers take to organize in the 1870s and 1880s?

> How did industrialization transform home life and leisure?

> How did cities respond to the challenges of growth?

> Conclusion: Who built the cities?

DID YOU KNOW?

More than 40 percent of Americans have ancestors who came through Ellis Island.

Brooklyn Bridge. Completed in 1883, the Brooklyn Bridge realized John Roebling's dream of creating "a great work of art" as well as a superbly engineered bridge.

509

Why did American cities grow so fast in the late nineteenth century?

Russian Immigrant Family   A Russian immigrant family is shown leaving Ellis Island in 1900. Notice the white slips of paper pinned to their coats indicating that they have been processed. An immigration official in uniform stands on the left. The original wooden structure burned down and was replaced with an elaborate stone building the year this photo was taken.
Keystone-Mast Collection, UCR/California Museum of Photography, University of California, Riverside.

"**WE CANNOT ALL LIVE IN CITIES,** yet nearly all seem determined to do so," New York editor Horace Greeley complained. The last three decades of the nineteenth century witnessed an urban explosion. Cities and towns grew more than twice as rapidly as the total population. Most of the nation's largest cities were east of the Mississippi, although St. Louis and San Francisco both ranked among the top ten urban areas in 1900. Patterns of global migration contributed to the surge in urban population. In the port cities of the East Coast, more than fourteen million people arrived, many from southern and eastern Europe.

The Urban Explosion, a Global Migration

Between 1870 and 1900, eleven million people moved into cities. Industrial centers such as Pittsburgh, Chicago, New York, and Cleveland acted as giant magnets, attracting workers from the countryside. But migrants to the cities were by no means only rural Americans. Worldwide in scope, the movement from rural areas to urban industrial centers attracted millions of immigrants to American shores.

By the 1870s, the world could be conceptualized as three interconnected geographic regions (**Map 19.1**). At the center stood an industrial core that included parts of North America and Europe. This core was surrounded by a vast agricultural domain. Capitalist development in the late nineteenth century shattered traditional patterns of economic activity in this rural periphery. As old patterns broke down, these rural areas exported, along with other raw materials, new recruits for the industrial labor force.

CHAPTER LOCATOR │ Why did American cities grow so fast in the late nineteenth century?

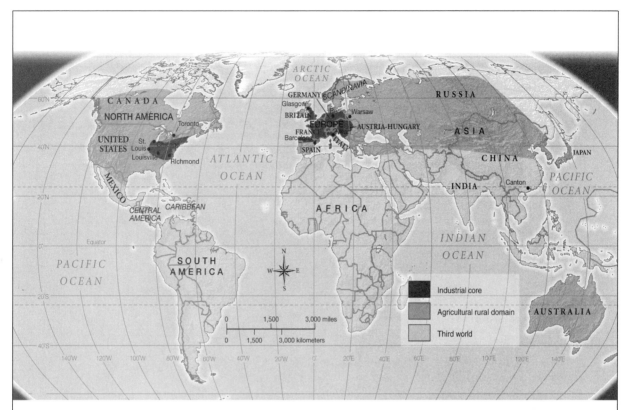

MAP 19.1 ▪ Economic Regions of the World, 1890s
The global nature of the world economy at the turn of the twentieth century is indicated by three interconnected geographic regions. At the center stands the industrial core—western Europe and the northeastern United States. The second region—the agricultural periphery—supplied immigrant laborers to the industries in the core. Beyond these two regions lay a vast area tied economically to the industrial core by colonialism.

Beyond this second circle lay an even larger third world. Ties between this part of the world and the industrial core strengthened in the late nineteenth century, but most of the people living there stayed put. They worked on plantations and railroads, in mines and ports, as part of a huge export network managed by foreign powers that staked out spheres of influence and colonies.

In the 1870s, railroad expansion and low steamship fares gave the world's peoples a newfound mobility that enabled industrialists to draw on a global population for cheap labor. When Andrew Carnegie opened his first steel mill in 1872, his superintendent hired workers he called "buckwheats"—young American boys just off the farm. By the 1890s, however, Carnegie's workforce included rural Hungarians and Slavs who had migrated to the United States, willing to work for low wages.

Altogether, more than 25 million immigrants came to the United States between 1850 and 1920 (**Map 19.2**, page 512). Part of a worldwide migration, immigrants traveled to South America and Australia as well as to the United States. Yet more than 70 percent of all European immigrants chose North America as their destination. (See "Global Comparison," page 513.)

At first, the largest number of immigrants to the United States came from the British Isles and from German-speaking lands. The vast majority of immigrants were white; Asians accounted for fewer than one million immigrants, and other people of color numbered even fewer. Yet ingrained racial prejudices increasingly influenced the country's perception of immigration patterns. One of the classic formulations of the history of European immigration divided immigrants into two distinct waves that have been called the "old" and the "new" immigration. According to this theory, before 1880 the majority of immigrants came from northern and western Europe. After 1880, the pattern shifted, with more and more

| What kinds of work did people do in industrial America? | What steps did workers take to organize in the 1870s and 1880s? | How did industrialization transform home life and leisure? | How did cities respond to the challenges of growth? | Conclusion: Who built the cities? |

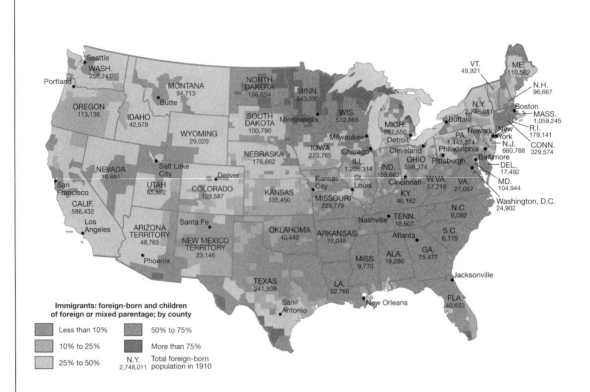

Immigrants: foreign-born and children of foreign or mixed parentage; by county

Less than 10%

10% to 25%

25% to 50%

50% to 75%

More than 75%

N.Y.
2,748,011   Total foreign-born population in 1910

MAP 19.2 ■ The Impact of Immigration, to 1910

Immigration flowed in all directions—south from Canada, north from Mexico and Latin America, east from Asia to Seattle and San Francisco, and west from Europe to East Coast port cities, including Boston and New York.

▶ FOR MORE HELP ANALYZING THIS MAP, see the map activity for this chapter in the Online Study Guide at bedfordstmartins.com/roarkunderstanding.

ships carrying passengers from southern and eastern Europe. Implicit in the distinction was an invidious comparison between "old" pioneer settlers and "new" unskilled proletarians. Yet this sweeping generalization spoke more to perception than to reality. In fact, many of the earlier immigrants from Ireland, Germany, and Scandinavia came not as settlers or farmers, but as wage laborers, much like the Italians and Slavs who followed them.

The "new" immigration resulted from a number of factors. Improved economic conditions in western Europe coupled with increased immigration to Australia and Canada slowed the flow of immigrants coming into the United States from northern and western Europe. At the same time, economic depression in southern Italy, the persecution of Jews in eastern Europe, and a general desire to avoid conscription into the Russian army led many people from southern and eastern Europe to move to the United States. The need of America's industries for cheap, unskilled labor during prosperous years also stimulated immigration.

Steamship companies courted immigrants with low fares. By the 1880s, the price of a ticket from Liverpool had dropped to less than $25. Would-be immigrants eager for information about the United States relied on letters from friends and relatives, advertisements, and word of mouth—sources that were not always dependable or truthful. No wonder people left for the United States believing, as one Italian immigrant observed, "that if they were ever fortunate enough to reach America, they would fall into a pile of manure and get up brushing the diamonds out of their hair."

CHAPTER LOCATOR | Why did American cities grow so fast in the late nineteenth century?

GLOBAL COMPARISON

European Emigration, 1870–1890

A comparison of European emigrants and their destinations between 1870 and 1890 shows that emigrants from Germany and the British Isles (including England, Ireland, Scotland, and Wales) formed the largest group of out-migrants. The United States, which took in 63 percent of these emigrants, was by far the most popular destination. After 1890, the origin of European emigrants would tilt south and east, with Italians and eastern Europeans growing in number. Argentina proved a particularly popular destination for Italian emigrants, who found the climate and geography to their liking. What factors might account for why Europeans immigrated to the port cities of the eastern United States rather than to South America or Australia?

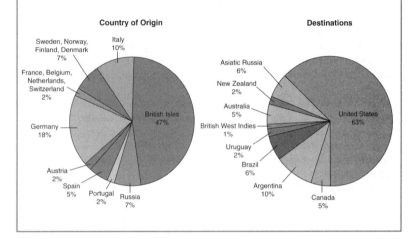

Country of Origin

- Sweden, Norway, Finland, Denmark 7%
- Italy 10%
- France, Belgium, Netherlands, Switzerland 2%
- Germany 18%
- British Isles 47%
- Austria 2%
- Spain 5%
- Portugal 2%
- Russia 7%

Destinations

- Asiatic Russia 6%
- New Zealand 2%
- Australia 5%
- British West Indies 1%
- Uruguay 2%
- Brazil 6%
- Argentina 10%
- United States 63%
- Canada 5%

Most of the newcomers stayed in the nation's cities. By 1900, almost two-thirds of the country's immigrant population resided in cities, many of the immigrants being too poor to move on. Although the foreign-born population rarely outnumbered the native-born population, taken together immigrants and their American-born children did constitute a majority, particularly in the nation's largest cities: Philadelphia, 55 percent; Boston, 66 percent; Chicago, 75 percent; and New York City, an amazing 80 percent in 1900.

Not all the newcomers came to stay. Perhaps eight million European immigrants—most of them young men—worked for a year or a season and then returned to their homelands. Immigration officers called these immigrants, many of them Italians, "birds of passage" because they followed a regular pattern of migration to and from the United States. By 1900, almost 75 percent of the new immigrants were young, single men. Women generally had less access to funds for travel and faced tighter family control. For these reasons, women most often came to the United States as wives, mothers, or daughters, not as single wage laborers. Only among the Irish did women immigrants outnumber men by a small margin.

Jews from eastern Europe most often came with their families and came to stay. Beginning in the 1880s, a wave of violent pogroms, or persecutions, in Russia and Poland prompted the departure of more than a million Jews in the next two decades. Most of the Jewish immigrants settled in the port cities of the East, creating distinct ethnic enclaves.

What kinds of work did people do in industrial America?	What steps did workers take to organize in the 1870s and 1880s?	How did industrialization transform home life and leisure?	How did cities respond to the challenges of growth?	Conclusion: Who built the cities?

CHRONOLOGY

1880s
- Immigration from southern and eastern Europe rises.

1890
- Jacob Riis publishes *How the Other Half Lives*, documenting in photographs the lives of tenement dwellers.

1890s
- African American migration from the South begins.

1892
- Ellis Island, a facility for processing new immigrants arriving in New York City, opens.

1896
- President Grover Cleveland vetoes immigrant literacy test.

Racism and the Cry for Immigration Restriction

Ethnic diversity and racism played a role in dividing skilled workers (those with a craft or specialized ability) from unskilled workers (those who supplied muscle or tended machines). As industrialists mechanized to replace skilled workers with lower-paid unskilled labor, they drew on immigrants, particularly those from southern and eastern Europe, who had come to the United States in the hope of bettering their lives. Skilled workers, frequently members of older immigrant groups, criticized the newcomers. Throughout the nineteenth century and into the twentieth, many Americans viewed ethnic and even religious differences as racial characteristics, referring to the Polish or the Jewish "race." Americans judged "new" immigrants of southern and eastern European "races" as inferior to those of Anglo-Teutonic "stock." Each wave of newcomers was deemed somehow inferior to the established residents.

In addition, the new immigrants brought their own religious and racial prejudices to the United States and also absorbed the popular prejudices of American culture. Social Darwinism, with its strongly racist overtones, decreed that whites stood at the top of the evolutionary ladder. But who was "white"? Skin color supposedly served as a marker for the "new" immigrants—"swarthy" Italians; dark-haired, olive-skinned Jews. But even blond, blue-eyed Poles were not considered white. The social construction of "race" is nowhere more apparent than in the testimony of an Irish dockworker who boasted that he hired only "white men," a category that he insisted excluded "Poles and Italians." For the new immigrants, Americanization and assimilation would prove inextricably part of becoming "white."

For African Americans, the cities of the North promised not just economic opportunity but also an end to institutionalized segregation and persecution. Jim Crow laws—restrictions that segregated blacks—became common throughout the South in the decades following Reconstruction. Intimidation and lynching terrorized blacks throughout the South (see chapter 18). "To die from the bite of frost is far more glorious than at the hands of a mob," proclaimed the *Defender*, Chicago's largest African American newspaper. In the 1890s, many blacks moved north, settling for the most part in the growing cities. Racism relegated them to poor jobs and substandard living conditions, but by 1900 New York, Philadelphia, and Chicago had the largest black communities in the nation.

On the West Coast, Asian immigrants became scapegoats of the changing economy. After California's gold rush, many Chinese who had come to work "on the gold mountain" found jobs on the country's transcontinental railroads. When the railroad work ended, they took work other groups shunned, including domestic service. But hard times in the 1870s made them a target for disgruntled workers. Prohibited from owning land, the Chinese migrated to the cities. The Chinese population of San Francisco continued to grow until passage of the Chinese Exclusion Act in 1882 (see chapter 17). For the first time in the nation's history, U.S. law excluded an immigrant group on the basis of race. In contrast, the nation's small Japanese community of about 3,000 expanded rapidly after 1890, until pressures to keep out all Asians led in 1910 to the creation of an immigration station at Angel Island in San Francisco Bay. Asian immigrants were detained there, sometimes for months, and many were deported as "undesirables."

On the East Coast, the volume of immigration from Europe in the last two decades of the century proved unprecedented. In 1888 alone, more than half a million Europeans landed in America, 75 percent of them in New York City. The Statue of Liberty, a gift from the people of France erected in 1886, stood sentinel

CHAPTER LOCATOR | Why did American cities grow so fast in the late nineteenth century?

in the harbor. The tide of immigrants to New York City soon swamped the immigration office at Castle Garden in lower Manhattan. A new facility opened on **Ellis Island** in New York harbor in 1892. Its overcrowded halls became the gateway to the United States for millions.

To many Americans, the "new" immigrants seemed impossible to assimilate. "These people are not Americans," editorialized the popular journal *Public Opinion*, "they are the very scum and offal of Europe." Terence V. Powderly, head of the broadly inclusive Knights of Labor, complained that the newcomers "herded together like animals and lived like beasts." Blue-blooded Yankees led by Senator Henry Cabot Lodge of Massachusetts formed an unlikely alliance with organized labor to press for immigration restrictions. In 1896, Congress approved a literacy test for immigrants, but President Grover Cleveland promptly vetoed it. "It is said," the president reminded Congress, "that the quality of recent immigration is undesirable. The time is quite within recent memory when the same thing was said of immigrants, who, with their descendants, are now numbered among our best citizens." Cleveland's veto forestalled immigration restriction but did not stop anti-immigrant forces from pressing for restrictions until they achieved their goal in the 1920s (see chapter 23).

Ellis Island
▶ Immigration facility opened in 1892 in New York harbor that processed new immigrants coming into New York City. In the late nineteenth century, some 75 percent of European immigrants to America came through New York.

The Social Geography of the City

During the Gilded Age, cities experienced demographic and technological changes that greatly altered the social geography of the city. Cleveland, Ohio, provides a good example. In the 1870s, Cleveland was a small city in both population and area. Oil magnate John D. Rockefeller could, and often did, walk from his large brick house to his office downtown. On his way, he passed the small homes of his clerks and other middle-class families. Behind these homes ran alleys crowded with the dwellings of Cleveland's working class. Farther out, on the shores of Lake Erie, close to the factories and foundries, clustered the shanties of the city's poorest laborers.

Within two decades, the coming of mass transit had transformed this walking city. In its place emerged a central business district surrounded by concentric rings of residences organized by ethnicity and income. First the horsecar in the 1870s and then the electric streetcar in the 1880s made it possible for those who could afford the fare to work downtown and live in the "cool green rim" of the city, with its single-family homes, lawns, gardens, and trees. Social segregation— the separation of rich and poor, and of ethnic and old-stock Americans—was one of the major social changes engendered by the rise of the industrial metropolis, evident not only in Cleveland but in cities across the nation.

Race and ethnicity affected the way cities evolved. Newcomers to the nation's cities faced hostility and not surprisingly sought out their kin and country folk as they struggled to survive. Distinct ethnic neighborhoods often formed around a synagogue or church. Blacks typically experienced the greatest residential segregation, but every large city had its ethnic enclaves where English was rarely spoken.

Poverty, crowding, dirt, and disease constituted the daily reality of New York City's immigrant poor—a plight documented by photojournalist Jacob Riis in his best-selling book *How the Other Half Lives* (1890). Riis's photographs opened the nation's eyes to conditions in the city's slums. Many middle-class Americans worried equally about the excesses of the wealthy. They feared the class antagonism fueled by the growing inequality so visible in the nation's cities and shared

| What kinds of work did people do in industrial America? | What steps did workers take to organize in the 1870s and 1880s? | How did industrialization transform home life and leisure? | How did cities respond to the challenges of growth? | Conclusion: Who built the cities? |

The gap between the rich and the poor documented in Jacob Riis's best seller, *How the Other Half Lives*, is underscored here by juxtaposing the photographs of two women. Riis took the photograph of a "scrub" or washerwoman (left) in one of the notorious Police Station lodging houses, the shelters of last resort for the city's poor. On the right is Alice Vanderbilt costumed as the "Spirit of Electricity" for her sister-in-law Alva Vanderbilt's costume ball in 1883. Washerwoman: Museum of the City of New York; Vanderbilt: Collection of the New-York Historical Society.

▶ FOR MORE HELP ANALYZING THIS IMAGE, see the visual activity for this chapter in the Online Study Guide at bedfordstmartins.com/roarkunderstanding.

Riis's view that "the real danger to society comes not only from the tenements, but from the ill-spent wealth which reared them."

Such excesses were nowhere more visible than in the lifestyle of the Vanderbilts. With a fortune amassed in the railroads, the Vanderbilts spent their money on residences that sought to rival the palaces of Europe. In 1883, Alva (Mrs. William) Vanderbilt launched herself into New York society by throwing a costume party so lavish that not even old New York society, which turned up its nose at the nouveau riche, could resist an invitation. Her sister-in-law Alice Vanderbilt stole the show by appearing as that miraculous new invention, the electric light, in a white satin evening dress studded with diamonds (see photo). The *New York World* speculated that Alva Vanderbilt's party cost more than a quarter of a million dollars (more than $4 million today).

Such ostentatious displays of wealth became especially alarming when they were coupled with disdain for the well-being of ordinary people. When a reporter in 1882 asked William Vanderbilt whether he considered the public good when running his railroads, he shot back, "The public be damned." The fear that America had become a society ruled by the rich gained credence from the fact that the wealthiest 1 percent of the population owned more than half the real and personal property in the country.

QUICK REVIEW

What global trends were reflected in the growth of American cities in the late nineteenth century?

CHAPTER LOCATOR | Why did American cities grow so fast in the late nineteenth century?

CHAPTER 19
516   THE GROWTH OF AMERICA'S CITIES, 1870–1900

Sweatshop Worker Sweatshop workers endured crowded and often dangerous conditions. Young working girls earned low wages but prided themselves on their independence. Notice the young woman's stylish hairdo, white shirtwaist, and necklace. George Eastman House.

What kinds of work did people do in industrial America?

THE NUMBER OF INDUSTRIAL WAGEWORKERS in the United States exploded in the second half of the nineteenth century, more than tripling from 5.3 million in 1860 to 17.4 million in 1900. These workers toiled in a variety of settings. Many skilled workers and artisans still earned a living in small workshops. But with the rise of corporate capitalism, large factories, mills, and mines increasingly dotted the landscape. The best way to get a sense of the diversity of workers and workplaces is to look at the industrial nation at work.

America's Diverse Workers

Common laborers formed the backbone of the American labor force. These "human machines" stood at the bottom of the country's economic ladder and generally came from the most recent immigrant groups. Initially, the Irish wielded the picks and shovels that built American cities, but by the turn of the twentieth century, as the Irish bettered their lot, Slavs and Italians took their place.

At the opposite end of labor's hierarchy stood skilled craftsmen like iron puddler James J. Davis, a Welsh immigrant who worked in the Pennsylvania mills. The job of iron puddler required intelligence and experience, and Davis drew good wages, up to $7 a day, when there was work. But most industry and manufacturing

| What kinds of work did people do in industrial America? | What steps did workers take to organize in the 1870s and 1880s? | How did industrialization transform home life and leisure? | How did cities respond to the challenges of growth? | Conclusion: Who built the cities? |

1860
– There are 5.3 million industrial workers in the United States.

1880s
– The number of foreign-born mill workers doubles.
– Mill workers in Fall River, Massachusetts, work twelve hours a day, six days a week, for about $1 a day.

1890
– Typical male worker earns $500 a year, equivalent to about $12,000 a year today.
– Twenty-five percent of married African American women work outside the home.
– Three percent of married white women work outside the home.

1900
– There are 17.4 million industrial workers in the United States.

work in the nineteenth century remained seasonal; few workers could count on year-round pay. In addition, two major depressions only twenty years apart, beginning in 1873 and 1893, spelled unemployment and hardship. In an era before unemployment insurance, workers' compensation, or old-age pensions, even the best worker could not guarantee security for his family. "The fear of ending in the poorhouse is one of the terrors that dog a man through life," Davis confessed.

Skilled workers like Davis wielded power on the shop floor. Employers attempted to limit workers' control by replacing people with machines, breaking down skilled work into ever-smaller tasks that could be performed by unskilled factory operatives. New England's textile mills provide a classic example of the effects of mechanized factory labor in the nineteenth century. Mary, a weaver at the mills in Fall River, Massachusetts, went to work in the 1880s at the age of twelve. By then, mechanization of the looms had reduced the job of the weaver to watching for breaks in the thread. "At first the noise is fierce, and you have to breathe the cotton all the time, but you get used to it," Mary told a reporter from the *Independent* magazine. "When the bobbin flies out and a girl gets hurt, you can't hear her shout—not if she just screams, you can't. She's got to wait, 'till you see her. . . . Lots of us is deaf."

During the 1880s, the number of foreign-born mill workers almost doubled. At Fall River, Mary and her Scots-Irish family resented the new immigrants. "The Polaks learn weavin' quick," she remarked. "They just as soon live on nothin' and work like that. But it won't do 'em much good for all they'll make out of it." Employers encouraged racial and ethnic antagonism because it inhibited labor organization.

The majority of factory operatives in the textile mills were young, unmarried women like Mary. They worked from six in the morning to six at night six days a week, and they took home about $1 a day. The seasonal nature of the work also drove wages down. "Like as not your mill will 'shut down' three months," and "some weeks you only get two or three days' work," Mary recounted.

Mechanization transformed the garment industry as well. With the introduction of the foot-pedaled sewing machine in the 1850s and the use of mechanical cloth-cutting knives in the 1870s, independent tailors were replaced with workers hired by contractors to sew pieces of cloth into suits and dresses. Working in sweatshops, small rooms hired for the season or even in the contractor's own tenement, women and children formed an important segment of garment workers. Discriminated against in the marketplace, where they earned less than men, women generally worked for wages only eight to ten years, until they married.

The Family Economy: Women and Children

In 1890, the typical male worker earned $500 a year, about $12,000 in today's dollars. Many working-class families, whether native-born or immigrant, lived in or near poverty, their economic survival dependent on the contributions of all family members, regardless of sex or age. The paid and unpaid work of women and children proved essential for family survival and economic advancement.

In the cities, boys as young as six years old plied their trades as bootblacks and newsboys. Often working under an adult contractor, these children earned as little as fifty cents a day. Many of them were homeless—orphaned or cast off by their families. "We wuz six, and we ain't got no father," a child of twelve told reporter Jacob Riis. "Some of us had to go."

CHAPTER LOCATOR | Why did American cities grow so fast in the late nineteenth century?

Bootblacks

The faces and hands of the two bootblacks shown here with a third boy on a New York City street in 1896 testify to their grimy trade. Boys as young as six worked on city streets as bootblacks and newsboys. For these child workers, education was a luxury they could not afford.

Alice Austin photo, Staten Island Historical Society.

Child labor increased decade by decade after 1870. The percentage of children under fifteen engaged in paid labor did not drop until after World War I. The number of women workers also rose sharply, with their most common occupation changing slowly from domestic service to factory work and then to office work. Between 1870 and 1890, the number of women working for wages in nonagricultural occupations more than doubled (**Figure 19.1**, page 520). Women's working patterns varied considerably according to race and ethnicity. White married women, even among the working class, rarely worked for wages outside the home. In 1890, only 3 percent were employed. Black women, married and unmarried, worked for wages in much greater numbers. The 1890 census showed that 25 percent of married African American women were employed, often as domestics in the houses of white families.

White-Collar Workers: Managers, "Typewriters," and Salesclerks

In the late nineteenth century, business expansion and consolidation led to a managerial revolution, creating a new class of white-collar workers who worked in offices and stores. As skilled workers saw their crafts replaced by mechanization, some moved into management positions. "The middle class is becoming a salaried class," a writer for the *Independent* magazine observed, "and is rapidly losing the economic and moral independence of former days." As large business organizations consolidated, corporate development separated management from

| What kinds of work did people do in industrial America? | What steps did workers take to organize in the 1870s and 1880s? | How did industrialization transform home life and leisure? | How did cities respond to the challenges of growth? | Conclusion: Who built the cities? |

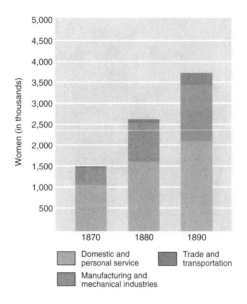

FIGURE 19.1 ■ Women and Work, 1870–1890
In 1870, close to 1.5 million women worked in nonagricultural occupations. By 1890, that number had more than doubled to 3.7 million. More and more women sought work in manufacturing and mechanical industries, although domestic service still constituted the largest employment arena for women.

ownership, and the job of directing the firm became the province of salaried executives and managers, the majority of whom were white men drawn from the 8 percent of Americans who held high school diplomas.

Until late in the century, when engineering schools began to supply recruits, many skilled workers moved from the shop floor to positions of considerable responsibility. William "Billy" Jones, the son of a Welsh immigrant, was one such worker. Beginning as an apprentice at the age of ten, Jones rose through the ranks to become plant superintendent at Andrew Carnegie's Pittsburgh steelworks in 1872.

The new white-collar workforce also included women "typewriters" and salesclerks. In the decades after the Civil War, as businesses became larger and more far-flung, the need for more elaborate and exact records, as well as the greater volume of correspondence, led to the hiring of more office workers. Mechanization transformed business as it had industry and manufacturing. The adding machine, the cash register, and the typewriter came into general use in the 1880s. Employers seeking literate workers soon turned to women. Educated men had many other career choices, but for middle-class white women, secretarial work constituted one of very few areas where they could put their literacy to use for wages.

Sylvie Thygeson was typical of the young women who went to work as secretaries. When her father died in 1884, Thygeson went to work as a country schoolteacher at the age of sixteen, after graduating high school. Realizing that teaching school did not pay a living wage, she mastered typing and stenography and found

CHAPTER LOCATOR | Why did American cities grow so fast in the late nineteenth century?

CHAPTER 19
520   THE GROWTH OF AMERICA'S CITIES, 1870–1900

work as a secretary to help support her family. According to her account, she made "a fabulous sum of money." Nevertheless, she gave up her job after a few years when she met and married her husband.

By the 1890s, secretarial work was the overwhelming choice of native-born white women, who constituted more than 90 percent of the female clerical force. Not only considered more genteel than factory work or domestic labor, office work also meant more money for shorter hours. Boston's clerical workers made more than $6 a week in 1883, compared with less than $5 for women working in manufacturing.

As a new consumer culture came to dominate American urban life in the late nineteenth century, department stores offered another employment opportunity for women in the cities. Stores such as Macy's in New York, Wanamaker's in Philadelphia, and Marshall Field in Chicago stood as monuments to the material promise of the era. Within these palaces of consumption, cash girls, stock clerks, and wrappers earned as little as $3 a week, while at the top of the scale, buyers like Belle Cushman of the fancy goods department at Macy's earned $25 a week. Salesclerks counted themselves a cut above factory workers. Their work was neither dirty nor dangerous, and even when they earned less than factory workers, they felt a sense of superiority.

Clerical Worker

A stenographer takes dictation in an 1890s office. In the 1880s, with the invention of the typewriter, many women put their literacy skills to use in the nation's offices. Brown Brothers.

QUICK REVIEW

How did business expansion and consolidation change workers' occupations in the late nineteenth century?

| What kinds of work did people do in industrial America? | What steps did workers take to organize in the 1870s and 1880s? | How did industrialization transform home life and leisure? | How did cities respond to the challenges of growth? | Conclusion: Who built the cities? |

What steps did workers take to organize in the 1870s and 1880s?

Destruction from the Great Railroad Strike of 1877

Pictures of the devastation caused in Pittsburgh during the strike shocked many Americans. When militiamen fired on striking workers, killing more than twenty strikers, the mob retaliated by destroying a two-mile area along the track. Carnegie Library of Pittsburgh.

BY THE LATE NINETEENTH CENTURY, industrial workers were losing ground in the workplace. In the fierce competition to reduce prices and cut costs, industrialists like Andrew Carnegie invested heavily in new machinery that enabled them to replace skilled workers with unskilled labor. The erosion of skills and the redefinition of labor as mere "machine tending" left the worker with a growing sense of individual helplessness that served as a spur to collective action. In the 1870s and 1880s, labor organizations grew, and the Knights of Labor and the American Federation of Labor attracted workers. Convinced of the inequity of the wage-labor system, labor organizers spoke eloquently of abolishing class privileges and monopoly.

The Great Railroad Strike of 1877

Economic depression following the panic of 1873 threw as many as three million people out of work. Those who were lucky enough to keep their jobs watched as pay cuts eroded their wages until they could no longer feed their families. In the summer of 1877, the Baltimore and Ohio (B&O) Railroad announced a 10 percent wage cut at the same time it declared a 10 percent dividend to its stockholders. Angry brakemen in West Virginia, whose wages had already fallen from $70 to $30 a month, walked out on strike.

The West Virginia brakemen's strike touched off the **Great Railroad Strike** of 1877, a nationwide uprising that spread rapidly to Pittsburgh and Chicago, St. Louis and San Francisco (**Map 19.3**). Within a few days, nearly 100,000 railroad workers walked off the job. An estimated 500,000 laborers soon joined the train workers. In Reading, Pennsylvania, militiamen refused to fire on the strikers,

Great Railroad Strike

▶ Strike that began in 1877 with a strike of West Virginia railroad brakemen and quickly spread to include roughly 600,000 workers. Responding to pressure from railroad owners and managers, President Rutherford B. Hayes used federal troops to break the strike. Despite the strike's failure, it led to a surge in union membership.

CHAPTER LOCATOR │ Why did American cities grow so fast in the late nineteenth century?

Strike activity

MAP 19.3 ▪ The Great Railroad Strike of 1877
Starting in West Virginia and Pennsylvania, the strike spread as far north as Albany, New York, and as far west as San Francisco, bringing rail traffic to a standstill. Called the Great Uprising, the strike heralded the beginning of a new era of working-class protest and trade union organization.

CHRONOLOGY

1869
– Knights of Labor is founded.

1873
– Panic on Wall Street touches off depression.

1877
– In Great Railroad Strike, more than 600,000 workers across the country go on strike.

1878
– Knights of Labor launches a campaign to organize all workers.

1886
– American Federation of Labor (AFL) is founded to represent skilled workers.
– Haymarket bombing in Chicago deals a death blow to the Knights of Labor.

saying, "We may be militiamen, but we are workmen first." Rail traffic ground to a halt; the nation lay paralyzed.

Violence erupted as the strike spread. In Pittsburgh, militia brought in from Philadelphia opened fire on a crowd, killing twenty people. Angry workers retaliated by reducing an area two miles long beside the tracks to rubble. Before the day ended, twenty more workers had been shot, and the railroad had sustained property damage totaling $2 million.

Within eight days, the governors of nine states, acting at the prompting of the railroad owners and managers, defined the strike as an "insurrection" and called for federal troops. President Rutherford B. Hayes, after hesitating briefly, called out the army. By the time the troops arrived, the violence had run its course. Federal troops did not shoot a single striker in 1877. But they struck a blow against labor by acting as strikebreakers—opening rail traffic, protecting nonstriking "scab" train crews, and maintaining peace along the line. In three weeks, the strike was over.

Although many middle-class Americans initially sympathized with the conditions that led to the strike, they condemned the strikers for the violence and property damage that occurred. The *Independent* magazine offered the following advice on how to deal with "rioters": "If the club of a policeman, knocking out the brains of the rioter, will answer then well and good; but if it does not promptly meet the exigency, then bullets and bayonets . . . constitutes [*sic*] the one remedy and one duty of the hour."

"The strikes have been put down by force," President Hayes noted in his diary on August 5. "But now for the real remedy. Can't something be done by education of the strikers, by judicious control of the capitalists, by wise general policy to end or diminish the evil? The railroad strikers, as a rule, are good men,

| What kinds of work did people do in industrial America? | **What steps did workers take to organize in the 1870s and 1880s?** | How did industrialization transform home life and leisure? | How did cities respond to the challenges of growth? | Conclusion: Who built the cities? |

sober, intelligent, and industrious." While Hayes acknowledged the workers' grievances, most businessmen and industrialists did not and fought the idea of labor unions. For their part, workers quickly recognized that they held little power individually and flocked to join unions. As labor leader Samuel Gompers noted, the strike served as an alarm bell to labor "that sounded a ringing message of hope to us all."

The Knights of Labor and the American Federation of Labor

Knights of Labor

▶ The first mass organization of America's working class. Founded in 1869, the Knights of Labor attempted to bridge the boundaries of ethnicity, gender, ideology, race, and occupation to build a brotherhood of all workers. The 1886 Haymarket bombing contributed to the Knights' decline and the ascendancy of trade unionism.

Terence V. Powderly

▶ Leader of the Knights of Labor during the 1880s. Under his leadership, the Knights became the dominant force in labor during the decade. Powderly's Knights called for one big union to create a cooperative commonwealth that would supplant the wage system and remove class distinctions.

Samuel Gompers

▶ Labor organizer who founded the Organized Trades and Labor Unions in 1881 and reorganized it in 1886 into the American Federation of Labor (AFL). Gompers organized skilled workers and focused on workplace issues such as wages and working conditions.

American Federation of Labor (AFL)

▶ Organization created by Samuel Gompers in 1886 that coordinated the activities of craft unions throughout the United States. Under Gompers's leadership, the AFL worked to achieve immediate benefits for skilled workers. In its early days, the AFL attracted fewer members than the Knights of Labor, but in time its approach to unionism came to prevail.

The **Knights of Labor**, the first mass organization of America's working class, proved the chief beneficiary of labor's newfound consciousness. Founded in 1869, the Knights were a secret society that envisioned a "universal brotherhood" of all workers, from common laborers to master craftsmen. Secrecy and ritual served to bind Knights together at the same time that it discouraged company spies and protected members from reprisals.

Although the Knights played no active role in the 1877 railroad strike, membership swelled as a result of the growing interest in labor organizing that followed the strike. In 1878, the Knights abandoned secrecy and launched an ambitious campaign to organize workers regardless of skill, sex, race, or nationality. The Knights attempted to bridge the boundaries of ethnicity, gender, ideology, race, and occupation. Leonora Barry served as general investigator for women's work from 1886 to 1890, helping the Knights recruit teachers, waitresses, housewives, and domestics along with factory and sweatshop workers. Women comprised perhaps 20 percent of the membership. The Knights also included African Americans, organizing more than 95,000 black workers. That the Knights of Labor often fell short of its goals to unify the working class proved less surprising than the scope of its efforts.

Under the direction of Grand Master Workman **Terence V. Powderly**, the Knights became the dominant force in labor during the 1880s. The organization advocated a kind of workers' democracy that embraced reforms including public ownership of the railroads, an income tax, equal pay for women workers, and the abolition of child labor. The Knights called for one big union to create a cooperative commonwealth that would supplant the wage system and remove class distinctions. Only the "parasitic" members of society—gamblers, stockbrokers, lawyers, bankers, and liquor dealers—were denied membership.

In theory, the Knights of Labor opposed strikes. Powderly championed arbitration and preferred to use boycotts. But in practice, much of the organization's appeal came from a successful strike the Knights mounted in 1885 against railroads controlled by Jay Gould. Despite the reservations of its leadership, the Knights became a militant labor organization that won support from working people with the slogan "An injury to one is the concern of all."

The Knights of Labor was not without rivals. Many skilled workers belonged to craft unions organized by trade. Trade unionists spurned the broad reform goals of the Knights and focused on workplace issues such as higher pay and better working conditions. **Samuel Gompers** promoted what he called "pure and simple" unionism. Gompers founded the Organized Trades and Labor Unions in 1881 and reorganized it in 1886 into the **American Federation of Labor (AFL)**, which coordinated the activities of craft unions throughout the United States.

CHAPTER LOCATOR | Why did American cities grow so fast in the late nineteenth century?

Gompers at first drew few converts. The AFL had only 138,000 members in 1886, compared with 730,000 for the Knights of Labor. But events soon brought down the Knights, and Gompers's brand of unionism came to prevail.

Haymarket and the Specter of Labor Radicalism

While the AFL and the Knights of Labor competed for members, more-radical labor groups, including socialists and anarchists, believed that reform was futile and called instead for social revolution. Both groups, sensitive to criticism that they preferred revolution in theory to improvements here and now, rallied around the popular issue of the eight-hour day.

Since the 1840s, labor had sought to end the twelve-hour workday, which was standard in industry and manufacturing. By the mid-1880s, it seemed clear to many workers that labor shared too little in the new prosperity of the decade, and pressure mounted for the eight-hour day. Labor rallied to the popular issue and launched major rallies in cities across the nation. Supporters of the movement set May 1, 1886, as the date for a nationwide general strike in support of the eight-hour workday.

All factions of the labor movement came together in Chicago on May Day. A group of labor radicals led by anarchist Albert Parsons, a *Mayflower* descendant, and August Spies, a German socialist, spearheaded the eight-hour movement in Chicago. Chicago's Knights of Labor rallied to the cause even though Terence Powderly and the union's national leadership refused to endorse the movement for shorter hours. Samuel Gompers was on hand, too, to lead the city's trade unionists, although he privately urged the AFL assemblies not to participate in the general strike.

Gompers's skilled workers were labor's elite. Many still worked in small shops where negotiations between workers and employers took place in an environment tempered by personal relationships. The AFL's skilled workers stood in sharp contrast to the dispossessed workers out on strike across town at Chicago's McCormick reaper works. There strikers watched helplessly as the company brought in strikebreakers to take their jobs and marched the "scabs" to work under the protection of the Chicago police and private security guards.

During the May Day rally, 45,000 workers paraded peacefully down Michigan Avenue in support of the eight-hour day. Trouble came two days later, when strikers attacked strikebreakers outside the McCormick works and police opened fire, killing or wounding six men. Angry radicals called on workers to "arm yourselves and appear in full force" at a rally in Haymarket Square.

"The Chicago Riot"

Inflammatory pamphlets like this one published in the wake of the Haymarket bombing presented a one-sided view of the incident and stirred public passion. Chicago Historical Society.

▶ FOR MORE HELP ANALYZING THIS IMAGE, see the visual activity for this chapter in the Online Study Guide at bedfordstmartins.com/roarkunderstanding.

| What kinds of work did people do in industrial America? | **What steps did workers take to organize in the 1870s and 1880s?** | How did industrialization transform home life and leisure? | How did cities respond to the challenges of growth? | Conclusion: Who built the cities? |

On the evening of May 4, the turnout at Haymarket was disappointing. No more than two or three thousand gathered to hear Spies, Parsons, and the other speakers. Mayor Carter Harrison, known as a friend of labor, mingled conspicuously in the crowd, pronounced the meeting peaceable, and went home. A short time later, police captain John "Blackjack" Bonfield marched his men into the crowd, by now fewer than three hundred people, and demanded that it disperse. Suddenly, someone threw a bomb into the police ranks. After a moment of stunned silence, the police drew their revolvers. "Fire and kill all you can," shouted a police lieutenant. When the melee ended, seven policemen and an unknown number of other people lay dead. An additional sixty policemen and thirty or forty civilians suffered injuries.

News of the "Haymarket riot" provoked a nationwide convulsion of fear and rage directed at anarchists, labor unions, strikers, immigrants, and the working class in general. Eight men, including Parsons and Spies, went on trial in Chicago. "Convict these men," thundered the state's attorney, Julius S. Grinnell, "make examples of them, hang them, and you save our institutions." Although the state could not link any of the defendants to the **Haymarket bombing**, the jury nevertheless found them all guilty. Four were executed, one committed suicide, and three received prison sentences.

The bomb blast at Haymarket had lasting repercussions. To commemorate the death of the Haymarket martyrs, labor made May 1 an annual international celebration of the worker. But the Haymarket bomb, in the eyes of one observer, proved "a godsend to all enemies of the labor movement." It effectively scotched the eight-hour day movement and dealt a blow to the Knights of Labor, already wracked by internal divisions. With the labor movement under attack, many skilled workers turned to the American Federation of Labor. Gompers's narrow economic strategy made sense at the time and enabled one segment of the workforce—the skilled—to organize effectively and achieve tangible gains. But the nation's unskilled workers remained untouched by the AFL's brand of trade unionism.

Haymarket bombing

▶ May 4, 1886, conflict between labor protesters and police in which both workers and policemen were killed or wounded. The violence began when an unknown person threw a bomb into the ranks of the police assigned to the labor gathering. The incident created a powerful backlash against labor activism.

QUICK REVIEW

What were the long-term effects of the Great Railroad Strike of 1877 and the Haymarket bombing in 1886?

CHAPTER LOCATOR | Why did American cities grow so fast in the late nineteenth century?

Beach Scene at Coney Island Opened in the 1870s, Coney Island came into its own at the turn of the twentieth century with the development of elaborate amusement parks. It became a symbol of commercialized leisure and mechanical excitement. This fanciful rendering captures the frenetic goings-on. Weekend crowds on the island reportedly reached one million. Library of Congress.

How did industrialization transform home life and leisure?

THE GROWTH OF URBAN INDUSTRIALISM not only dramatically altered the workplace but also transformed home and family life and gave rise to new forms of commercialized leisure. Industrialization redefined the very concepts of work and home. Increasingly, men went out to work for wages, while most white married women stayed home, either working in the home without pay—cleaning, cooking, and rearing children—or supervising paid domestic servants who did the housework.

Domesticity and "Domestics"

The separation of the workplace and the home that marked the shift to industrial society led to a new ideology, one that sentimentalized the home and women's role in it. The cultural ideology that dictated woman's place in the home has been called the cult of domesticity, a phrase used to prescribe an ideal of middle-class, white womanhood that dominated the period from 1820 to the end of the nineteenth century (see chapter 11).

The cult of domesticity and the elaboration of the middle-class home led to a major change in patterns of hiring household help. The live-in servant, or domestic, became a fixture in the North, replacing the hired girl of the previous century. (The South continued to rely on black female labor, first slave and later free.) In American cities by 1870, 15 to 30 percent of all households included live-in domestic servants, more than 90 percent of them women. By the mid-nineteenth century, native-born women increasingly took up other work and left domestic service to immigrants.

Servants by all accounts resented the long hours and lack of privacy. "She is liable to be rung up at all hours," one study reported. "Her very meals are not secure from interruption, and even her sleep is not sacred." Domestic service

| What kinds of work did people do in industrial America? | What steps did workers take to organize in the 1870s and 1880s? | **How did industrialization transform home life and leisure?** | How did cities respond to the challenges of growth? | Conclusion: Who built the cities? |

CHRONOLOGY

1869

– Cincinnati Red Stockings becomes the first professional baseball team. By the 1870s, baseball is the "national pastime" for men.

1870

– Between 15 and 30 percent of urban households employ live-in domestic servants, some 90 percent of them women.

1890s

– Coney Island, New York, becomes one of the largest and most elaborate amusement parks in the country, attracting as many as one million visitors a weekend.

Coney Island

▶ Popular leisure destination for New York City's residents, particularly its working class. In the 1890s, Coney Island became the site of some of the largest and most elaborate amusement parks in the country. Coney Island embodied the commercialization of entertainment in the late nineteenth century.

became the occupation of last resort, a "hard and lonely life" in the words of one servant girl.

For women of the white middle class, domestics were a boon, freeing them from household drudgery and giving them more time to spend with their children or to pursue club work or reform. Thus, while domestic service supported the cult of domesticity, it created, for those women who could afford it, opportunities to expand their horizons outside the home in areas such as women's clubs and the temperance and suffrage movements.

Cheap Amusements

Growing class divisions manifested themselves in patterns of leisure as well as in work and home life. The poor and working class took their leisure, not in the crowded tenements that housed their families, but increasingly in the cities' new dance halls, music houses, ballparks, and amusement arcades, which by the 1890s formed a familiar part of the urban landscape.

The growing anonymity of urban industrial society posed a challenge to traditional rituals of courtship. Adolescent working girls no longer met prospective husbands only through their families. Fleeing crowded tenements, the young sought each other's company in dance halls and other commercial retreats. Young workingwomen, who rarely could afford more than trolley fare when they went out, counted on being "treated" by men, a transaction that often implied sexual payback. Young women's need to negotiate sexual encounters if they wished to participate in commercial amusements blurred the line between respectability and promiscuity and made the dance halls a favorite target of reformers who feared they lured girls into prostitution.

For men, baseball became a national pastime in the 1870s, one force in urban life capable of uniting a city across class lines. Cincinnati mounted the first entirely paid team, the Red Stockings, in 1869. Soon professional teams proliferated in cities across the nation, and Mark Twain hailed baseball as "the very symbol, the outward and visible expression, of the drive and push and rush and struggle of the raging, tearing, booming nineteenth century."

The increasing commercialization of entertainment in the late nineteenth century can best be seen at **Coney Island**, New York. Long a center for popular amusements, in the 1890s Coney Island was transformed into the site of some of the largest and most elaborate amusement parks in the country. Promoter George Tilyou built Steeplechase Park in 1897, advertising "10 hours of fun for 10 cents." With its mechanical thrills and fun-house laughs, the amusement park encouraged behavior that one schoolteacher aptly described as "everyone with the brakes off." By 1900, as many as a million New Yorkers flocked to Coney Island on any given weekend, making the amusement park the unofficial capital of a new mass culture.

QUICK REVIEW

How did urban industrialism shape the world of leisure?

CHAPTER LOCATOR | Why did American cities grow so fast in the late nineteenth century?

CHAPTER 19
528 THE GROWTH OF AMERICA'S CITIES, 1870–1900

Central Park Lake

Looking south across Central Park Lake, this photograph shows boaters and well-dressed New Yorkers taking their leisure on Bethesda Terrace. The bronze figure in the center of the photograph, *Angel of the Waters*, was the work of sculptor Emma Stebbins. Calvert Vaux, who along with Frederick Law Olmsted designed the landscaping, considered Bethesda Terrace the "drawing room of the park." People of all ages, from children floating toy sailboats (inset) to grandparents out for a stroll, found something to enjoy in the park.
Photo: Culver Pictures; Boat: Picture Research Consultants & Archives.

PRIVATE ENTERPRISE, not planners, built the cities of the United States. With a few notable exceptions, cities simply mushroomed, formed by the dictates of private enterprise and the exigencies of local politics. With the rise of the city came the need for public facilities, transportation, and services that would tax the imaginations of America's architects and engineers and set the scene for the rough-and-tumble of big-city government, politics, and politicians.

Building Cities of Stone and Steel

In the late nineteenth century, Americans rushed to embrace new technology of all kinds, making their cities the most modern in the world. Structural steel made enormous advances in building possible. The Brooklyn Bridge, a soaring monument to the New York City, opened in 1883. As the age of steel supplanted the age of stone and iron, skyscrapers and mighty bridges dominated the imagination and the urban landscape.

Chicago, not New York, gave birth to the modern skyscraper. Rising from the ashes of the Great Fire of 1871, which destroyed three square miles and left eighteen thousand people homeless, Chicago offered a generation of skilled architects and engineers the chance to experiment. A group of architects known as the "Chicago school," whose members included Louis Sullivan and John Wellborn Root, gave Chicago some of the world's finest commercial buildings. Employing the dictum "Form follows function," they built startlingly modern structures.

| What kinds of work did people do in industrial America? | What steps did workers take to organize in the 1870s and 1880s? | How did industrialization transform home life and leisure? | **How did cities respond to the challenges of growth?** | Conclusion: Who built the cities? |

529

CHRONOLOGY

1871
– Boss Tweed's rule in New York ends.
– Chicago's Great Fire destroys three square miles and leaves eighteen thousand people homeless.

1873
– New York's Central Park is completed.

1883
– Brooklyn Bridge opens.

1893
– World's Columbian Exposition is held in Chicago.
– Panic on Wall Street touches off major economic depression.

1895
– Boston Public Library opens.

Frederick Law Olmsted
▶ Landscape architect who designed numerous urban parks in the late nineteenth century. Olmsted is best known for New York's Central Park, completed in 1873. His parks were meant to provide city residents with a place where they could retreat from crowded, noisy city streets.

William Marcy "Boss" Tweed
▶ The most notorious city boss. In the mid-nineteenth century, Tweed was the leader of New York's Democratic machine, Tammany Hall. Through the use of bribery and graft, Tweed kept the Democratic Party in power and ran New York City. Tweed's excesses produced demands for reform and led to his fall from power in 1871.

Across the United States, municipal governments undertook public works on a scale never before seen. They paved streets, built sewers and water mains, installed electric lights, ran trolley tracks, and dug underground to build subways. Cities became more beautiful with the creation of urban public parks. Much of the credit for America's greatest parks goes to one man—landscape architect **Frederick Law Olmsted**. Olmsted designed parks for many cities, but he is best remembered for the creation of New York City's Central Park. Completed in 1873, it became the first land-scaped public park in the United States. Olmsted's goal for the eight hundred acres between 59th and 110th streets was to create a place where people "may stroll for an hour, seeing, hearing, and feeling nothing of the bustle and jar of the streets."

American cities did not overlook the mind in their efforts at improvement. In the late nineteenth century, American cities created the most extensive free public library system in the world. In 1895, the Boston Public Library opened with more than 700,000 books available to the reading public. Cities also created a comprehensive free public school system that educated everyone from the children of the middle class to the sons and daughters of immigrant workers. The exploding urban population strained the system and led to crowded and inadequate facilities. In 1899, more than 544,000 pupils attended school in New York's five boroughs.

The parks, the libraries, and even the subways and sewers benefited some city dwellers more than others. Few library cards were held by Boston's laborers, who worked six days a week and found the library closed on Sunday. And in the 1890s, there was nothing central about New York's Central Park. It was a four-mile walk from the tenements of Hester Street to the park's entrance at 59th Street and Fifth Avenue.

Any story of the American city, it seems, must be a tale of two cities—or, given the cities' great diversity, a tale of many cities within each metropolis. At the turn of the twentieth century, a central paradox emerged: The enduring monuments of America's cities—the bridges, skyscrapers, parks, and libraries—stood as the undeniable achievements of the same system of municipal government that reformers dismissed as boss-ridden, criminal, and corrupt.

City Government and the "Bosses"

The physical growth of the cities required the expansion of public services and the creation of entirely new facilities: streets, subways, elevated trains, bridges, docks, sewers, and public utilities. With work to be done and money to be made, the professional politician—the colorful big-city boss—became a phenomenon of urban growth. Though corrupt and often criminal, the boss saw to the building of the city and provided needed social services for the new residents. Yet not even the big-city boss could be said to rule the city. The governing of America's cities resembled more a tug-of-war than boss rule.

The most notorious of all the city bosses was **William Marcy "Boss" Tweed** of New York. At midcentury, Boss Tweed's Democratic Party "machine" held sway. A machine was really no more than a political party organized at the grass-roots level. Its purpose was to win elections and reward its followers, often with jobs on the city's payroll. New York's citywide Democratic machine, Tammany Hall, commanded an army of party functionaries. They formed a shadow government more powerful than the city's elected officials.

The only elected office Tweed ever held was alderman. But as chairman of the Tammany general committee, he wielded more power than the mayor. Through the use

CHAPTER LOCATOR | Why did American cities grow so fast in the late nineteenth century?

of bribery and graft, he kept the Democratic Party together and ran the city. "As long as I count the votes," he shamelessly boasted, "what are you going to do about it?"

The excesses of the Tweed ring soon led to a clamor for reform. Cartoonist Thomas Nast pilloried Tweed in the pages of *Harper's Weekly*. His cartoons, easily understood even by those who could not read, did the boss more harm than hundreds of outraged editorials. Tweed's rule ended in 1871. Eventually, he was tried and convicted and later died in jail.

New York was not the only city to experience bossism and corruption. More than 80 percent of the nation's thirty largest cities experienced some form of boss rule in the decades around the turn of the twentieth century. However, infighting among powerful ward bosses often meant that no single boss enjoyed exclusive power in the big cities.

Urban reformers and proponents of good government (derisively called "goo goos" by their rivals) challenged machine rule and sometimes succeeded in electing reform mayors, but they rarely managed to stay in office for long. The bosses enjoyed continued success largely because the urban political machines helped the cities' immigrants and poor, who remained machine rule's staunchest allies. "What tells in holding your district," a Tammany ward boss observed, "is to go right down among the poor and help them in the different ways they need help. It's philanthropy, but it's politics, too—mighty good politics."

Tammany Bank

This cast-iron bank, a campaign novelty, bears the name of the New York City Democratic machine. It conveys its political reform message graphically: When you put a penny in the politician's hand, he puts it in his pocket. Collection of Janice L. and David J. Frent.

The big-city boss, through the skillful orchestration of rewards, exerted powerful leverage and lined up support for his party from a broad range of constituents, from the urban poor to wealthy industrialists. In 1902, when journalist Lincoln Steffens began "The Shame of the Cities," a series of articles exposing city corruption, he found that business leaders who refused to mingle socially with the bosses nevertheless struck deals with them. "He is a self-righteous fraud, this big businessman," Steffens concluded. "I found him buying boodlers [bribers] in St. Louis, defending grafters in Minneapolis, originating corruption in Pittsburgh, sharing with bosses in Philadelphia, deploring reform in Chicago, and beating good government with corruption funds in New York."

For all the color and flamboyance of the big-city boss, he was simply one of many players in municipal government. Old-stock aristocrats, new professionals, saloonkeepers, pushcart peddlers, and politicians all fought for their interests. They didn't much like each other, and they sometimes fought savagely. But they learned to live with one another. Compromise and accommodation—not boss rule—best characterized big-city government by the turn of the twentieth century, although the cities' reputation for corruption left an indelible mark on the consciousness of the American public.

What kinds of work did people do in industrial America?	What steps did workers take to organize in the 1870s and 1880s?	How did industrialization transform home life and leisure?	**How did cities respond to the challenges of growth?**	Conclusion: Who built the cities?

White City or City of Sin?

Americans have always been of two minds about the city. They like to boast of its skyscrapers and bridges, its culture and sophistication, and they pride themselves on its bigness and bustle. At the same time, they fear it as the city of sin, the home of immigrant slums, the center of vice and crime. Nowhere did the divided view of the American city take form more graphically than in Chicago in 1893.

World's Columbian Exposition

▶ World's fair held in Chicago in 1893. Millions of fairgoers visited the fabulous grounds that came to be known as the White City. The White City embodied the American urban ideal and offered a stark contrast to the realities of Chicago life.

In that year, Chicago hosted the **World's Columbian Exposition**, the grandest world's fair in the nation's history. The fairground, called the White City and built on the shores of Lake Michigan, offered a lesson in what Americans on the eve of the twentieth century imagined a city might be. Only five miles down the shore from downtown Chicago, the White City seemed light-years away. Its very name celebrated a harmony and pristine beauty unknown in Chicago, with its stock-yards, slums, and bustling terminals. Frederick Law Olmsted and architect Daniel Burnham supervised the creation of a paradise of lagoons, fountains, wooded islands, gardens, and imposing buildings.

Visitors from home and abroad strolled the elaborate grounds and visited the exhibits—everything from a model of the Brooklyn Bridge carved in soap to the latest goods and inventions. Half carnival, half culture, the great fair offered something for everyone. On the Midway Plaisance, crowds thrilled to the massive wheel built by Mr. Ferris and watched agog as Little Egypt danced the hootchy-kootchy.

In October, the fair closed its doors in the midst of the worst depression the country had yet seen. During the winter of 1894, Chicago's unemployed and homeless took over the grounds, vandalized the buildings, and frightened the city's comfortable citizens. When reporters asked Daniel Burnham what should be done with the moldering remains of the White City, he responded, "It should be torched." And it was. In July 1894, in a clash between federal troops and striking railway workers, incendiaries set fires that leveled the fairgrounds.

In the end, the White City remained what it had always been, a dreamscape. Perhaps it was not so strange, after all, that the legacy of the White City could be found on Coney Island, where two new amusement parks, Luna and Dreamland, sought to combine, albeit in a more tawdry form, the beauty of the White City and the thrill of the Midway Plaisance. More enduring than the White City itself was what it represented: the emergent industrial might of the United States, at home and abroad, with its inventions, manufactured goods, and growing consumer culture.

QUICK REVIEW

How did American cities change
in the late nineteenth century?

CHAPTER LOCATOR | Why did American cities grow so fast in the late nineteenth century?

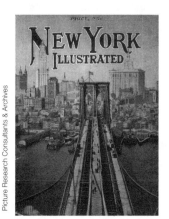

Picture Research Consultants & Archives

Conclusion: Who built the cities?

AS MUCH AS THE GREAT INDUSTRIALISTS and financiers, common workers, most of them immigrants, built the nation's cities. The unprecedented growth of urban, industrial America resulted from the labor of millions of men, women, and children who toiled in workshops and factories, in sweatshops and mines, on railroads and construction sites across America.

America's cities in the late nineteenth century teemed with life. Americans from all walks of life lived in the cities and contributed to their growth. Town houses and tenements jostled for space with skyscrapers and great department stores, while parks, ball fields, amusement arcades, and public libraries provided the city masses with recreation and entertainment. Municipal governments, straining to build the new cities, experienced the rough-and-tumble of machine politics as bosses and their constituents looked to profit from city growth.

For America's workers, urban industrialism, along with the rise of big business and corporate consolidation, drastically changed the workplace. Industrialists replaced skilled workers with new machines that could be operated by cheaper unskilled labor. And during hard times, employers did not hesitate to cut workers' already meager wages. Organization held out the best hope for the workers; first the Knights of Labor and later the American Federation of Labor won converts among the nation's working class.

The rise of urban industrialism challenged the American promise, which for decades had been dominated by Jeffersonian agrarian ideals. Could such a promise exist in the changing world of cities, tenements, immigrants, and huge corporations? In the great depression that came in the 1890s, mounting anger and frustration would lead workers and farmers to join forces and create a grassroots movement to fight for change under the banner of a new People's Party.

SO NOW YOU KNOW

The late nineteenth century witnessed an influx of "new" immigrants into the United States, most of them from Southern and Eastern Europe. Ellis Island, the destination of many new immigrants to the East Coast, was just the first stop for the newcomers who would provide critical labor in building America's growing cities.

| What kinds of work did people do in industrial America? | What steps did workers take to organize in the 1870s and 1880s? | How did industrialization transform home life and leisure? | How did cities respond to the challenges of growth? | **Conclusion: Who built the cities?** |

CHAPTER 19 STUDY GUIDE

Online Study Guide
bedfordstmartins.com/roarkunderstanding

STEP 1

GETTING STARTED

Below are basic terms from this period in American history. Can you identify each term below and explain why it matters? To do this exercise online or to download this chart, visit bedfordstmartins.com/roarkunderstanding.

TERM	WHO OR WHAT & WHEN	WHY IT MATTERS
Ellis Island, p. 515		
Great Railroad Strike, p. 522		
Knights of Labor, p. 524		
Terrence V. Powderly, p. 524		
Samuel Gompers, p. 524		
American Federation of Labor, p. 524		
Haymarket bombing, p. 526		
Coney Island, p. 528		
Frederick Law Olmsted, p. 530		
William Marcy "Boss" Tweed, p. 530		
World's Columbian Exposition, p. 532		

STEP 2

MOVING BEYOND THE BASICS

The exercise below represents a more advanced understanding of the chapter material. Describe the key characteristics of American cities at the turn of the twentieth century and the impact that these characteristics had on city life. How did growth contribute to changes in work and social relationships? How did the influx of immigrants in the late nineteenth century shape city politics? How did the relationship among work, domestic life, and leisure activities change over the course of the late nineteenth and early twentieth centuries? To do this exercise online or to download this chart, visit bedfordstmartins.com/roarkunderstanding.

Characteristic	The American city, ca. 1900	Impact on city life
Population		
Diversity		
Social structure		
Work and labor relations		
Politics		
Domestic life		
Leisure		

STEP

3

PUTTING IT ALL TOGETHER

Now that you have reviewed key elements of the chapter, take a step back and try to explain the big picture by answering these questions. Remember to use specific examples from the chapter in your answers. To do this exercise online, visit bedfordstmartins.com/roarkunderstanding.

URBANIZATION

▶ What factors led immigrants to American cities in the late nineteenth century? How did their arrival change the cities in which they settled?

▶ How and why did the social geography of the American city change in the late nineteenth century?

INDUSTRY AND LABOR

▶ What new social divisions accompanied business expansion and industrialization?

▶ What kinds of organizations did workers form in the late nineteenth century, and why did they start them? How successful were they?

CITY LIFE

▶ How did urban industrialism transform home and family life?

▶ What led to the rise of the big-city boss? Whose interests did late-nineteenth-century city governments serve?

LOOKING BACKWARD, LOOKING AHEAD

▶ How did early-twentieth-century American cities differ from their early-nineteenth-century counterparts?

▶ How did the rise of urban industrialism change Americans' sense of themselves as a people?

IN YOUR OWN WORDS

Imagine that you must explain chapter 19 to someone who hasn't read it. What would be the most important points to include and why?

Practicing Your Textbook Reading Skills

1. Which of the following sentences from the first paragraph on page 510 introduces the main topic of the chapter?

    a. "'We cannot all live in cities, yet nearly all seem determined to do so,' New York editor Horace Greeley complained."

    b. "The last three decades of the nineteenth century witnessed an urban explosion."

    c. "Cities and towns grew more than twice as rapidly as the total population."

    d. "Most of the nation's largest cities were east of the Mississippi, although St. Louis and San Francisco both ranked among the top ten urban areas in 1900."

2. Examine Map 19.2 on page 512. Which region had the highest percentage of immigrant residents in late-nineteenth-century America?

    a. the West Coast

    b. New England

    c. the upper Midwest

    d. the South

3. Where can you find help interpreting the cover of *The Chicago Riot* pictured on page 525?

    a. in the printed study guide for *Understanding the American Promise*

    b. online at www.bedfordstmartins.com/roarkunderstanding

    c. in the library

    d. in the section of the chapter titled "Haymarket and the Specter of Labor Radicalism"

4. Which of the following sentences from the section "Racism and the Cry for Immigration Restriction" (pages 514–15) is a fact?

    a. "Throughout the nineteenth century and into the twentieth, many Americans viewed ethnic and even religious differences as racial characteristics, referring to the Polish or the Jewish 'race.'"

    b. "But who was 'white'?"

    c. "The social construction of race is nowhere more apparent than in the testimony of an Irish dockworker who boasted that he hired only 'white men,' a category that he insisted excluded 'Poles and Italians.'"

    d. "'These people are not Americans.'"

5. Which of the following sentences from the section "Racism and the Cry for Immigration Restriction" (pages 514–15) is an opinion?

a. "On the West Coast, Asian immigrants became scapegoats of the changing economy."

b. "After California's gold rush, many Chinese who had come to work 'on the gold mountain' found jobs on the country's transcontinental railroads."

c. "The Chinese population of San Francisco continued to grow until passage of the Chinese Exclusion Act in 1882."

d. "For the first time in the nation's history, U.S. law excluded an immigrant group on the basis of race."

6. The photograph of three boys on page 519 illustrates

   a. nineteenth-century fashion.

   b. the shoe-shining process.

   c. child labor.

   d. labor politics.

7. According to Figure 19.1 (page 520), what was the most common source of employment for women from 1870 to 1890?

   a. trade and transportation

   b. manufacturing and mechanical industries

   c. domestic and personal service

   d. agriculture

8. What inference about nineteenth-century city politicians can be drawn from the Tammany bank pictured on page 531?

   a. They were lazy.

   b. They were known to take bribes.

   c. They believed that if they worked together they could win reform.

   d. They wanted more authority.

9. Throughout the chapter, a row of six questions runs across the bottom of the pages. Why?

   a. to make the book longer

   b. to provide practice quizzes

   c. to highlight major events

   d. to indicate what topic is under discussion

10. Read the short blurbs titled "Did You Know?" on page 509 and "So Now You Know" on page 533. What is their purpose?

    a. to interpret the image of a steamer trunk

    b. to provide a study aid

c. to highlight the relevance of history to contemporary life

d. They serve no purpose.

Testing Your Understanding

Identify the following statements as *true* or *false*.

1. The first modern skyscrapers were built in Chicago.

   T _____   F _____

2. Child labor was rare in the 1800s.

   T _____   F _____

3. American troops were called in to control striking railroad workers in 1877.

   T _____   F _____

4. By 1890, most married women worked in paying jobs.

   T _____   F _____

5. On an average weekend in 1900, as many as one million people went to professional baseball games.

   T _____   F _____

Select the best answer to each of the following questions.

6. In the 1890s, most of the world's farming was centered in

   a. South America, Africa, and southern Asia.

   b. western Europe.

   c. North America, eastern Europe, and Russia.

   d. Mexico and Central America.

7. Which of the following was *not* a type of industrial worker?

   a. skilled craftsman

   b. common laborer

   c. factory worker

   d. miner

8. Which of the following were introduced in the late nineteenth century?

   a. public libraries

   b. public parks

   c. public schools

   d. all of the above

9. What percentage of the country's property was possessed by the wealthiest 1 percent of Americans in the late nineteenth century?

   a. less than 10 percent

   b. approximately 25 percent

   c. more than 50 percent

   d. a little less than 90 percent

10. Of the following popular sources of recreation, which was considered least respectable for young women?

    a. beer gardens

    b. dance halls

    c. baseball parks

    d. amusement parks

11. The Great Railroad Strike of 1877 resulted in

    a. the deaths of more than twenty militiamen.

    b. increased tensions between workers and the middle and upper classes.

    c. middle-class sympathy for the strikers.

    d. substantially improved working conditions for railroad employees.

12. Terence V. Powderly was

    a. the owner of the Pennsylvania Railroad.

    b. the founder of the Knights of Labor.

    c. the Grand Master Workman of the Knights of Labor.

    d. the president of the American Federation of Labor.

13. The eight-hour workday was a primary goal of

    a. the American Federation of Labor.

    b. radical socialists and anarchists.

    c. Terence V. Powderly.

    d. clerical workers.

14. Tammany Hall was a

    a. popular dance club.

    b. socialite known for throwing expensive parties.

    c. group of New York City politicians.

    d. labor reform organization.

15. Which of the following events happened first?

    a. Haymarket bombing

    b. Great Railroad Strike

    c. World's Columbian Exposition

    d. Chicago's Great Fire

Using your own words, define the following terms as they are used in the chapter.

16. *birds of passage*

    _____

    _____

    _____

17. *cult of domesticity*

    _____

    _____

    _____

    _____

18. *political machines*

    _____

    _____

    _____

19. *Jim Crow*

    _____

    _____

    _____

    _____

20. *mechanization*

    _____

    _____

    _____

    _____

Answer each of the following questions using the space provided.

21. Identify at least three causes for the rapid growth of American cities in the late nineteenth century.

_____

_____

_____

_____

22. Describe the typical nineteenth-century industrial worker.

_____

_____

_____

_____

23. Briefly explain the differences between the Knights of Labor and the American Federation of Labor.

_____

_____

_____

_____

_____

_____

24. What was the Haymarket "riot," and how did it affect the labor movement?

_____

_____

_____

_____

_____

_____

_____

_____

25. How does the World's Columbian Exposition in 1893 illustrate major changes in nineteenth-century cities?

_____

_____

_____

_____

_____

_____

_____

_____

Making Thematic Connections

The college success chapter reprinted at the beginning of this reader, "Majors & Career Choices," describes working conditions in the early twenty-first century (see pages 148–49 of Unit 1). Its authors explain that because we live in a global economy, modern workers need to be flexible, creative, and willing to continually improve their skills in order to stay employed. In particular, they point out that jobs and manufacturing facilities are often shifted to developing countries such as India because such outsourcing saves companies money—a practice that angers many American workers and labor organizations. In what ways does this contemporary development parallel the late-nineteenth-century influx of immigrants to the United States described on pages 510–15 of *Understanding the American Promise*? How do the two situations differ?

Psychology

"Stress, Health, and Coping"

Introduction

If you've ever wondered why somebody behaved a certain way, how your brain works, or where emotions come from, you've asked yourself a question about psychology. A very popular subject for undergraduate study, psychology is the science of the human mind. And as the authors of the following textbook chapter see it, psychology is "the most fascinating and personally relevant science that exists." It's easy to see why: The topics explored by psychologists include memory, sexuality, personality, dreams, and therapy. You can apply just about anything you learn in a psychology class to yourself, to your friends and acquaintances, and to your family. Psychologists might work with patients in a clinical or school setting, but more often they focus on research and teaching. Their findings are applied by people in many other fields, including business, advertising and marketing, history, literature, education, medicine, and urban planning.

Psychology, Fifth Edition, by Don H. Hockenbury and Sandra E. Hockenbury, is a best-selling introduction to the science. The authors actively seek feedback from their students and have been careful to respond to what those new learners suggest. The chapter you're about to read, as a result, is easy to follow and relevant to your own experiences. Many of its elements will help you identify what is important and understand psychological concepts:

- A narrative—or story-telling—style begins with real-life examples, then explains how those stories illustrate what psychologists have learned.

- The "Chapter Outline" provides you with a sense of the chapter's main ideas and supporting details.

- Each section begins with a feature the authors call an "Advance Organizer": It includes a "Key Theme" to consider and "Key Questions" that identify the section's most important points (see, for example, "What Is Stress?" on page 541).

- Key terms and the names of important psychologists are highlighted in bold and reviewed at the end of the chapter.

- The "Concept Reviews" that end each section help you think carefully about what you've just learned as you answer the questions. (You can even find the authors' answers to these questions at the end of the chapter.)

- Boxes in the text—"In Focus," "Critical Thinking," "Culture and Human Behavior," and "Focus on Neuroscience"—pinpoint particularly interesting topics. (As you learned earlier, you can read these boxes either before or after you read the discussion in the text; don't feel you have to interrupt your reading because of where they appear on the page.)

- An "Application" feature suggests how you can use what you have learned in your own life.

This unit's textbook reading comes from *Psychology*, Fifth Edition, by Don H. Hockenbury and Sandra E. Hockenbury, Worth Publishers, 2010, Chapter 13, pages 538–69.

- Finally, a "Chapter Review" helps you check your understanding and study for a test or quiz by summarizing the chapter's key points, terms, and people.

The chapter that follows will help you understand how people (yourself included) respond—and why they respond in certain ways—to difficult situations in the workplace, in school, and in life in general. If you read the chapter attentively, you will come away from it armed with new and useful ideas about how to cope with stress.

Preparing to Read the Textbook Chapter

1. What makes you feel stressed? What do you do when you start to feel overwhelmed? Is there anything you can do to deal with pressure and conflict more effectively?

2. Flip through the chapter and note the various headings within it. Before you read, convert those headings into questions. What do you think the answers might be?

3. Some kinds of work are naturally more stressful than others. Air traffic controllers, doctors, and firefighters, for example, take other people's lives into their hands. But even in jobs where lives are not at stake, many people suffer from the emotional and physical effects of stress. Why? What can people and their employers do to minimize or control stress?

CHAPTER 13

Stress, Health, and Coping

prologue

Katie's Story

A beautiful, crystal-clear New York morning. In her high-rise apartment at 1 West Street, our 20-year-old niece Katie was fixing herself some breakfast. From the street below, Katie could hear the muted sound of sirens, but she thought nothing of it. The phone rang. It was Lydia, her roommate, calling from her job in midtown Manhattan. "Katie, you're not going to believe this. A plane hit the World Trade Center. Go up on the roof and take a look!"

Katie hung up the phone and scurried up the fire escape stairwell, joining other residents already gathered on the roof. Down below, sirens were blaring and she could see emergency vehicles, fire engines, and people racing from all directions toward the World Trade Center, just a few blocks away. There was a gaping hole in the north tower. Thick black smoke was billowing out, drifting upward, and filling the sky. She thought she could see the flames. *What a freaky accident.*

After watching for a few minutes, Katie turned to go back downstairs and get ready for her dance class. Then, "Look at that plane!" someone yelled. Seconds later, a massive jet roared overhead and slammed into the World Trade Center's south tower, exploding into a huge fireball.

Katie froze in terror. Then: People screaming. Panic. Pushing and shoving at the stairwell door. *Get back to the apartment.* The television. Live views of the burning towers. Newscaster shouting: "Terrorist attack! New York is being attacked!" The TV went dead. *Don't panic. What am I going to do? Are we being bombed?*

Two thousand miles away. A sunny Colorado morning. Phone ringing. Judy was sound asleep. Ringing. Answer the phone. "Katie? What's wrong? Is someone in your apartment? Calm down, I can't understand...."

"Mom, New York is being attacked! I don't know what to do! What should I do?" Katie sobbed uncontrollably.

Judy flipped on the television. Bizarre scenes of chaos in New York. *Oh my God, Katie's only a few blocks from the World Trade Center.* "Katie, stay in your apartment! Don't. . . ." The phone connection went dead.

Katie dropped the phone. *Worthless. Don't panic.* Lights flickered off, then on. Pounding on the door. "Evacuate the building! Get out!" a man's voice shouted. "Get out now! Use the stairwell!" *Gotta get out of here. Get out.*

Putting on her shoes and pulling a T-shirt over her pajamas, Katie grabbed her cell phone and raced out of her apartment toward the crowded stairwell. On the street was a scene of mass confusion. *Cross the street.* She joined a throng of people gathering in Battery Park. *Breathe. Stay calm.* As the crowd watched the towers burn, people shouted out more news. *Pentagon has been hit. White House is on fire. More planes in the air. President on Air Force One.*

Shaking, she couldn't take her eyes off the burning towers. *What's falling?* Figures falling from the windows of the Trade Center, a hundred stories high. *On fire. That person was on fire. Oh my God, they're*

❯ Chapter Outline

● Prologue: Katie's Story

● Introduction: What Is Stress?

  CULTURE AND HUMAN BEHAVIOR: The Stress of Adapting to a New Culture

● Physical Effects of Stress: The Mind–Body Connection

  FOCUS ON NEUROSCIENCE: The Mysterious Placebo Effect

● Individual Factors That Influence the Response to Stress

  CRITICAL THINKING: Do Personality Factors Cause Disease?

  IN FOCUS: Providing Effective Social Support

● Coping: How People Deal with Stress

  IN FOCUS: Gender Differences in Responding to Stress: "Tend and Befriend" or "Fight-or-Flight?"

● Closing Thoughts

  APPLICATION: Minimizing the Effects of Stress

jumping out of the buildings! Don't look!
Firefighters, EMT workers, police, media
people swarming on the plaza at the base
of the buildings. *This is not real. It's a
movie. It's not real.*

Suddenly, unbelievably, the south tower
crumbled. Onlookers screaming. *It's col-
lapsing! It's coming down.* A vast ball of
smoke formed, mushrooming in the sky.
Like everyone else in the park, Katie turned
and started running blindly. Behind her, a
huge cloud of black smoke, ash, and de-
bris followed, howling down West Street
like a tornado.

Running. Cops shouting. "Go north!
Don't go back! Get out of here!" *Don't go
north. Go toward the ferry.* Choking on
the smoke and dust, Katie covered her
face with her T-shirt and stumbled down
the street, moving toward the harbor. *I'm
going to choke . . . can't breathe.* She saw
a group of people near the Staten Island
Ferry. *Get on the ferry, get out of Manhattan.* Another explosion. Panic. More people
running.

Katie is still not certain how, dazed and
disoriented, she ended up on a boat—a
commuter ferry taking people to Atlantic

Highlands, New Jersey. *Stop shaking. I'm
safe. Stop shaking.* Covered with soot.
Filthy. Standing in her pajamas amid
stunned Wall Street workers in their suits
and ties. Call anyone. Trying to call people.
Cell phone dead . . . no, please work!
"Here, Miss, use mine, it's working." Call
anyone. Crying. *They're dead. Those fire-
men, the EMT workers on the plaza.
They're all dead.* From the boat, she got a
call through to her dance teacher, Pam,
who lived in New Jersey. Pam would come
and get her. She could stay with Pam.

Katie survived, but the next few weeks
were difficult ones. Like the other residents
of buildings near the World Trade Center,
Katie wasn't allowed back into her apartment for many days. She had no money,
no clothes, none of her possessions. And
the reminders were everywhere. Fire station shrines, signs for the subway stop that
didn't exist anymore, photographs of the
missing on fences and walls. And the
haunting memories—images of people
jumping, falling, the faces of the rescue
workers, the plane ripping through the
building.

Eventually, like millions of other New
Yorkers, Katie regained her equilibrium.
"Are things back to normal?" Katie says,
"No, things will never be normal again,
not in a hundred years. But it's okay. I'm
fine. And I'm not going to leave New York.
This is where I am, this is where I live, this
is where I can dance."

>> Introduction: What Is Stress?

Key Theme

• **When events are perceived as exceeding your ability to cope with them, you experience an unpleasant emotional and physical state called stress.**

Key Questions

• **What is health psychology, and what is the biopsychosocial model?**
• **How do life events, daily hassles, and conflict contribute to stress?**
• **What are some social and cultural sources of stress?**

stress
A negative emotional state occurring in response to events that are perceived as taxing or exceeding a person's resources or ability to cope.

health psychology
The branch of psychology that studies how biological, behavioral, and social factors influence health, illness, medical treatment, and health-related behaviors.

When you think of the causes of psychological stress, your initial tendency is probably to think of events and issues directly related to yourself, such as school, work, or family pressures. And, indeed, we don't want to minimize those events as stressors. If you're like most of our students, you probably have ample firsthand experience with the stress of juggling the demands of college, work, and family responsibilities. Those pressures represent very real and personal concerns for many of us as we negotiate the challenges of daily life.

But as the terrorist attacks of September 11, 2001, unfolded, our entire nation was thrown into an extraordinary state of shared psychological stress as we watched, minute by minute, reeling in disbelief. It is impossible, of course, to convey the anguish, grief, and despair experienced by the thousands of people who lost loved ones as a result of the attacks. It is equally impossible to convey the sense of relief that thousands of other people felt when they eventually learned that their loved ones—like our niece Katie—had survived the attack.

What exactly is *stress*? It's one of those words that is frequently used but is hard to define precisely. Early stress researchers, who mostly studied animals, defined stress in terms of the physiological response to harmful or threatening events (e.g., Selye, 1956). However, people are far more complex than animals in their response to potentially stressful events. Two people may respond very differently to the same potentially stressful event.

Since the 1960s, psychologists have been studying the human response to stress, including the effects of stress on health and how people cope with stressful events. It has become clear that psychological and social factors, as well as biological factors, are involved in the stress experience and its effects.

Today, **stress** is widely defined as a negative emotional state occurring in response to events that are perceived as taxing or exceeding a person's resources or ability to cope. This definition emphasizes the important role played by a person's perception or appraisal of events in the experience of stress. Whether we experience stress depends largely on our *cognitive appraisal* of an event and the resources we have to deal with the event (Lazarus & Folkman, 1984; Storch & others, 2007; Tomaka & others, 1993).

If we think that we have adequate resources to deal with a situation, it will probably create little or no stress in our lives. But if we perceive our resources as being inadequate to deal with a situation we see as threatening, challenging, or even harmful, we'll experience the effects of stress. If our coping efforts are effective, stress will decrease. If they are ineffective, stress will increase.

The study of stress is a key topic in **health psychology,** one of the most rapidly growing specialty areas in psychology. Health psychology is also sometimes referred to as *behavioral medicine*. Health psychologists are interested in how biological, psychological, and social factors influence health, illness, and treatment. Along with developing strategies to foster emotional and physical well-being, they investigate issues such as the following:

How Do You Define Stress? Juggling babies and bags, motherhood and a career is certainly stressful. However, stressors come in all sizes. Any event can produce stress— if you think you don't have the resources to cope with it.

biopsychosocial model
The belief that physical health and illness are determined by the complex interaction of biological, psychological, and social factors.

stressors
Events or situations that are perceived as harmful, threatening, or challenging.

daily hassles
Everyday minor events that annoy and upset people.

- How to promote health-enhancing behaviors
- How people respond to being ill
- How people respond in the patient–health practitioner relationship
- Why some people don't follow medical advice

Health psychologists work with many different health care professionals, including physicians, dentists, nurses, social workers, and occupational and physical therapists. In their research and clinical practice, health psychologists are guided by the **biopsychosocial model.** According to this model, health and illness are determined by the complex interaction of biological factors (e.g., genetic predispositions), psychological and behavioral factors (e.g., health beliefs and attitudes, lifestyle, stress), and social conditions (e.g., family relationships, social support, cultural influences). Throughout this chapter, we'll look closely at the roles that different biological, psychological, and social factors play in our experience of stress.

○ **Table 13.1**

The Social Readjustment Rating Scale: Sample Items

Life Change	Life Event Units
Death of spouse	100
Divorce	73
Marital separation	65
Death of close family member	63
Major personal injury or illness	53
Marriage	50
Fired at work	47
Retirement	45
Pregnancy	40
Change in financial state	38
Death of close friend	37
Change to different line of work	36
Mortgage or loan for major purchase	31
Foreclosure on mortgage or loan	30
Change in work responsibilities	29
Outstanding personal achievement	28
Begin or end school	26
Trouble with boss	23
Change in work hours or conditions	20
Change in residence	20
Change in social activities	18
Change in sleeping habits	16
Vacation	13
Christmas	12
Minor violations of the law	11

Source: Holmes & Rahe (1967).

The Social Readjustment Rating Scale, developed by Thomas Holmes and Richard Rahe (1967), was an early attempt to quantify the amount of stress experienced by people in a wide range of situations. Holmes and Rahe reasoned that any life event that required some sort of adaptation or change would create stress, whether the life event was pleasant or unpleasant.

Sources of Stress

Life is filled with potential **stressors**—events or situations that produce stress. Virtually any event or situation can be a source of stress if you question your ability or resources to deal effectively with it (Lazarus & Folkman, 1984). In this section, we'll survey some of the most important and common sources of stress.

Life Events and Change
Is *Any* Change Stressful?

Early stress researchers Thomas Holmes and Richard Rahe (1967) believed that any change that required you to adjust your behavior and lifestyle would cause stress. In an attempt to measure the amount of stress people experienced, they developed the *Social Readjustment Rating Scale.* The scale included 43 life events that are likely to require some level of adaptation. Each life event was assigned a numerical rating that estimates its relative impact in terms of *life change units.* Sample items from the original Social Readjustment Rating Scale are shown in Table 13.1.

Life event ratings range from 100 life change units for the most stress-producing to 11 life change units for the least stress-producing events. Cross-cultural studies have shown that people in many different cultures tend to rank the magnitude of stressful events in a similar way (McAndrew & others, 1998; Wong & Wong, 2006). Notice that some of the life events are generally considered to be positive events, such as a vacation. According to the life events approach, *any* change, whether positive or negative, is inherently stress-producing.

To measure their level of stress, people simply check off the life events they have experienced in the past year and total the life change units. Holmes and Rahe found that people who had accumulated more than 150 life change units within a year had an increased rate of physical or psychological illness (Holmes & Masuda, 1974; Rahe, 1972).

Despite its initial popularity, several problems with the life events approach have been noted. First, the link between scores on the Social Readjustment Rating Scale and the development of physical and psychological problems is relatively weak. In general, scores on the Social Readjustment Rating Scale are *not* very good predictors of poor physical or mental health. Instead, researchers have found that most people weather major life events without developing serious physical or psychological problems (Coyne & Downey, 1991; Kessler & others, 1985).

Second, the Social Readjustment Rating Scale does not take into account a person's subjective appraisal of an event, response to that event, or ability to cope with the event (Hammen, 2005; Lazarus, 1999). Instead, the number of life change units on the scale is preassigned, reflecting the assumption that a given life event will have the same impact on virtually everyone. But clearly, the stress-producing potential of an event might vary widely from one person to another. For instance, if you are in a marriage that is filled with conflict, tension, and unhappiness, getting divorced (73 life change units) might be significantly less stressful than remaining married.

Third, the life events approach assumes that change in itself, whether good or bad, produces stress. However, researchers have found that negative life events have greater adverse effects on health, especially when they're unexpected and uncontrollable (Dohrenwend & others, 1993). In contrast, positive or desirable events are much *less* likely to affect your health adversely. Today, most researchers agree that undesirable events are significant sources of stress but that change in itself is not necessarily stressful.

Nonetheless, the Social Readjustment Rating Scale is still often used in stress research (Lynch & others, 2005; Scully & others, 2000). Efforts have been made to revise and update the scale so that it more fully takes into account the influences of gender, age, marital status, and other characteristics (C. Hobson & Delunas, 2001).

Major Life Events and Stress Would the birth of a child or losing your home in a fire both produce damaging levels of stress? According to the life events approach, any event that required you to change or adjust your lifestyle would produce significant stress—whether the event was positive or negative, planned or unexpected. How was the life events approach modified by later research?

Daily Hassles
That's Not What I Ordered!

What made you feel "stressed out" in the last week? Chances are it was not a major life event. Instead, it was probably some unexpected but minor annoyance, such as splotching ketchup on your new white T-shirt, misplacing your keys, or discovering that you've been standing in the wrong line.

Stress researcher **Richard Lazarus** and his colleagues suspected that such ordinary irritations in daily life might be an important source of stress. To explore this idea, they developed a scale measuring **daily hassles**—everyday occurrences that annoy and upset people (DeLongis & others, 1982; Kanner & others, 1981). The *Daily Hassles Scale* measures the occurrence of everyday annoyances, such as losing something, getting stuck in traffic, and even being inconvenienced by lousy weather.

Are there gender differences in the frequency of daily hassles? One study measured the daily hassles experienced by married couples (Almeida & Kessler, 1998). The women experienced both more daily hassles and higher levels of psychological stress than their husbands did. For men, the most common sources of daily stress were financial and job-related problems. For women, family demands and interpersonal conflict were the most frequent causes of stress. However, when women *do* experience a stressful day in the workplace, the stress is more likely to spill over into their interactions with their husbands and other family members (Schulz & others, 2004). Men, on the other hand, are more likely to simply withdraw.

How important are daily hassles in producing stress? The frequency of daily hassles is linked to both psychological distress and physical symptoms, such as headaches and backaches (Bottos & Dewey, 2004; DeLongis & others, 1988). In fact, the number of daily hassles people experience is a better predictor of physical illness and symptoms than is the number of major life events experienced (Burks & Martin, 1985).

Why do daily hassles take such a toll? One explanation is that such minor stressors are *cumulative* (Repetti, 1993). Each hassle may be relatively unimportant in itself, but after a day filled with minor hassles, the effects add up. People feel drained, grumpy, and stressed out. Daily hassles also contribute to the stress produced by major life events. Any major life change, whether positive or negative, can create a ripple effect, generating a host of new daily hassles (Maybery & others, 2007; Pillow & others, 1996).

Richard Lazarus (1922–2002) Psychologist Richard Lazarus has made several influential contributions to the study of stress and coping. His definition of stress emphasizes the importance of cognitive appraisal in the stress response. He also demonstrated the significance of everyday hassles in producing stress.

Major Life Events, Daily Hassles, and Stress After the collapse of the two World Trade Center towers, people who lived in nearby apartments were evacuated. More than a week after the disaster, these lower Manhattan residents are waiting to be escorted by members of the National Guard to retrieve some of their possessions. Even after people were allowed to return to their homes, they had to deal with damaged apartments, air filled with smoke and dust, and a lack of basic services, like telephone service. The daily hassles created by major disasters add to the level of stress felt by those affected.

For example, like many other New Yorkers, our niece Katie had to contend with a host of daily hassles after the terrorist attacks. She had no place to live, could not get access to her clothing or other possessions, and was unable to get money from the Red Cross because her roommate's father's name was on the lease. After pleading with the National Guardsmen patroling the area, Katie and her roommate, Lydia, were allowed to get some of their belongings out of their apartment. They loaded as much as they could into a shopping cart, dragging and pushing the cart some 30 blocks north to a friend's home. Katie had to take a second waitress job to pay for the new, more expensive apartment.

Social and Cultural Sources of Stress

Social conditions can also be an important source of stress. Racism and discrimination, whether real or suspected, can create stress (Contrada & others, 2000; Townes, 2007). Crowding, crime, unemployment, poverty, inadequate health care, and substandard housing are all associated with increased stress (Gallo & Matthews, 2003). When people live in an environment that is inherently stressful, they often experience ongoing, or *chronic*, stress (Krantz & McCeney, 2002).

People in the lowest socioeconomic levels of society tend to have the highest levels of psychological distress, illness, and death (Mays & others, 2007). Researcher Sheldon Cohen found that people with low SES tend to have higher levels of certain stress hormones (Cohen & others, 2006). This finding remained consistent regardless of other variables, including race, gender, and age. In a poverty-stricken neighborhood, people are likely to be exposed to more negative life events and to have fewer resources available to cope with those events. Daily hassles are also more common.

Stress can also result when cultures clash. For refugees, immigrants, and their children, adapting to a new culture can be extremely stress-producing (Berry, 2003; Chun & others, 2003; Jamil, 2007). In the Culture and Human Behavior box we describe the stress that can result from adapting to a different culture.

Conflict
Torn Between Two Choices

Another common source of stress is **conflict**—feeling pulled between two opposing desires, motives, or goals (Mellers, 2000). There are three basic types of conflict, each with a different potential to produce stress. These conflicts are described in terms of *approach* and *avoidance*. An individual is motivated to *approach* desirable or pleasant outcomes and to *avoid* undesirable or unpleasant outcomes.

An *approach–approach conflict* represents a win–win situation—you're faced with a choice between two equally appealing outcomes. Approach–approach conflicts are usually easy to resolve and don't produce much stress. Much more stressful are *avoidance–avoidance conflicts*—choosing between two unappealing or undesirable outcomes. A common response is to avoid both outcomes by delaying the decision (Tversky & Shafir, 1992; Bello, 2006).

Most stressful are *approach–avoidance conflicts*. Here, a goal has both desirable and undesirable aspects. When faced with an approach–avoidance conflict, people often *vacillate*, unable to decide whether to approach or avoid the goal. From a distance, the desirable aspects of the goal can exert a strong pull. But as you move toward or approach the goal, the negative aspects loom more vividly in your mind, and you pull back. Not surprisingly, people facing approach–avoidance conflicts often find themselves "stuck"—unable to resolve the conflict but unable to stop thinking about it, either (Emmons & King, 1988). The result is a significant increase in feelings of stress and anxiety.

How can you get "unstuck"? There are several things you can do to resolve an approach–avoidance conflict. First, accept the reality that very few of life's major decisions are likely to be simple, with one alternative standing head and shoulders above the others. Second, see if you can adopt a *partial-approach strategy*, in which

conflict
A situation in which a person feels pulled between two or more opposing desires, motives, or goals.

acculturative stress
(ah-KUL-chur-uh-tiv) The stress that results from the pressure of adapting to a new culture.

CULTURE AND HUMAN BEHAVIOR

The Stress of Adapting to a New Culture

Refugees, immigrants, and even international students are often unprepared for the dramatically different values, language, food, customs, and climate that await them in their new land. Coping with a new culture can be extremely stress-producing (Johnson & Sandhu, 2007). The process of changing one's values and customs as a result of contact with another culture is referred to as *acculturation*. Thus, the term **acculturative stress** describes the stress that results from the pressure of adapting to a new culture (Berry, 1994, 2003, 2006).

Many factors can influence the degree of acculturative stress that a person experiences. For example, when the new society is one that accepts ethnic and cultural diversity, acculturative stress is reduced (Shuval, 1993). The ease of transition is also enhanced when the person has some familiarity with the new language and customs, advanced education, and social support from friends, family members, and cultural associations (Finch & Vega, 2003).

Cross-cultural psychologist John Berry has found that a person's attitudes are important in determining how much acculturative stress is experienced. When people encounter a new cultural environment, they are faced with two fundamental questions: (1) Should I seek positive relations with the dominant society? (2) Is my original cultural identity of value to me, and should I try to maintain it?

The answers to these questions result in one of four possible patterns of acculturation: integration, assimilation, separation, or marginalization (see the diagram). Each pattern represents a different way of coping with the stress of adapting to a new culture (Berry, 1994, 2003).

Integrated individuals continue to value their original cultural customs but also seek to become part of the dominant society. Ideally, the integrated individual feels comfortable in both her culture of origin and the culture of the dominant society, moving easily from one to the other (LaFromboise, Coleman, & Gerton, 1993). The successfully integrated individual's level of acculturative stress will be low (Ward & Rana-Deuba, 1999).

Assimilated individuals give up their old cultural identity and try to become part of the new society. They may adopt the new clothing, religion, and social values of the new environment and abandon their old customs and language.

Assimilation usually involves a moderate level of stress, partly because it involves a psychological loss—one's previous cultural identity. People who follow this pattern also face the possibility of being rejected either by members of the majority culture or by members of their original culture (LaFromboise & others, 1993).

Acculturative Stress Adapting to a new culture is a stressful process. However, acculturative stress can be reduced when immigrants learn the language and customs of their newly adopted home. Here, two friends, one from China, one from Cuba, help one another in an English language class in Miami, Florida.

The process of learning new behaviors and suppressing old behaviors can also be moderately stressful.

Individuals who follow the pattern of *separation* maintain their cultural identity and avoid contact with the new culture. They may refuse to learn the new language, live in a neighborhood that is primarily populated by others of the same ethnic background, and socialize only with members of their own ethnic group.

In some instances, such withdrawal from the larger society is self-imposed. However, separation can also be the result of discrimination by the dominant society, as when people of a particular ethnic group are discouraged from fully participating in the dominant society. Not surprisingly, the level of acculturative stress associated with separation is likely to be very high.

Finally, the *marginalized* person lacks cultural and psychological contact with *both* his traditional cultural group and the culture of his new society. By taking the path of marginalization, he has lost the important features of his traditional culture but has not replaced them with a new cultural identity.

Marginalized individuals are likely to experience the greatest degree of acculturative stress, feeling as if they don't really belong anywhere. Essentially, they are stuck in an unresolved conflict between the traditional culture and the new social environment. They are also likely to experience feelings of alienation and a loss of identity (Berry & Kim, 1988; Castillo & others, 2007).

	Question 1: Should I seek positive relations with the dominant society?	
	Yes	**No**
Question 2: Is my original cultural identity of value to me, and should I try to maintain it? **Yes**	Integration	Separation
No	Assimilation	Marginalization

Patterns of Adapting to a New Culture According to cross-cultural psychologist John Berry (1994, 2003), there are four basic patterns of adapting to a new culture. Which pattern is followed depends on how the person responds to the two key questions shown.

CATHY

you test the waters but leave yourself an "out" before making a final decision or commitment.

Third, get as much information as you can about each option. Try to analyze objectively the pros and cons of every option. (We described this strategy of decision making in Chapter 7.) Finally, discuss the issue with a friend or someone outside the conflict. Doing so may help you see other possible rewards or pitfalls that your own analysis might have missed.

Physical Effects of Stress
The Mind–Body Connection

> **Key Theme**
> - The effects of stress on physical health were demonstrated in research by Walter Cannon and Hans Selye.
>
> **Key Questions**
> - What endocrine pathways are involved in the fight-or-flight response and the general adaptation syndrome?
> - What is psychoneuroimmunology, and how does the immune system interact with the nervous system?
> - What kinds of stressors affect immune system functioning?

From headaches to heart attacks, stress contributes to a wide range of disorders, especially when it is long-term, or chronic (Cass, 2006; Krantz & McCeney, 2002). Basically, stress appears to undermine physical well-being in two ways: indirectly and directly (Schneiderman & others, 2005).

First, stress can *indirectly* affect a person's health by prompting behaviors that jeopardize physical well-being, such as not eating or sleeping properly (see Figure 13.1). For example, among residents of Manhattan, there was a sharp rise in substance abuse during the weeks after the September 11 attacks. Almost 30 percent of residents participating in a New York Academy of Medicine survey reported that they had increased their level of alcohol consumption, cigarette smoking, or marijuana use (Vlahov & others, 2002). High levels of stress can also interfere with cognitive abilities, such as attention, concentration, and memory (Mandler, 1993). In turn, such cognitive disruptions can increase the likelihood of accidents and injuries.

Second, stress can *directly* affect physical health by altering body functions, leading to symptoms, illness, or disease (Kiecolt-Glaser & others, 2002). Here's a very common example: When people are under a great deal of stress, their neck and head muscles can contract and tighten, resulting in stress-induced tension headaches. But exactly how do stressful events influence bodily processes, such as muscle contractions?

fight-or-flight response
A rapidly occurring chain of internal physical reactions that prepare people either to fight or take flight from an immediate threat.

catecholamines
(*cat*-eh-COLE-uh-meens) Hormones secreted by the adrenal medulla that cause rapid physiological arousal; include adrenaline and noradrenaline.

Percent of American Adults Who Have Had Sleep Problems Prior to and Following September 11

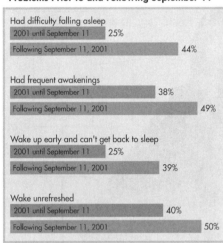

Had difficulty falling asleep
2001 until September 11   25%
Following September 11, 2001   44%

Had frequent awakenings
2001 until September 11   38%
Following September 11, 2001   49%

Wake up early and can't get back to sleep
2001 until September 11   25%
Following September 11, 2001   39%

Wake unrefreshed
2001 until September 11   40%
Following September 11, 2001   50%

Source: National Sleep Foundation (2002).

Figure 13.1 **Disrupted Sleep: One Indicator of Stress** In the weeks immediately following the 9/11 terrorist attacks, the psychological stress caused by those events was evident in the increased sleep disruptions experienced by millions of Americans. Even years after the attacks, many firefighters, police officers, and other rescue and recovery workers continue to experience insomnia, recurring nightmares, and other sleep problems (Farfel & others, 2008; Stellman & others, 2008).

Stress and the Endocrine System

To explain the connection between stress and health, researchers have focused on how the nervous system, including the brain, interacts with two other important body systems: the endocrine and immune systems. We'll first consider the role of the endocrine system in our response to stressful events and then look at the connections between stress and the immune system.

Walter Cannon
Stress and the Fight-or-Flight Response

Any kind of immediate threat to your well-being is a stress-producing experience that triggers a cascade of changes in your body. As we've noted in previous chapters, this rapidly occurring chain of internal physical reactions is called the **fight-or-flight response.** Collectively, these changes prepare us either to fight or to take flight from an immediate threat.

The fight-or-flight response was first described by American physiologist **Walter Cannon,** one of the earliest contributors to stress research. Cannon (1932) found that the fight-or-flight response involved both the sympathetic nervous system and the endocrine system (see Chapter 2).

With the perception of a threat, the hypothalamus and lower brain structures activate the sympathetic nervous system (see left side of Figure 13.2). The sympathetic nervous system stimulates the adrenal medulla to secrete hormones called **catecholamines,** including *adrenaline* and *noradrenaline.* Circulating through the blood, catecholamines trigger the rapid and intense bodily changes associated with the fight-or-flight response. Once the threat is removed, the high level of bodily arousal subsides gradually, usually within about 20 to 60 minutes.

As a short-term reaction, the fight-or-flight response helps ensure survival by swiftly mobilizing internal physical resources to defensively attack or flee an immediate threat. Without question, the fight-or-flight response is very useful if you're suddenly faced with a life-threatening situation, such as a guy pointing a gun at you in a deserted parking lot. However, when exposure to an unavoidable threat is prolonged, the intense arousal of the fight-or-flight response can also become prolonged. Under these conditions, Cannon believed, the fight-or-flight response could prove harmful to physical health.

Walter B. Cannon (1875–1945) Cannon made many lasting contributions to psychology, including an influential theory of emotion, which we discussed in Chapter 8. During World War I, Cannon's research on the effects of stress and trauma led him to recognize the central role of the adrenal glands in mobilizing the body's resources in response to threatening circumstances—the essence of the *fight-or-flight response.* Cannon also coined the term *homeostasis,* which is the tendency of the body to maintain a steady internal state (see page 336).

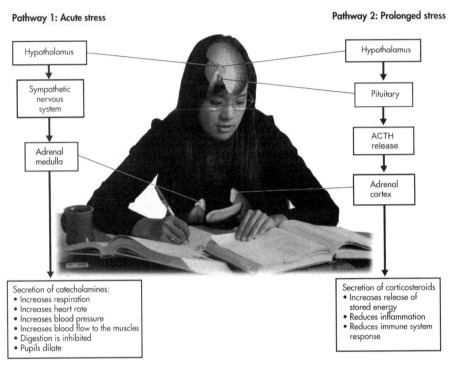

Pathway 1: Acute stress

Hypothalamus → Sympathetic nervous system → Adrenal medulla → Secretion of catecholamines:
• Increases respiration
• Increases heart rate
• Increases blood pressure
• Increases blood flow to the muscles
• Digestion is inhibited
• Pupils dilate

Pathway 2: Prolonged stress

Hypothalamus → Pituitary → ACTH release → Adrenal cortex → Secretion of corticosteroids:
• Increases release of stored energy
• Reduces inflammation
• Reduces immune system response

Figure 13.2 Endocrine System Pathways in Stress Two different endocrine system pathways are involved in the response to stress. Walter Cannon identified the endocrine pathway shown on the left side of this diagram. This is the pathway involved in the fight-or-flight response to immediate threats. Hans Selye identified the endocrine pathway shown on the right. This second endocrine pathway plays an important role in dealing with prolonged, or chronic, stressors.

general adaptation syndrome
Selye's term for the three-stage progression of physical changes that occur when an organism is exposed to intense and prolonged stress. The three stages are alarm, resistance, and exhaustion.

A Pioneer in Stress Research With his tie off and his feet up, Canadian endocrinologist Hans Selye (1907–1982) looks the very picture of relaxation. Selye's research at the University of Montreal documented the physical effects of exposure to prolonged stress. His popular book *The Stress of Life* (1956) helped make *stress* a household word.

Hans Selye
Stress and the General Adaptation Syndrome

Cannon's suggestion that prolonged stress could be physically harmful was confirmed by Canadian endocrinologist **Hans Selye.** Most of Selye's pioneering research was done with rats that were exposed to prolonged stressors, such as electric shock, extreme heat or cold, or forced exercise. Regardless of the condition that Selye used to produce prolonged stress, he found the same pattern of physical changes in the rats. First, the adrenal glands became enlarged. Second, stomach ulcers and loss of weight occurred. And third, there was shrinkage of the thymus gland and lymph glands, two key components of the immune system. Selye believed that these distinct physical changes represented the essential effects of stress—the body's response to any demand placed on it.

Selye discovered that if the bodily "wear and tear" of the stress-producing event continued, the effects became evident in three progressive stages. He called these stages the **general adaptation syndrome.** During the initial *alarm stage,* intense arousal occurs as the body mobilizes internal physical resources to meet the demands of the stress-producing event. Selye (1976) found that the rapidly occurring changes during the alarm stage result from the release of catecholamines by the adrenal medulla, as Cannon had previously described.

In the *resistance stage,* the body actively tries to resist or adjust to the continuing stressful situation. The intense arousal of the alarm stage diminishes, but physiological arousal remains above normal and resistance to new stressors is impaired.

If the stress-producing event persists, the *exhaustion stage* may occur. In this third stage, the symptoms of the alarm stage reappear, only now irreversibly. As the body's energy reserves become depleted, adaptation begins to break down, leading to exhaustion, physical disorders, and, potentially, death.

Selye (1956, 1976) found that prolonged stress activates a second endocrine pathway (see Figure 13.2) that involves the hypothalamus, the pituitary gland, and the adrenal cortex. In response to a stressor, the hypothalamus signals the pituitary gland to secrete a hormone called *adrenocorticotropic hormone,* abbreviated *ACTH.* In turn, ACTH stimulates the adrenal cortex to release stress-related hormones called **corticosteroids,** the most important of which is *cortisol.*

In the short run, the corticosteroids provide several benefits, helping protect the body against the harm caused by stressors. For example, corticosteroids reduce inflammation of body tissues and enhance muscle tone in the heart and blood vessels. However, unlike the effects of catecholamines, which tend to diminish rather quickly, corticosteroids have long-lasting effects. If a stressor is prolonged, continued high levels of corticosteroids can weaken important body systems, lowering immunity and increasing susceptibility to physical symptoms and illness. There is mounting evidence that chronic stress can lead to increased vulnerability to acute and chronic diseases, including cardiovascular disease, and even to premature aging (Robles & others, 2005; Segerstrom & Miller, 2004). Chronic stress can also lead to depression and other psychological problems (Hammen, 2005).

Selye's pioneering studies are widely regarded as the cornerstone of modern stress research. His description of the general adaptation syndrome firmly established some of the critical biological links between stress-producing events and their potential impact on physical health. But as you'll see in the next section, the endocrine system is not the only body system affected by stress: The immune system, too, is part of the mind–body connection.

Stress and the Immune System

The **immune system** is your body's surveillance system. It detects and battles foreign invaders, such as bacteria, viruses, and tumor cells. Your immune system comprises several organs, including bone marrow, the spleen, the thymus, and lymph nodes (see Figure 13.3). The most important elements of the immune system are **lymphocytes**—the specialized white blood cells that fight bacteria, viruses, and other foreign invaders. Lymphocytes are initially manufactured in the bone marrow. From the bone marrow, they migrate to other immune system organs, such as the thymus and spleen, where they develop more fully and are stored until needed.

Psychoneuroimmunology

Until the 1970s, the immune system was thought to be completely independent of other body systems, including the nervous and endocrine systems. Thus, most scientists believed that psychological processes could not influence the immune system response.

That notion was challenged in the mid-1970s, when psychologist **Robert Ader** teamed up with immunologist Nicholas Cohen. Ader (1993) recalls, "As a psychologist, I was not aware of the general position of immunology that there were no connections between the brain and the immune system." But Ader and Cohen showed that the immune system response in rats could be classically conditioned (see Chapter 5). After repeatedly pairing flavored water with a drug that suppressed immune system functioning, Ader and Cohen (1975) demonstrated that the flavored water *alone* suppressed the immune system.

Ader and Cohen's research helped establish a new interdisciplinary field called *psychoneuroimmunology.* **Psychoneuroimmunology** is the scientific study of the connections among psychological processes (*psycho-*), the nervous system (*-neuro-*) and the immune system (*-immunology*).

corticosteroids
(core-tick-oh-STAIR-oydz) Hormones released by the adrenal cortex that play a key role in the body's response to long-term stressors.

immune system
Body system that produces specialized white blood cells that protect the body from viruses, bacteria, and tumor cells.

lymphocytes
(LIMF-oh-sites) Specialized white blood cells that are responsible for immune defenses.

psychoneuroimmunology
An interdisciplinary field that studies the interconnections among psychological processes, nervous and endocrine system functions, and the immune system.

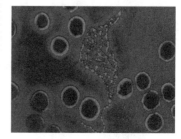

Lymphocytes in Action In this color-enhanced photo, you can see white blood cells, or lymphocytes, attacking and ingesting the beadlike chain of streptococcus bacteria, which can cause diseases such as pneumonia and scarlet fever.

Conditioning the Immune System Psychologist Robert Ader *(left)* teamed with immunologist Nicholas Cohen *(right)* and demonstrated that immune system responses could be classically conditioned. Ader and Cohen's groundbreaking research helped lead to the new field of psychoneuroimmunology—the study of the connections among psychological processes, the nervous system, and the immune system.

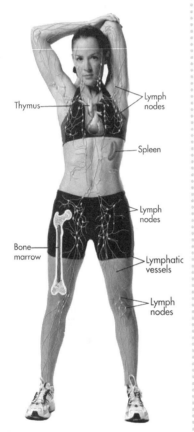

Figure 13.3 The Immune System Your immune system battles bacteria, viruses, and other foreign invaders that try to set up housekeeping in your body. The specialized white blood cells that fight infection are manufactured in the bone marrow and are stored in the thymus, spleen, and lymph nodes until needed.

Ron Glaser and Janice Kiecolt-Glaser Two of the leading researchers in psychoneuroimmunology are psychologist Janice Kiecolt-Glaser and her husband, immunologist Ron Glaser. Their research has shown that the effectiveness of the immune system can be lowered by many common stressors—from marital arguments to caring for sick relatives (see Glaser & Kiecolt-Glaser, 2005).

Today, it is known that there are many interconnections among the immune system, the endocrine system, and the nervous system, including the brain (Ader, 2001; Segerstrom & Miller, 2004). First, the central nervous system and the immune system are *directly* linked via sympathetic nervous system fibers, which influence the production and functioning of lymphocytes.

Second, the surfaces of lymphocytes contain receptor sites for neurotransmitters and hormones, including catecholamines and cortisol. Thus, rather than operating independently, the activities of lymphocytes and the immune system are directly influenced by neurotransmitters, hormones, and other chemical messengers from the nervous and endocrine systems.

Third, psychoneuroimmunologists have discovered that lymphocytes themselves *produce* neurotransmitters and hormones. These neurotransmitters and hormones, in turn, influence the nervous and endocrine systems. In other words, there is ongoing interaction and communication among the nervous system, the endocrine system, and the immune system. Each system influences *and* is influenced by the other systems (Ader, 2001).

Stressors That Can Influence the Immune System

When researchers began studying how stress affects the immune system, they initially focused on extremely stressful events (see Kiecolt-Glaser & Glaser, 1993). For example, researchers looked at how the immune system was affected by such intense stressors as the reentry and splashdown of returning *Skylab* astronauts, being forced to stay awake for days, and fasting for a week (Kimzey, 1975; Leach & Rambaut, 1974; Palmblad & others, 1979). Each of these highly stressful events, it turned out, was associated with reduced immune system functioning.

Could immune system functioning also be affected by more common negative life events, such as the death of a spouse, divorce, or marital separation? In a word, yes. Researchers consistently found that the stress caused by the end or disruption of important interpersonal relationships impairs immune function, putting people at greater risk for health problems (Kiecolt-Glaser, 1999; Kiecolt-Glaser & Newton, 2001). And perhaps not surprisingly, chronic stressors that continue for years, such as caring for a family member with Alzheimer's disease, also diminish immune system functioning (Cass, 2006; Robles & others, 2005).

What about the ordinary stressors of life, such as the pressure of exams? Do they affect immune system functioning? Since the 1980s, psychologist **Janice Kiecolt-Glaser** and her husband, immunologist Ronald Glaser, have collected immunological and psychological data from medical students. Several times each academic year, the medical students face three-day examination periods. Kiecolt-Glaser and Glaser have consistently found that even commonplace stress of exams can adversely affect the immune system (Glaser & Kiecolt-Glaser, 2005; Kiecolt-Glaser & Glaser, 1991, 1993).

What are the practical implications of reduced immune system functioning? One consistent finding is that psychological stress can increase the length of time it takes for a wound to heal. In one study, dental students volunteered to receive two small puncture wounds on the roofs of their mouths (Marucha & others, 1998). To

FOCUS ON NEUROSCIENCE

The Mysterious Placebo Effect

The *placebo effect* is perhaps one of the most dramatic examples of how the mind influences the body. A *placebo* is an inactive substance with no known effects, like a sugar pill or an injection of sterile water. Placebos are often used in biomedical research to help gauge the effectiveness of an actual medication or treatment. But after being given a placebo, many research participants, including those suffering from pain or diseases, experience benefits from the placebo treatment. How can this be explained?

In Chapter 2 we noted that one possible way that placebos might reduce pain is by activating the brain's own natural painkillers—the *endorphins*. (The endorphins are structurally similar to opiate painkillers, like morphine.) One reason for believing this is that a drug called *naloxone*, which blocks the brain's endorphin response, also blocks the painkilling effects of placebos (Fields & Levine, 1984). Might placebos reduce pain by activating the brain's natural opioid network?

A brain-imaging study by Swedish neuroscientist Predrag Petrovic and his colleagues (2002) tackled this question. In the study, painfully hot metal was placed on the back of each volunteer's hand. Each volunteer was then given an injection of either an actual opioid painkiller or a saline solution placebo. About 30 seconds later, positron emission tomography (PET) was used to scan the participants' brain activity.

Both the volunteers who received the painkilling drug *and* the volunteers who received the placebo treatment reported that the injection provided pain relief. In the two PET scans shown here, you can see that the genuine painkilling drug *(left)* and the placebo *(right)* activated the same brain area, called the *anterior cingulate cortex* (marked by the cross). The anterior cingulate

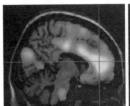 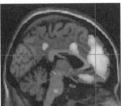

Received opiate painkiller   Received placebo

cortex is known to contain many opioid receptors. Interestingly, the level of brain activity was directly correlated with the participants' subjective perception of pain relief. The PET scan on the right shows the brain activity of those participants who had strong placebo responses.

Many questions remain about exactly how placebos work, but the PET scan study by Petrovic and his colleagues (2002) vividly substantiates the biological reality of the placebo effect. In a recent study, Jon-Kar Zubieta and his colleagues (2005) showed that a placebo treatment activated opioid receptors in several brain regions associated with pain. Further, the greater the activation, the higher the level of pain individual volunteers were able to tolerate. As these studies show, cognitive expectations, learned associations, and emotional responses can have a profound effect on the perception of pain. Other studies have shown that placebos produce measurable effects on other types of brain processes, including those of people experiencing Parkinson's disease or major depression (Fuente-Fernández & others, 2001; Leuchter & others, 2002).

compare the impact of stress on wound healing, the students received the first wound when they were on summer vacation and the second wound three days before their first major exam during the fall term. The results? The wounds inflicted before the major test healed an average of 40 percent more slowly—an extra three days—than the wounds inflicted on the same volunteers during summer vacation. Other studies have shown similar findings (Glaser & Kiecolt-Glaser, 2005).

What about the relationship between stress and infection? In a series of carefully controlled studies, psychologist Sheldon Cohen and his colleagues (1991, 1993, 1998, 2006) demonstrated that people who are experiencing high levels of stress are more susceptible to infection by a cold virus than people who are not under stress (see Figure 13.4). Subjects who experienced *chronic* stressors that lasted a month or longer were most likely to develop colds after being exposed to a cold virus. One reason may be that, as Selye showed, chronic stress triggers the secretion of corticosteroids, which influence immune system functioning (G. E. Miller & others, 2002). For example, one study showed that stress interfered with the

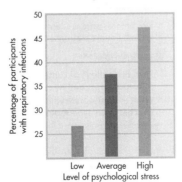

Figure 13.4 Stress and the Common Cold Are you more likely to catch a cold if you're under a great deal of stress? In a classic series of studies, Sheldon Cohen and his colleagues (1991, 1993) measured levels of psychological stress in healthy volunteers, then exposed them to a cold virus. While quarantined in apartments for a week, the participants were monitored for signs of respiratory infection. The results? As shown in the graph, the researchers found an almost perfect relationship between the level of stress and the rate of infection. The higher the volunteers' psychological stress level, the higher the rate of respiratory infection.

long-term effectiveness of vaccinations against influenza in young adults (Burns & others, 2003). In the short term, stress was associated with a strong immune system response to the flu vaccine. But after five months, the stressed-out young adults were virtually unprotected against the flu.

Health psychologists have found that a wide variety of stressors are associated with diminished immune system functioning, increasing the risk of health problems and slowing recovery times (Kiecolt-Glaser & others, 2002; Robles & others, 2005). However, while stress-related decreases in immune system functioning may heighten our susceptibility to health problems, exposure to stressors does not automatically translate into poorer health. Physical health is affected by the interaction of many factors, including heredity, nutrition, health-related habits, and access to medical care. Of course, your level of exposure to bacteria, viruses, and other sources of infection or disease will also influence your likelihood of becoming sick.

Finally, the simple fact is that some people are more vulnerable to the negative effects of stress than others (Adler & Matthews, 1994; Gunnar & Quevedo, 2007). Why? As you'll see in the next section, researchers have found that a wide variety of psychological factors can influence people's reactions to stressors.

CONCEPT REVIEW 13.1

Sources and Effects of Stress

Indicate whether each of the following items is true or false. Rewrite each false statement to correct it.

1. According to the biopsychosocial model, physical well-being is wholly determined by stress and social adjustment.

2. In the past year, Andrea has gotten divorced, changed jobs, moved three times, and lost her closest friend in an auto accident. Because of the number of stress-producing life events Andrea has experienced, she is certain to develop a major illness in the next six months.

3. The level of stress due to daily hassles is measured by the Social Readjustment Rating Scale.

4. During periods of prolonged stress, the adrenal medulla secretes stress-related hormones called catecholamines.

5. Shelley's manager has just unexpectedly informed her that she is being laid off, effective immediately. Shelley is probably experiencing the exhaustion stage of the general adaptation syndrome.

6. The study of interconnections among the nervous system, immune system, endocrine system, and psychological factors is called *psychoneuroimmunology*.

Individual Factors That Influence the Response to Stress

Key Theme

- Psychologists have identified several psychological factors that can modify an individual's response to stress and affect physical health.

Key Questions

- How do feelings of control, explanatory style, and negative emotions influence stress and health?
- What is Type A behavior, and what role does hostility play in the relationship between Type A behavior and health?

People vary a great deal in the way they respond to a distressing event, whether it's a parking ticket or a pink slip. In part, individual differences in reacting to stressors result from how people appraise an event and their resources for coping with the event. However, psychologists and other researchers have identified several factors that influence an individual's response to stressful events. In this section, we'll take a look at some of the most important psychological and social factors that seem to affect an individual's response to stress.

Psychological Factors

It's easy to demonstrate the importance of psychological factors in the response to stressors. Sit in any airport waiting room during a busy holiday travel season and observe how differently people react to news of flight cancellations or delays. Some people take the news calmly, while others become enraged and indignant. Psychologists have confirmed what common sense suggests: Psychological processes play a key role in determining the level of stress experienced.

Personal Control

Who is more likely to experience more stress, a person who has some control over a stressful experience or a person who has no control? Psychological research has consistently shown that having a sense of control over a stressful situation reduces the impact of stressors and decreases feelings of anxiety and depression (Dickerson & Kemeny, 2004; Taylor, Kemeny, & others, 2000). Those who can control a stress-producing event often show no more psychological distress or physical arousal than people who are not exposed to the stressor at all.

Psychologists Judith Rodin and Ellen Langer (1977) demonstrated the importance of a sense of control in a classic series of studies with nursing home residents. One group of residents—the "high-control" group—was given the opportunity to make choices about their daily activities and to exercise control over their environment. In contrast, residents assigned to the "low-control" group had little control over their daily activities. Decisions were made for them by the nursing home staff. Eighteen months later, the high-control residents were more active, alert, sociable, and healthier than the low-control residents. And, twice as many of the low-control residents had died (Langer & Rodin, 1976; Rodin & Langer, 1977).

How does a sense of control affect health? If you feel that you can control a stressor by taking steps to minimize or avoid it, you will experience less stress, both subjectively and physiologically (Heth & Somer, 2002; Thompson & Spacapan, 1991). Having a sense of personal control also works to our benefit by enhancing positive emotions, such as self-confidence and feelings of self-efficacy, autonomy, and self-reliance (Taylor, Kemeny, & others, 2000). In contrast, feeling a lack of control over events produces all the hallmarks of the stress response. Levels of catecholamines and corticosteroids increase, and the effectiveness of immune system functioning decreases (see Maier & Watkins, 2000; Rodin, 1986).

However, the perception of personal control in a stressful situation must be *realistic* to be adaptive (Heth & Somer, 2002). Studies of people with chronic diseases, like heart disease and arthritis, have shown that unrealistic perceptions of personal control contribute to stress and poor adjustment (Affleck, Tennen, & Croog, 1987; Affleck, Tennen, Pfeiffer, & others, 1987).

Further, not everyone benefits from feelings of enhanced personal control. Cross-cultural studies have shown that a sense of control is more highly valued in individualistic, Western cultures than in collectivistic, Eastern cultures. Comparing Japanese and British participants, Darryl O'Connor and Mikiko Shimizu (2002) found that a heightened sense of personal control *was* associated with a lower level of perceived stress—but *only* among the British participants.

Uncontrollable Events Literally hundreds of thousands of passengers were stranded when more than a thousand planes were grounded in April of 2008 because of a suspected wiring problem. Long lines, chaotic crowds, and uncertainty about when they might be able to fly to their destination contributed to the passengers' frustration. Psychological research has shown that events and situation that are perceived as being beyond your control are especially likely to cause stress (Heth & Somer, 2002). Given that, how might you be able to lessen the stressful impact of such situations?

optimistic explanatory style
Accounting for negative events or situations with external, unstable, and specific explanations.

pessimistic explanatory style
Accounting for negative events or situations with internal, stable, and global explanations.

Explanatory Style
Optimism Versus Pessimism

We all experience defeat, rejection, or failure at some point in our lives. Yet despite repeated failures, rejections, or defeats, some people persist in their efforts. In contrast, some people give up in the face of failure and setbacks—the essence of *learned helplessness*, which we discussed in Chapter 5. What distinguishes between those who persist and those who give up?

According to psychologist **Martin Seligman** (1990, 1992), how people characteristically explain their failures and defeats makes the difference. People who have an **optimistic explanatory style** tend to use *external, unstable,* and *specific* explanations for negative events. In contrast, people who have a **pessimistic explanatory style** use *internal, stable,* and *global* explanations for negative events. Pessimists are also inclined to believe that no amount of personal effort will improve their situation. Not surprisingly, pessimists tend to experience more stress than optimists.

Let's look at these two explanatory styles in action. Optimistic Olive sees an attractive guy at a party and starts across the room to introduce herself and strike up a conversation. As she approaches him, the guy glances at her, then abruptly turns away. Hurt by the obvious snub, Optimistic Olive retreats to the buffet table. Munching on some fried zucchini, she mulls the matter over in her mind. At the same party, Pessimistic Pete sees an attractive female across the room and approaches her. He, too, gets a cold shoulder and retreats to the chips and clam dip. Standing at opposite ends of the buffet table, here is what each of them is thinking:

> **OPTIMISTIC OLIVE:** *What's his problem?* (External explanation: The optimist blames other people or external circumstances.)

> **PESSIMISTIC PETE:** *I must have said the wrong thing. She probably saw me stick my elbow in the clam dip before I walked over.* (Internal explanation: The pessimist blames self.)

> **OPTIMISTIC OLIVE:** *I'm really not looking my best tonight. I've just got to get more sleep.* (Unstable, temporary explanation)

> **PESSIMISTIC PETE:** *Let's face it, I'm a pretty boring guy and really not very good-looking.* (Stable, permanent explanation)

> **OPTIMISTIC OLIVE:** *He looks pretty preoccupied. Maybe he's waiting for his girlfriend to arrive. Or his boyfriend! Ha!* (Specific explanation)

> **PESSIMISTIC PETE:** *Women never give me a second look, probably because I dress like a nerd and I never know what to say to them.* (Global, pervasive explanation)

> **OPTIMISTIC OLIVE:** *Whoa! Who's that hunk over there?! Okay, Olive, turn on the charm! Here goes!* (Perseverance after a rejection)

> **PESSIMISTIC PETE:** *Maybe I'll just hold down this corner of the buffet table . . . or go home and soak up some TV.* (Passivity and withdrawal after a rejection)

Most people, of course, are neither as completely optimistic as Olive nor as totally pessimistic as Pete. Instead, they fall somewhere along the spectrum of optimism and pessimism, and their explanatory style may vary somewhat in different situations (Peterson & Bossio, 1993). Even so, a person's characteristic explanatory style, particularly for negative events, is relatively stable across the lifespan (Burns & Seligman, 1989).

Like personal control, explanatory style is related to health consequences (Gilham & others, 2001; Wise & Rosqvist, 2006). One study showed that explanatory style in early adulthood predicted physical health status decades later. On the basis of interviews conducted at age 25, explanatory style was evaluated for a large group of Harvard graduates. At the time of the interviews, all the young men were in excellent physical and mental health. Thirty-five years later, however, those who had an optimistic explanatory style were significantly healthier than those with a pessimistic explanatory style (Peterson & others, 1988; Peterson & Park, 2007).

Other studies have shown that a pessimistic explanatory style is associated with poorer physical health (Bennett & Elliott, 2005; Jackson & others, 2002; Peterson & Bossio, 2001). For example, first-year law school students who had an optimistic, confident, and generally positive outlook experienced fewer negative moods than did pessimistic students (Segerstrom & others, 1998). And, in terms of their immune system measures, the optimistic students had significantly higher levels of lymphocytes, T cells, and helper T cells. Explaining the positive relationship between optimists and good health, Suzanne Segerstrom and her colleagues (2003) suggest that optimists are more inclined to persevere in their efforts to overcome obstacles and challenges. Optimists are also more likely to cope effectively with stressful situations than pessimists, perhaps because they attribute their failures to their coping strategies and adjust them accordingly (Iwanaga & others, 2004).

Chronic Negative Emotions
The Hazards of Being Grouchy

Some people seem to have been born with a sunny, cheerful disposition. But other people almost always seem to be unhappy campers—they frequently experience bad moods and negative emotions (Marshall & others, 1992). Are people who are prone to chronic negative emotions more likely to suffer health problems?

Howard S. Friedman and Stephanie Booth-Kewley (1987, 2003) set out to answer this question. After systematically analyzing more than 100 studies investigating the potential links between personality factors and disease, they concluded that people who are habitually anxious, depressed, angry, or hostile *are* more likely to develop a chronic disease such as arthritis or heart disease.

How might chronic negative emotions predispose people to develop disease? Not surprisingly, tense, angry, and unhappy people experience more stress than do happier people. They also report more frequent and more intense daily hassles than people who are generally in a positive mood (Bolger & Schilling, 1991; Bolger & Zuckerman, 1995). And they react much more intensely, and with far greater distress, to stressful events (Marco & Suls, 1993).

Of course, everyone occasionally experiences bad moods. Are transient negative moods also associated with health risks? One series of studies investigated the relationship between daily mood and immune system functioning (Stone & others, 1987, 1994). For three months, participants recorded their moods every day. On the days on which they experienced negative events and moods, the effectiveness of their immune systems dipped. But their immune systems improved on the days on which they experienced positive events and good moods. And in fact, other studies have found that higher levels of hope and other positive emotions are associated with a decreased likelihood of developing health problems (Richman & others, 2005).

How Do You Explain Your Setbacks and Failures? Everyone experiences setbacks, rejection, and failure at some point. The way you explain your setbacks has a significant impact on motivation and on mental and physical health. If this store owner blames his business failure on temporary and external factors, such as a short-lived downturn in the economy, he may be more likely to try opening a new store in the future.

Calvin and Hobbes by Bill Watterson

The Type A Behavior Pattern The original formulation of the Type A behavior pattern included hostility, ambition, and a sense of time urgency. Type A people always seem to be in a hurry. They hate wasting time, and often try to do two or more things at once. However, later research showed that hostility, anger, and cynicism were far more damaging to physical health than ambition or time urgency (Suls & Bunde, 2005).

Type A Behavior and Hostility

The concept of Type A behavior originated about 35 years ago, when two cardiologists, Meyer Friedman and Ray Rosenman, noticed that many of their patients shared certain traits. The original formulation of the **Type A behavior pattern** included a cluster of three characteristics: (1) an exaggerated sense of time urgency, often trying to do more and more in less and less time; (2) a general sense of hostility, frequently displaying anger and irritation; and (3) intense ambition and competitiveness. In contrast, people who were more relaxed and laid back were classified as displaying the *Type B behavior pattern* (Hock, 2007; Janisse & Dyck, 1988; Rosenman & Chesney, 1982).

Friedman and Rosenman (1974) interviewed and classified more than 3,000 middle-aged, healthy men as either Type A or Type B. They tracked the health of these men for eight years and found that Type A men were twice as likely to develop heart disease as Type B men. This held true even when the Type A men did not display other known risk factors for heart disease, such as smoking, high blood pressure, and elevated levels of cholesterol in their blood. The conclusion seemed clear: The Type A behavior pattern was a significant risk factor for heart disease.

Although early results linking the Type A behavior pattern to heart disease were impressive, studies soon began to appear in which Type A behavior did *not* reliably predict the development of heart disease (see Myrtek, 2007; Krantz & McCeney, 2002). These findings led researchers to question whether the different components of the Type A behavior pattern were equally hazardous to health. After all, many people thrive on hard work, especially when they enjoy their jobs. And, high achievers don't necessarily suffer from health problems (Robbins & others, 1991).

When researchers focused on the association between heart disease and each separate component of the Type A behavior pattern—time urgency, hostility, and achievement striving—an important distinction began to emerge (Suls & Bunde, 2005). Feeling a sense of time urgency and being competitive or achievement oriented did *not* seem to be associated with the development of heart disease. Instead, the critical component that emerged as the strongest predictor of cardiac disease was hostility (Miller & others, 1996). *Hostility* refers to the tendency to feel anger, annoyance, resentment, and contempt and to hold cynical and negative beliefs about human nature in general. Hostile people are also prone to believing that the disagreeable behavior of others is intentionally directed against them. Thus, hostile people tend to be suspicious, mistrustful, cynical, and pessimistic.

Hostile people are much more likely than other people to develop heart disease, even when other risk factors are taken into account (Niaura & others, 2002). In one study that covered a 25-year span, hostile men were five times as likely to develop heart disease and nearly seven times as likely to die as nonhostile men (Barefoot & others, 1983). The results of this prospective study are shown in Figure 13.5. Subsequent research has found that high hostility levels increase the likelihood of dying from *all* natural causes, including cancer (Miller & others, 1996).

Figure 13.5 Hostility and Mortality Beginning when they were in medical school, more than 250 doctors were monitored for their health status for 25 years. In this prospective study, those who had scored high in hostility in medical school were seven times more likely to die by age 50 than were those who had scored low in hostility.

Source: Based on Barefoot & others (1983), p. 61.

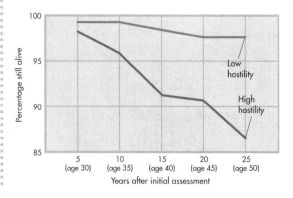

How does hostility predispose people to heart disease and other health problems? First, hostile Type As tend to react more intensely to a stressor than other people do (Lyness, 1993). They experience greater increases in blood pressure, heart rate, and the production of stress-related hormones. Because of their attitudes and behavior, hostile men and women also tend to *create* more stress in their own lives (Suls & Bunde, 2005). They experience more frequent, and more severe, negative life events and daily hassles than other people (Smith, 1992).

In general, the research evidence demonstrating the role of personality factors in the development of stress-related disease is impressive. Nevertheless, it's important to keep this evidence in perspective: Personality characteristics are just *some* of the many factors involved in the overall picture of health and disease. We look at this issue in more detail in the Critical Thinking box. And, in the chapter Application, we describe some of the steps that you can take to help you minimize the effects of stress on your health.

Type A behavior pattern
A behavioral and emotional style characterized by a sense of time urgency, hostility, and competitiveness.

CRITICAL THINKING

Do Personality Factors Cause Disease?

● You overhear a co-worker saying, "I'm not surprised he had a heart attack—the guy is a workaholic!"

● An acquaintance casually remarks, "She's been so depressed since her divorce. No wonder she got cancer."

● A tabloid headline hails, "New Scientific Findings: Use Your Mind to Cure Cancer!"

Statements like these make health psychologists, physicians, and psychoneuroimmunologists extremely uneasy. Why? Throughout this chapter, we've presented scientific evidence that emotional states can affect the functioning of the endocrine system and the immune system. Both systems play a significant role in the development of various physical disorders. We've also shown that personality factors, such as hostility and pessimism, are associated with an increased likelihood of developing poor health. But saying that "emotions affect the immune system" is a far cry from making such claims as "a positive attitude can cure cancer."

Psychologists and other scientists are cautious in the statements they make about the connections between personality and health for several reasons. First, many studies investigating the role of psychological factors in disease are *correlational*. That is, researchers have statistical evidence that two factors happen together so often that the presence of one factor reliably predicts the occurrence of the other. However, correlation does not necessarily indicate causality—it indicates only that two factors occur together. It's completely possible that some third, unidentified factor may have caused the other two factors to occur.

Second, personality factors might indirectly lead to disease via poor health habits. Low control, pessimism, chronic negative emotions, and hostility are each associated with poor health habits (Anton & Miller, 2005; Herbert & Cohen, 1993; Peterson, 2000). In turn, poor health habits are associated with higher rates of illness. That's why psychologists who study the role of personality factors in disease are typically careful to measure and consider the possible influence of the participants' health practices.

Third, it may be that the disease influences a person's emotions, rather than the other way around. After being diagnosed with advanced cancer or heart disease, most people would probably find it difficult to feel cheerful, optimistic, or in control of their lives.

*"What do you mean, I have an ulcer?
I give ulcers, I don't get them!"*

One way researchers try to disentangle the relationship between personality and health is to conduct carefully controlled prospective studies. A *prospective study* starts by assessing an initially healthy group of participants on variables thought to be risk factors, such as certain personality traits. Then the researchers track the health, personal habits, health habits, and other important dimensions of the participants' lives over a period of months, years, or decades. In analyzing the results, researchers can determine the extent to which each risk factor contributed to the health or illness of the participants. Thus, prospective studies provide more compelling evidence than do correlational studies that are based on people who are already in poor health.

CRITICAL THINKING QUESTIONS

▶ Given that health professionals frequently advise people to change their health-related behaviors to improve physical health, should they also advise people to change their psychological attitudes, traits, and emotions? Why or why not?

▶ What are the advantages and disadvantages of correlational studies? Prospective studies?

CONCEPT REVIEW 13.2

Psychological Factors and Stress

Identify the psychological characteristic that is best illustrated by each of the examples below. Choose from the following:

   a. high level of personal control
   b. optimistic explanatory style
   c. Type A behavior pattern
   d. Type B behavior pattern
   e. pessimistic explanatory style
   f. chronic negative emotions

1. No matter what happens to her, Lucy is dissatisfied and grumpy. She constantly complains about her health, her job, and how awful her life is. She dislikes most of the people she meets.

2. Cheryl was despondent when she received a low grade on her algebra test. She said, "I never do well on exams because I'm not very smart. I might as well drop out of school now before I flunk out."

3. In order to deal with the high levels of stress associated with returning to college full-time, Pat selected her courses carefully, arranged her work and study schedules to make the best use of her time, and scheduled time for daily exercise and social activities.

4. Richard is a very competitive, ambitious stockbroker who is easily irritated by small inconveniences. If he thinks that someone is wasting his time, he blows up and becomes completely enraged.

5. Max flubbed an easy free throw in the big basketball game but told his coach, "My game was off today because I'm still getting over the flu and I pulled a muscle in practice yesterday. I'll do better in next week's game."

Social Factors: A Little Help from Your Friends

"A Sense of Being Loved by Our Community . . ." Author Philip Simmons had been an English professor for nine years when he learned that he had Lou Gehrig's disease, a fatal neuromuscular condition that usually kills its victims in two to five years. But Simmons beat those odds and lived an incredibly productive life for almost ten years, in part by learning to ask for—and accept—help from his friends. For several years, some thirty friends and neighbors helped the Simmons family with the routine chores of daily life, such as fixing dinner and chauffeuring kids. Said Philip's wife, Kathryn, "It gives us a sense of being loved by our community."

> **Key Theme**
> • Social support refers to the resources provided by other people.
>
> **Key Questions**
> • How has social support been shown to benefit health?
> • How can relationships and social connections sometimes increase stress?
> • What gender differences have been found in social support and its effects?

Psychologists have become increasingly aware of the importance that close relationships play in our ability to deal with stressors and, ultimately, in our physical health. Consider the following research evidence:

- Patients with advanced breast cancer who attended weekly support-group sessions survived twice as long as a matched group of patients with equally advanced cancer who did not attend support groups. Both groups of women received comparable medical treatment. The added survival time for those who attended support-group sessions was longer than that which could have been provided by any known medical treatment (Spiegel, 1993b; Spiegel & others, 1989).

- After monitoring the health of 2,800 people for seven years, researchers found that people who had no one to talk to about their problems were three times as likely to die after being hospitalized for a heart attack than were those who had at least one person to provide such support (Berkman & others, 1992).

- The health of nearly 7,000 adults was tracked for nine years. Those who had few social connections were twice as likely to die from all causes than were those who had numerous social contacts, even when risk factors such as cigarette smoking, obesity, and elevated cholesterol levels were taken into account (Berkman, 1995; Berkman & Syme, 1979).

- In a study begun in the 1950s, college students rated their parents' level of love and caring. More than 40 years later, 87 percent of those who had rated their parents as being "low" in love and caring had been diagnosed with a serious physical disease. In contrast, only 25 percent of those who had rated their parents as being "high" in love and caring had been diagnosed with a serious physical disease (Russek & Schwartz, 1997).

These are just a few of the hundreds of studies exploring how interpersonal relationships influence our health and ability to tolerate stress. To investigate the role played by personal relationships in stress and health, psychologists measure the level of **social support**—the resources provided by other people in times of need (Hobfoll & Stephens, 1990). Repeatedly, researchers have found that socially isolated people have poorer health and higher death rates than people who have many social contacts or relationships (Southwick & others, 2005; Uchino & others, 1996). In fact, social isolation seems to be just as potent a health risk as smoking, high blood cholesterol, obesity, or physical inactivity (Cohen & others, 2000).

How Social Support Benefits Health

Social support may benefit our health and improve our ability to cope with stressors in several ways (Cohen & others, 2000). First, the social support of friends and relatives can modify our appraisal of a stressor's significance, including the degree to which we perceive it as threatening or harmful. Simply knowing that support and assistance are readily available may make the situation seem less threatening.

Second, the presence of supportive others seems to decrease the intensity of physical reactions to a stressor. Thus, when faced with a painful medical procedure or some other stressful situation, many people find the presence of a supportive friend to be calming.

Third, social support can influence our health by making us less likely to experience negative emotions (Cohen & Herbert, 1996). Given the well-established link between chronic negative emotions and poor health, a strong social support network can promote positive moods and emotions, enhance self-esteem, and increase feelings of personal control. In contrast, loneliness and depression are unpleasant emotional states that increase levels of stress hormones and adversely affect immune system functioning (Irwin & Miller, 2007).

The flip side of the coin is that relationships with others can also be a significant *source* of stress (McKenny & Price, 2005; Swickert & others, 2002). In fact, negative interactions with other people are often more effective at creating psychological distress than positive interactions are at improving well-being (Lepore, 1993; Rook, 1992). And, although married people tend to be healthier than unmarried people overall, marital conflict has been shown to have adverse effects on physical health, especially for women (Kiecolt-Glaser & Newton, 2001; Liu & Chen, 2006).

Clearly, the quality of interpersonal relationships is an important determinant of whether those relationships help or hinder our ability to cope with stressful events. When other people are perceived as being judgmental, their presence may increase the individual's physical reaction to a stressor. In two clever studies, psychologist Karen Allen and her colleagues (1991, 2002) demonstrated that the presence of a favorite dog or cat was more effective than the presence of a spouse or friend in lowering reactivity to a stressor. Why? Perhaps because the pet was perceived as being nonjudgmental, nonevaluative, and unconditionally supportive. Unfortunately, the same is not always true of friends, family members, and spouses.

Stress may also increase when well-meaning friends or family members offer unwanted or inappropriate social support. The In Focus box offers some suggestions on how to provide helpful social support and avoid inappropriate support behaviors.

Gender Differences in the Effects of Social Support

Women may be particularly vulnerable to some of the problematic aspects of social support, for a couple of reasons. First, women are more likely than men to serve as providers of support, which can be a very stressful role (Ekwall & Hallberg, 2006;

social support
The resources provided by other people in times of need.

Pets as a Source of Social Support Pets can provide both companionship and social support, especially for people with limited social contacts. Can the social support of pets buffer the negative effects of stress? One study showed that elderly people with pets had fewer doctor visits and reported feeling less stress than elderly people without pets (Siegel, 1990). Other studies have found that the presence of a pet cat or dog can lower blood pressure and lessen the cardiovascular response to acute stress (Allen & others, 2002).

IN FOCUS

Providing Effective Social Support

A close friend turns to you for help in a time of crisis or personal tragedy. What should you do or say? As we've noted in this chapter, appropriate social support can help people weather crises and can significantly reduce the amount of distress that they feel. Inappropriate support, in contrast, may only make matters worse.

Researchers generally agree that there are three broad categories of social support: emotional, tangible, and informational. Each provides different beneficial functions (Peirce & others, 1996; Taylor & Aspinwall, 1993).

Emotional support includes expressions of concern, empathy, and positive regard. *Tangible support* involves direct assistance, such as providing transportation, lending money, or helping with meals, child care, or household tasks. When people offer helpful suggestions, advice, or possible resources, they are providing *informational support*.

It's possible that all three kinds of social support might be provided by the same person, such as a relative, spouse, or very close friend. More commonly, we turn to different people for different kinds of support (Masters & others, 2007).

Research by psychologist Stevan Hobfoll and his colleagues (1992) has identified several support behaviors that are typically perceived as helpful by people under stress. In a nutshell, you're most likely to be perceived as helpful if you:

- are a good listener and show concern and interest
- ask questions that encourage the person under stress to express his or her feelings and emotions
- express understanding about why the person is upset
- express affection for the person, whether with a warm hug or simply a pat on the arm
- are willing to invest time and attention in helping
- can help the person with practical tasks, such as housework, transportation, or responsibilities at work or school

Just as important is knowing what *not* to do or say. Here are several behaviors that, however well intentioned, are often perceived as unhelpful:

- Giving advice that the person under stress has not requested

- Telling the person, "I know exactly how you feel." It's a mistake to think that you have experienced distress identical to what the other person is experiencing
- Talking about yourself or your own problems
- Minimizing the importance of the person's problem by saying things like, "Hey, don't make such a big deal out of it," "It could be a lot worse," or "Don't worry, everything will turn out okay."
- Joking or acting overly cheerful
- Offering your philosophical or religious interpretation of the stressful event by saying things like, "It's just fate," "It's God's will," or "It's your karma"

Finally, remember that although social support is helpful, it is *not* a substitute for counseling or psychotherapy. If a friend seems overwhelmed by problems or emotions, or is having serious difficulty handling the demands of everyday life, you should encourage him or her to seek professional help. Most college campuses have a counseling center or a health clinic that can provide referrals to qualified mental health workers. Sliding fee schedules, based on ability to pay, are usually available. Thus, you can assure the person that cost need not be an obstacle to getting help—or an additional source of stress!

Hobfoll & Vaux, 1993). Consider the differences found in one study. When middle-aged male patients were discharged from the hospital after a heart attack, they went home and their wives took care of them. But when middle-aged female heart attack patients were discharged from the hospital, they went home and fell back into the routine of caring for their husbands (Coyne & others, 1990).

Second, women may be more likely to suffer from the *stress contagion effect*, becoming upset about negative life events that happen to other people whom they care about (Belle, 1991). Since women tend to have larger and more intimate social networks than men, they have more opportunities to become distressed by what happens to people who are close to them. And women are more likely than men to be upset about negative events that happen to their relatives and friends.

For example, when Judy was unable to reach her daughter Katie by phone on the morning of September 11, she quickly called two family members for advice and comfort: her mother, Fern, in Chicago, and her sister, your author Sandy, in Tulsa. Of course, there was nothing Sandy or Fern could do to help Katie escape the chaos of lower Manhattan. Like Judy, Sandy and Fern became increasingly upset and worried as they watched the events of the day unfold from hundreds of miles away with no news of Katie's fate. When stressful events strike, women tend to reach out to one another for support and comfort (Taylor, Klein, & others, 2000).

In contrast, men are more likely to be distressed only by negative events that happen to their immediate family—their wives and children (Wethington & others, 1987). Men tend to rely heavily on a close relationship with their spouse, placing less importance on relationships with other people. Women, in contrast, are more likely to list close friends along with their spouse as confidants (Ackerman & others, 2007; Shumaker & Hill, 1991). Because men tend to have a much smaller network of intimate others, they may be particularly vulnerable to social isolation, especially if their spouse dies. Thus, it's not surprising that the health benefits of being married are more pronounced for men than for women (Kiecolt-Glaser & Newton, 2001).

The Health Benefits of Companionship
This married couple in their seventies are enjoying an afternoon outdoors. Numerous research studies have shown that married people and couples live longer than people who are single, divorced, or widowed (Burman & Margolin, 1992). Because men tend to have fewer close friends than women, they often depend on their spouse or partner for social support.

Coping
How People Deal with Stress

> **Key Theme**
> - Coping refers to the ways in which we try to change circumstances, or our interpretation of circumstances, to make them less threatening.
>
> **Key Questions**
> - What are the two basic forms of coping, and when is each form typically used?
> - What are some of the most common coping strategies?
> - How does culture affect coping style?

Think about some of the stressful periods that have occurred in your life. What kinds of strategies did you use to deal with those distressing events? Which strategies seemed to work best? Did any of the strategies end up working against your ability to reduce the stressor? If you had to deal with the same events again today, would you do anything differently?

Katie survived a terrorist attack on her neighborhood by being resourceful and, as she would be the first to admit, through sheer good luck. But how did she survive the months following? Along with having a good support system—friends, relatives, and a dance teacher who could offer her emotional and tangible help—she used a number of different strategies to cope with the stress that she continued to experience.

Two Ways of Coping
Problem-Focused and Emotion-Focused Coping

The strategies that you use to deal with distressing events are examples of coping. **Coping** refers to the ways in which we try to change circumstances, or our interpretation of circumstances, to make them more favorable and less threatening (Folkman & Lazarus, 1991; Folkman & Moskowitz, 2007; R. S. Lazarus, 1999, 2000).

coping
Behavioral and cognitive responses used to deal with stressors; involves our efforts to change circumstances, or our interpretation of circumstances, to make them more favorable and less threatening.

Ways of Coping Like the stress response itself, adaptive coping is a dynamic and complex process. Imagine that you had lost your home and most of your possessions in a fire. What kinds of coping strategies might prove most helpful?

problem-focused coping
Coping efforts primarily aimed at directly changing or managing a threatening or harmful stressor.

emotion-focused coping
Coping efforts primarily aimed at relieving or regulating the emotional impact of a stressful situation.

Coping tends to be a dynamic, ongoing process. We may switch our coping strategies as we appraise the changing demands of a stressful situation and our available resources at any given moment. We also evaluate whether our efforts have made a stressful situation better or worse and adjust our coping strategies accordingly (see Cheng, 2003).

When coping is effective, we adapt to the situation and stress is reduced. Unfortunately, coping efforts do not always help us adapt. Maladaptive coping can involve thoughts and behaviors that intensify or prolong distress or that produce self-defeating outcomes (Bolger & Zuckerman, 1995). The rejected lover who continually dwells on her former companion, passing up opportunities to form new relationships and letting her studies slide, is demonstrating maladaptive coping.

Adaptive coping responses serve many functions (Lazarus, 2000; Folkman & Moskowitz, 2007). Most important, adaptive coping involves realistically evaluating the situation and determining what can be done to minimize the impact of the stressor. But adaptive coping also involves dealing with the emotional aspects of the situation. In other words, adaptive coping often includes developing emotional tolerance for negative life events, maintaining self-esteem, and keeping emotions in balance. Finally, adaptive coping efforts are directed toward preserving important relationships during stressful experiences.

Psychologists Richard Lazarus and Susan Folkman (1984) have described two basic types of coping, each of which serves a different purpose. **Problem-focused coping** is aimed at managing or changing a threatening or harmful stressor. Problem-focused coping strategies tend to be most effective when you can exercise some control over the stressful situation or circumstances (Park & others, 2004). But if you think that nothing can be done to alter a situation, you tend to rely on **emotion-focused coping:** You direct your efforts toward relieving or regulating the emotional impact of the stressful situation. Although emotion-focused coping doesn't change the problem, it can help you feel better about the situation. People are flexible in the coping styles they adopt, often relying on different coping strategies for different stressors (Park & others, 2004).

Problem-Focused Coping Strategies
Changing the Stressor

Problem-focused coping strategies represent actions that have the goal of changing or eliminating the stressor. When people use aggressive or risky efforts to change the situation, they are engaging in *confrontive coping.* Ideally, confrontive coping is direct and assertive without being hostile. When it is hostile or aggressive, confrontive coping may well generate negative emotions in the people being confronted, damaging future relations with them (Folkman & Lazarus, 1991).

In contrast, *planful problem solving* involves efforts to rationally analyze the situation, identify potential solutions, and then implement them. In effect, you take the attitude that the stressor represents a problem to be solved. Once you assume that mental stance, you follow the basic steps of problem solving (see Chapter 7).

Problem-Focused Coping People rely on different coping strategies at different times in dealing with the same stressor. After dealing with the emotional impact of losing their homes to a hurricane, these Florida neighbors engaged in problem-focused coping as they help clear the site before rebuilding.

Emotion-Focused Coping Strategies
Changing Your Reaction to the Stressor

When the stressor is one over which we can exert little or no control, we often focus on dimensions of the situation that we *can* control—the emotional impact of the stressor on us (Thompson & others, 1994). All the different forms of emotion-focused coping share the goal of reducing or regulating the emotional impact of a stressor.

When you shift your attention away from the stressor and toward other activities, you're engaging in the emotion-focused coping strategy called *escape–avoidance*. As the name implies, the basic goal is to escape or avoid the stressor and neutralize distressing emotions. Excessive sleeping and the use of drugs and alcohol are maladaptive forms of escape–avoidance, as are escaping into fantasy or wishful thinking. More constructive escape–avoidance strategies include exercising or immersing yourself in your studies, hobbies, or work.

For example, Katie found that returning to her daily dance class was the most helpful thing she did to cope with her feelings. During those two hours, Katie was able to let go of her memories of death and destruction. Doing what she loved, surrounded by people she loved, Katie began to feel whole again.

Because you are focusing your attention on something other than the stressor, escape–avoidance tactics provide emotional relief in the short run. Thus, avoidance strategies can be helpful when you are facing a stressor that is brief and has limited consequences. But avoidance strategies such as wishful thinking tend to be counterproductive when the stressor is a severe or long-lasting one, like a serious or chronic disease (Stanton & Snider, 1993; Vollman & others, 2007). Escape–avoidance strategies are also associated with increased psychological distress in facing other types of stressors, such as adjusting to college (Aspinwall & Taylor, 1992).

In the long run, escape–avoidance tactics are associated with poor adjustment and symptoms of depression and anxiety (Stanton & Snider, 1993). That's not surprising if you think about it. After all, the problem *is* still there. And if the problem is one that needs to be dealt with promptly, such as a pressing medical concern, the delays caused by escape–avoidance strategies can make the stressful situation worse.

Seeking social support is the coping strategy that involves turning to friends, relatives, or other people for emotional, tangible, or informational support. As we discussed earlier in the chapter, having a strong network of social support can help buffer the impact of stressors (Brissette & others, 2002; Finch & Vega, 2003). Confiding in a trusted friend gives you an opportunity to vent your emotions and better understand the stressful situation.

When you acknowledge the stressor but attempt to minimize or eliminate its emotional impact, you're engaging in the coping strategy called *distancing*. Downplaying or joking about the stressful situation is one form of distancing (Abel, 2002). Sometimes people emotionally distance themselves from a stressor by discussing it in a detached, depersonalized, or intellectual way. Among Katie's circle of young friends, distancing was common. They joked about the soot, the dust, and the National Guard troops guarding the subway stations.

In certain high-stress occupations, distancing can help workers cope with painful human problems. Clinical psychologists, social workers, rescue workers, police officers, and medical personnel often use distancing to some degree to help them deal with distressing situations without falling apart emotionally themselves.

In contrast to distancing, *denial* is a refusal to acknowledge that the problem even exists. Like escape–avoidance strategies, denial can compound problems in situations that require immediate attention.

Perhaps the most constructive emotion-focused coping strategy is *positive reappraisal*. When we use positive reappraisal, we not only try to minimize the negative emotional aspects of the situation, but we also try to create positive meaning by focusing on personal growth. Even in the midst of deeply disturbing situations, positive reappraisal can help people experience positive emotions and minimize the

Transcending Personal Tragedy: Choosing Hope In the case of a few extraordinary people, like the late actor, director, and social activist Christopher Reeve, tragedy becomes the motivator for personal growth. After a horseback-riding accident in 1995 left him paralyzed from the shoulders down, Reeve established the nonprofit Christopher Reeve Paralysis Foundation and raised millions of dollars for research on spinal cord injuries. Refusing to accept the conventional scientific dogma that recovery of function was impossible, he also embarked on an intensive exercise program that eventually led to his recovering limited movement and sensation—revolutionizing the thinking on recovery from and treatment of spinal cord injury. As neurosurgeon Philip Steig (2004) said, "Christopher used his injury as an opportunity to help mankind." The title of his book, *Nothing Is Impossible: Reflections on a New Life*, reflects Reeve's personal philosophy. As he said, "When we have hope, we discover powers within ourselves we may have never known—the power to make sacrifices, to endure, to heal, and to love. Once we choose hope, everything is possible."

potential for negative aftereffects (Dasgupta & Sanyal, 2007; Updegraff & others, 2008). For example, Katie noted that in the days following the collapse of the two towers, "It was really beautiful. Everyone was pulling together, New Yorkers were helping each other."

IN FOCUS

Gender Differences in Responding to Stress: "Tend-and-Befriend" or "Fight-or-Flight"?

Physiologically, men and women show the same hormonal and sympathetic nervous system activation that Walter Cannon described as the "fight-or-flight" response to stress (1932). Yet *behaviorally,* the two sexes react very differently.

To illustrate, consider this finding: When fathers come home after a stressful day at work, they tend to withdraw from their families, wanting to be left alone—an example of the "flight" response (Schulz & others, 2004). If their workday was filled with a lot of interpersonal conflicts, they tend to initiate conflicts with family members—evidence of the "fight" response. In contrast, when mothers experience high levels of stress at work, they come home and are *more* nurturing toward their children (Repetti, 1989; Repetti & Wood, 1997).

As we have noted in this chapter, women tend to be much more involved in their social networks than men. And, as compared to men, women are much more likely to seek out and use social support when they are under stress (Glynn & others, 1999). Throughout their lives, women tend to mobilize social support—especially from other women—in times of stress (Taylor, Klein, & others, 2000). We saw this pattern in our story about Katie. Just as Katie called her mother, Judy, when her neighborhood came under attack, Judy called her sister, Sandy, and her *own* mother when she feared that her daughter's life was in danger.

Why the gender difference in coping with stress? Health psychologists Shelley Taylor, Laura Klein, and their colleagues (2000, 2002) believe that evolutionary theory offers some insight. According to the evolutionary perspective, the most adaptive response in virtually any situation is one that promotes the survival of both the individual *and* the individual's offspring. Given that premise, neither fighting nor fleeing is likely to have been an adaptive response for females, especially females who were pregnant, nursing, or caring for their offspring. According to Taylor and her colleagues (2000), "Stress responses that enabled the female to simultaneously protect herself and her offspring are likely to have resulted in more surviving offspring." Rather than fighting or fleeing, they argue, women developed a *tend-and-befriend* behavioral response to stress.

What is the "tend-and-befriend" pattern of responding? *Tending* refers to "quieting and caring for offspring and blending into the environment," Taylor and her colleagues (2000) write. That is, rather than confronting or running from the threat, females take cover and protect their young. Evidence supporting this behavior pattern includes studies of nonhuman animals showing that many female animals adopt a "tending" strategy when faced by a threat (Francis & others, 1999; Liu & others, 1997).

The "befriending" side of the equation relates to women's tendency to seek social support during stressful situations. Taylor and her colleagues (2000) describe *befriending* as "the creation of networks of associations that provide resources and protection for the female and her offspring under conditions of stress."

However, both males and females show the same neuroendocrine responses to an acute stressor—the sympathetic nervous system activates, stress hormones pour into the bloodstream, and, as those hormones reach different organs, the body kicks into high gear. So why do women "tend and befriend" rather than "fight or flee," as men do? Taylor points to the effects of another hormone, *oxytocin.* Higher in females than in males, oxytocin is associated with maternal behaviors in all female mammals, including humans. Oxytocin also tends to have a calming effect on both males and females (see Southwick & others, 2005).

Taylor speculates that oxytocin might simultaneously help calm stressed females and promote affiliative behavior. Supporting this speculation is research showing that oxytocin increases affiliative behaviors and reduces stress in many mammals (Carter & DeVries, 1999; Light & others, 2000). For example, one study found that healthy men who received a dose of oxytocin before being subjected to a stressful procedure were less anxious and had lower cortisol levels than men who received a placebo (Heinrichs & others, 2003).

In humans, oxytocin is highest in nursing mothers. Pleasant physical contact, such as hugging, cuddling, and touching, stimulates the release of oxytocin. In combination, all of these oxytocin-related changes seem to help turn down the physiological intensity of the fight-or-flight response for women. And perhaps, Taylor and her colleagues suggest, they also promote the tend-and-befriend response.

"*I'm somewhere between O. and K.*"

Similarly, a study by Barbara Fredrickson and her colleagues (2003) found that some college students "looked for the silver lining" after the September 11 terrorist attacks, reaching out to others and expressing gratitude for the safety of their loved ones. Those who found a positive meaning in the aftermath of the attacks were least likely to develop depressive symptoms and other problems in the following weeks. As Fredrickson and her colleagues (2003) observed, "Amidst the emotional turmoil generated by the September 11 terrorist attacks, subtle and fleeting experiences of gratitude, interest, love, and other positive emotions appeared to hold depressive symptoms at bay and fuel postcrisis growth."

Katie, too, was able to creatively transform the meaning of her experience. As part of her application to a college dance conservatory, she choreographed and performed an original dance expressing sadness, fear, hope, and renewal—all the emotions that she experienced on that terrible day. Her ability to express her feelings artistically has helped her come to terms with her memories.

However, it's important to note that there is no single "best" coping strategy. In general, the most effective coping is flexible, meaning that we fine-tune our coping strategies to meet the demands of a particular stressor (Cheng, 2003; Park & others, 2004). And, people often use multiple coping strategies, combining problem-focused and emotion-focused forms of coping. In the initial stages of a stressful experience, we may rely on emotion-focused strategies to help us step back emotionally from a problem. Once we've regained our equilibrium, we may use problem-focused coping strategies to identify potential solutions.

Dancing in Central Park Katie will never forget the events of that September day or the weeks that followed. She still struggles with the occasional nightmare, and certain smells and sounds—smoke, sirens—can trigger feelings of panic and dread. But Katie persevered. After graduating from a college dance conservatory, Katie moved back to New York City, where she is a dancer, choreographer, and producer.

Culture and Coping Strategies

Culture seems to play an important role in the choice of coping strategies. Americans and other members of individualistic cultures tend to emphasize personal autonomy and personal responsibility in dealing with problems. Thus, they are *less* likely to seek social support in stressful situations than are members of collectivistic cultures, such as Asian cultures (Marsella & Dash-Scheuer, 1988). Members of collectivistic cultures tend to be more oriented toward their social group, family, or community and toward seeking help with their problems.

Individualists also tend to emphasize the importance and value of exerting control over their circumstances, especially circumstances that are threatening or stressful (O'Connor & Shimizu, 2002). Thus, they favor problem-focused strategies, such as confrontive coping and planful problem solving. These strategies involve directly changing the situation to achieve a better fit with their wishes or goals (Wong & Wong, 2006).

In collectivistic cultures, however, a greater emphasis is placed on controlling your personal reactions to a stressful situation rather than trying to control the situation itself. This emotion-focused coping style emphasizes gaining control over inner feelings by accepting and accommodating yourself to existing realities (O'Connor & Shimizu, 2002).

For example, the Japanese emphasize accepting difficult situations with maturity, serenity, and flexibility (Gross, 2007). Common sayings in Japan are "The true tolerance is to tolerate the intolerable" and "Flexibility can control rigidity". Along with controlling inner feelings, many Asian cultures also stress the goal of controlling the outward expression of emotions, however distressing the situation (Johnson & others, 1995).

These cultural differences in coping underscore the point that there is no formula for effective coping in all situations. That we use multiple coping strategies throughout almost every stressful situation reflects our efforts to identify what will work best at a given moment in time. To the extent that any coping strategy helps us identify realistic alternatives, manage our emotions, and maintain important relationships, it is adaptive and effective.

CONCEPT REVIEW 13.3

Psychological Factors and Stress Coping Strategies

Identify the coping strategy that is being illustrated in each of the scenarios below. Choose from:

    a. confrontive coping   e. distancing

    b. planful problem solving   f. denial

    c. escape–avoidance   g. positive reappraisal

    d. seeking social support

1. In trying to contend with her stormy marriage, Emily often seeks the advice of her best friend, Caitlin.

2. Lionel was disappointed that he did not get the job, but he concluded that the knowledge he gained from the application and interview process was very beneficial.

3. Whenever Dr. Mathau has a particularly hectic and stressful shift in the emergency room, she finds herself making jokes and facetious remarks to the other staff members.

4. Jake's job as a public defender is filled with long days and little thanks. To take his mind off his job, Jake jogs every day.

5. Faced with low productivity and mounting financial losses, the factory manager bluntly told all his workers, "You people had better start getting more work done in less time, or you will be looking for jobs elsewhere."

6. Because of unavoidable personal problems, Chris did very poorly on his last two tests and was very concerned about his GPA. Chris decided to talk with his professor about the possibility of writing an extra paper or taking a makeup exam.

7. Although she failed her midterm exam and got a D on her term paper, Olivia insists that she is going to get a B in her economics course.

>> Closing Thoughts

From national tragedies and major life events to the minor hassles and annoyances of daily life, stressors come in all sizes and shapes. Any way you look at it, stress is an unavoidable part of life. Stress that is prolonged or intense can adversely affect both our physical and psychological well-being. Fortunately, most of the time people deal effectively with the stresses in their lives. As Katie's story demonstrates, the effects of even the most intense stressors can be minimized if we cope with them effectively.

    Ultimately, the level of stress that we experience is due to a complex interaction of psychological, biological, and social factors. We hope that reading this chapter has given you a better understanding of how stress affects your life and of how you can reduce its impact on your physical and psychological well-being. In the chapter Application, we'll suggest some concrete steps that you can take to minimize the harmful impact of stress in *your* life.

APPLICATION

Minimizing the Effects of Stress

Sometimes stressful situations persist despite our best efforts to resolve them. Knowing that chronic stress can jeopardize your health, what can you do to minimize the adverse impact of stress on your physical well-being? Here are four practical suggestions.

Suggestion 1: Avoid or Minimize the Use of Stimulants

In dealing with stressful situations, people often turn to stimulants to help keep them going, such as coffee or caffeinated energy drinks. If you know someone who smokes, you've probably observed that most smokers react to stress by increasing their

smoking (Ng & Jeffery, 2003; Todd, 2004). The problem is that common stimulants like caffeine and nicotine actually work *against* you in coping with stress. They increase the physiological effects of stress by raising heart rate and blood pressure. In effect, users of stimulant drugs are already primed to respond with greater reactivity, exaggerating the physiological consequences of stress (B. Smith & others, 2001; Lovallo & others, 1996).

    The best advice? Avoid stimulant drugs altogether. If that's not possible, make a conscious effort to monitor your use of stimulants, especially when you're under stress. You'll find it easier to deal with stressors when your nervous system is not

already in high gear because of caffeine, nicotine, or other stimulants. Minimizing your use of stimulants will also make it easier for you to implement the next suggestion.

Suggestion 2: Exercise Regularly

Numerous studies all point to the same conclusion: Regular exercise, particularly aerobic exercise like walking, swimming, or running, is one of the best ways to reduce the impact of stress (Bass & others, 2002; Ensel & Lin, 2004; Wijndaele & others, 2007). The key word here is *regular*. Try walking briskly for 20 minutes four or five times a week. It will improve your physical health and help you cope with stress. In fact, just about any kind of physical exercise helps buffer the negative effects of stress. (Rapidly right-clicking your computer mouse doesn't count.) Compared to sofa slugs, physically fit people are less physiologically reactive to stressors and produce lower levels of stress hormones (Rejeski & others, 1991, 1992). Psychologically, regular exercise reduces anxiety and depressed feelings and increases self-confidence and self-esteem (Berk, 2007).

Suggestion 3: Get Enough Sleep

With the ongoing push to get more and more done, people often stretch their days by short-changing themselves on sleep. But sleep deprivation just adds to your feelings of stress. "Without sufficient sleep it is more difficult to concentrate, make careful decisions, and follow instructions," explains researcher Mark Rosekind (2003). "You are more likely to make mistakes or errors, and are more prone to being impatient and lethargic. And, your attention, memory and reaction time are all adversely affected."

The stress–sleep connection also has the potential to become a vicious cycle. School, work, or family-related pressures contribute to reduced or disturbed sleep, leaving you less than adequately rested and making efforts to deal with the situation all the more taxing and distressful (Akerstedt & others, 2002). And, inadequate sleep, even for just a few nights, takes a physical toll on the body, leaving us more prone to health problems (Colten & Altevogt, 2007; National Sleep Foundation, 2004).

Fortunately, research indicates that the opposite is also true: Getting adequate sleep promotes resistance and helps buffer the effects of stress (Hamilton & others, 2007; Mohr & others, 2003). For some suggestions to help promote a good night's sleep, see the Application at the end of Chapter 4.

Suggestion 4: Practice a Relaxation Technique

You can significantly reduce stress-related symptoms by regularly using any one of a variety of relaxation techniques (Benson,

1993). One effective technique is *progressive muscle relaxation* (McCallie & others, 2006; Pawlow & others, 2003). This technique involves systematically tensing and then relaxing the major muscle groups of your body while lying down or sitting in a comfortable chair.

You begin by tensing your facial and jaw muscles, paying careful attention to the feeling of muscle tightness. Then take a deep breath, hold it for a few seconds, and exhale slowly as you relax your facial and jaw muscles as completely as possible. As you do so, notice the difference between the sensations of tension and the warm feelings of relaxation. Progressively work your way down your body, tensing and then relaxing muscle groups.

A very effective relaxation technique is *meditation,* which we discussed in Chapter 4. Meditation involves focusing your attention on an object, word, or phrase. Shown in the list below are the instructions for a simple meditation technique that we encourage you to try. Numerous studies have demonstrated the physical and psychological benefits of meditation (Barnes & others, 2001; Siegel, 2007; Waelde & others, 2004; Walton & others, 2002).

How to Meditate

Here is a simple but effective meditation technique developed by British psychologist and meditation researcher Michael A. West. Practice the technique for 15 to 20 minutes twice a day for at least two weeks.

1   Sit quietly in an upright position in a room where you are not likely to be disturbed.

2   Close your eyes and relax your body. Sit quietly for about half a minute.

3   Begin to repeat the word *one* easily and silently to yourself, or choose some other simple word, such as *peace* or *calm*.

4   Don't concentrate too hard on the sound. The word need only be a faint idea at times—you don't have to keep repeating it clearly.

5   Think the word easily. It may change by getting louder or softer, longer or shorter, or it may not change at all. In every case, just take it as it comes.

6   Remember, the word has no special meaning or special significance. It is a simple device that helps in meditation.

7   Continue the meditation in this way for about 15 minutes. Don't worry about achieving a deep level of meditation or about whether you are concentrating on the sound.

8   Don't try to control thoughts. If thoughts come during meditation, don't worry about it. When you become aware that you have slipped into a train of thought, just go very easily back to the sound. Don't make great efforts to exclude thoughts—just favor the sound.

9   If you become aware of outside noises or other distracting sounds, go easily back to the word; don't fight to exclude those distractions. Do the same as you would with thoughts. Accept them, but favor the sound.

10   Above all, you are meant to enjoy the meditation, so don't try too hard; just take it easily as it comes.

Source: West (1987).

CHAPTER REVIEW

STRESS, HEALTH, AND COPING

Key Points

Introduction: What Is Stress?

- **Stress** can be defined as a negative emotional state that occurs in response to events that are appraised as taxing or exceeding a person's resources.
- **Health psychologists** study stress and other psychological factors that influence health, illness, and treatment. Health psychologists are guided by the **biopsychosocial model.**
- **Stressors** are events or situations that produce stress. According to the life events approach, any event that requires adaptation produces stress. The Social Readjustment Rating Scale is one way to measure the impact of life events. The life events approach does not take into account a person's subjective appraisal of an event. It also assumes that any change, whether good or bad, produces stress.
- **Daily hassles** are a significant source of stress and also contribute to the stress produced by major life events.
- Stress can also be caused by approach–approach, avoidance–avoidance, or approach–avoidance **conflicts.** Approach–avoidance conflicts tend to create the most stress.
- Social factors, such as unemployment, crime, and racism, can be significant sources of stress, often producing chronic stress. Stress can also result when people encounter different cultural values.

Physical Effects of Stress: The Mind–Body Connection

- Stress can affect health indirectly, by influencing health-related behaviors, and directly, by influencing the body's functioning.
- Walter Cannon identified the endocrine pathway involved in the **fight-or-flight response.** This endocrine pathway includes the sympathetic nervous system, the adrenal medulla, and the release of **catecholamines.**
- In studying the physical effects of prolonged stressors, Hans Selye identified the three-stage **general adaptation syndrome,** which includes the alarm, resistance, and exhaustion stages. Selye found that prolonged stress involves a second endocrine pathway, which includes the hypothalamus, the pituitary gland, the adrenal cortex, and the release of **corticosteroids.**
- Stress affects the functioning of the **immune system.** The most important elements of the immune system are **lymphocytes.** Ader and Cohen's discovery that the immune system could be classically conditioned helped launch the new field of **psychoneuroimmunology.** Subsequent research has discovered that the nervous, endocrine, and immune systems are directly linked and continually influence one another.
- Stressors that affect immune system functioning include both unusual and common life events, along with everyday pressures. Although stress may increase susceptibility to infection and illness, many other factors are involved in physical health.

Individual Factors That Influence the Response to Stress

- The impact of stressors is reduced when people feel a sense of control over the stressful situation. Feelings of control have both physical and psychological benefits.
- The way people explain negative events often determines whether they will persist or give up after failure. People with an **optimistic explanatory style** use external, unstable, and specific explanations for negative events. People with a **pessimistic explanatory style** use internal, stable, and global explanations for negative events. A pessimistic explanatory style contributes to stress and undermines health.
- Chronic negative emotions are related to the development of some chronic diseases. People who frequently experience negative emotions experience more stress than other people. Transient negative moods have also been shown to diminish immune system functioning.
- The **Type A behavior pattern** can predict the development of heart disease. The most critical health-compromising component of Type A behavior is hostility. Hostile people react more intensely to stressors and experience stress more frequently than do nonhostile people.
- Social isolation contributes to poor health. **Social support** improves the ability to deal with stressors by modifying the appraisal of a stressor, decreasing the physical reaction to a stressor, and making people less likely to experience negative emotions. When the quality of relationships is poor, or when social support is inappropriate or unwanted, relationships may increase stress.
- Women are more likely than men to be the providers of social support and tend to be more vulnerable to the stress contagion effect. Men are less likely to be upset by negative events that happen to people outside their immediate family.

Coping: How People Deal with Stress

- **Coping** refers to the way in which people try to change either their circumstances or their interpretations of circumstances in order to make them more favorable and less threatening. Coping may be either maladaptive or adaptive.
- When people think that something can be done to change a situation, they tend to use **problem-focused coping** strategies, which involve changing a harmful stressor.
- When people think that a situation cannot be changed, they tend to rely on **emotion-focused coping** strategies, which involve changing their emotional reactions to the stressor.
- Problem-focused coping strategies include confrontive coping and planful problem solving.

- Emotion-focused coping strategies include escape–avoidance, seeking social support, distancing, denial, and positive reappraisal. Effective coping is flexible, and people often rely on multiple coping strategies in stressful situations.

- Culture affects the choice of coping strategies. People in individualistic cultures tend to favor problem-focused strategies. People in collectivistic cultures are more likely to seek social support, and they emphasize emotion-focused coping strategies more.

Key Terms

stress, p. 541

health psychology, p. 541

biopsychosocial model, p. 542

stressors, p. 542

daily hassles, p. 543

conflict, p. 544

acculturative stress, p. 545

fight-or-flight response, p. 547

catecholamines, p. 547

general adaptation syndrome, p. 548

corticosteroids, p. 549

immune system, p. 549

lymphocytes, p. 549

psychoneuroimmunology, p. 549

optimistic explanatory style, p. 554

pessimistic explanatory style, p. 554

Type A behavior pattern, p. 556

social support, p. 559

coping, p. 561

problem-focused coping, p. 562

emotion-focused coping, p. 562

Key People

Robert Ader (b. 1932) American psychologist who, with immunologist Nicholas Cohen, first demonstrated that immune system responses could be classically conditioned; helped establish the new interdisciplinary field of psychoneuroimmunology. (p. 549)

Walter B. Cannon (1871–1945) American physiologist who made several important contributions to psychology, especially in the study of emotions. Described the fight-or-flight response, which involves the sympathetic nervous system and the endocrine system (also see Chapter 8). (p. 547)

Janice Kiecolt-Glaser (b. 1951) American psychologist who, with immunologist Ronald Glaser, has conducted extensive research on the effects of stress on the immune system. (p. 550)

Richard Lazarus (1922–2002) American psychologist who helped promote the cognitive perspective on emotion and stress; developed the cognitive appraisal model of stress and coping with co-researcher Susan Folkman (also see Chapter 8). (p. 543)

Martin Seligman (b. 1942) American psychologist who conducted research on explanatory style and the role it plays in stress, health, and illness. (p. 554)

Hans Selye (1907–1982) Canadian endocrinologist who was a pioneer in stress research; defined stress as "the nonspecific response of the body to any demand placed on it" and described a three-stage response to prolonged stress that he termed the general adaptation syndrome. (p. 548)

Concept Review Answers

13.1 page 552

1. False. The biopsychosocial model holds that health and illness are determined by the interaction of biological, psychological, and social factors.
2. False. Exposure to life events is only one of many factors that influence health and illness.
3. False. The Social Readjustment Rating Scale measures stress due to life events.
4. False. During periods of prolonged stress, the adrenal cortex secretes corticosteroids.

5. False. Shelley is probably experiencing the alarm stage of the general adaptation syndrome.
6. True.

13.2 page 558

1. f   2. e   3. a   4. c   5. b

13.3 page 566

1. d	3. e	5. a	7. f
2. g	4. c	6. b	

 ## Web Companion Review Activities

You can find additional review activities at **www.worthpublishers.com/hockenbury.** The *Psychology* 4th edition Web Companion has self-scoring practice quizzes, flashcards, interactive crossword puzzles, and other activities to help you master the material in this chapter.

References

Abel, Millicent H. (2002). Humor, stress, and coping strategies. *Humor, 15,* 365–381.

Ackerman, Joshua M.; Kenrick, Douglas T.; & Schaller, Mark. (2007). Is friendship akin to kinship?; *Evolution and Human Behavior, 28*(5), 365–374.

Ader, Robert. (1993). Conditioned responses. In Bill Moyers & Betty Sue Flowers (Eds.), *Healing and the mind.* New York: Doubleday.

Ader, Robert. (2001). Psychoneuroimmunology. *Current Directions in Psychological Science, 10,* 94–98.

Ader, Robert, & Cohen, Nicholas. (1975). Behaviorally conditioned immunosuppression. *Psychosomatic Medicine, 37,* 333–340.

Adler, Nancy, & Matthews, Karen. (1994). Health psychology: Why do some people get sick and some stay well? *Annual Review of Psychology, 45,* 229–259.

Affleck, Glenn; Tennen, Howard; & Croog, Sydney. (1987). Causal attribution, perceived control, and recovery from a heart attack. *Journal of Social and Clinical Psychology, 5,* 399–455.

Affleck, Glenn; Tennen, Howard; Pfeiffer, Carol; & Fifield, Judith. (1987a). Appraisals of control and predictability in reacting to a chronic disease. *Journal of Personality and Social Psychology, 53,* 273–279.

Akerstedt, T.; Knutsson, A.; Westerholm, P.; Theorell, T.; Alfredsson, L.; & Kecklund, G. (2002). Sleep disturbances, work stress and work hours: A cross-sectional study. *Journal of Psychosomatic Research, 53,* 741–748.

Allen, Karen M.; Blascovich, Jim; & Mendes, Wendy B. (2002). Cardiovascular reactivity and the presence of pets, friends, and spouses: The truth about cats and dogs. *Psychosomatic Medicine, 64,* 727–739.

Allen, Karen M.; Blascovich, Jim; Tomaka, Joe; & Kelsey, Robert M. (1991). Presence of human friends and pet dogs as moderators of autonomic responses to stress in women. *Journal of Personality and Social Psychology, 61,* 582–589.

Almeida, David M., & Kessler, Ronald C. (1998). Everyday stressors and gender differences in daily distress. *Journal of Personality and Social Psychology, 75,* 670–680.

Anton, Stephen D., & Miller, Peter M. (2005). Do negative emotions predict alcohol consumption, saturated fat intake, and physical activity in older adults? *Behavior Modification, 29*(4), 677–688.

Aspinwall, Lisa G., & Taylor, Shelley E. (1992). Modeling cognitive adaptation: A longitudinal investigation of the impact of individual differences and coping on college adjustment and performance. *Journal of Personality and Social Psychology, 63,* 989–1003.

Barefoot, John C.; Dahlstrom, W. Grant; & Williams, Redford B. (1983). Hostility, CHD incidence, and total mortality: A 25-year follow-up study of 255 physicians. *Psychosomatic Medicine, 45,* 59–63.

Barnes, Thomas R. E., & Joyce, Eileen M. (2001). Antipsychotic drug treatment: Recent advances. *Current Opinion in Psychiatry, 14,* 25–37.

Bass, Martha A.; Enochs, Wendy K.; & DiBrezzo, Ro. (2002). Comparison of two exercise programs on general well-being of college students. *Psychological Reports, 91,* 1195–1201.

Belle, Deborah. (1991). Gender differences in the social moderators of stress. In Alan Monat & Richard S. Lazarus (Eds.), *Stress and coping: An anthology* (3rd ed.). New York: Columbia University Press.

Bello, Richard. (2006). Causes and paralinguistic correlates of interpersonal equivocation. *Journal of Pragmatics, 38*(9), 1430–1441.

Bennett, Kymberley K., & Elliott, Marta. (2005). Pessimistic explanatory style and cardiac health: What is the relation and the mechanism that links them? *Basic and Applied Social Psychology, 27*(3), 239–248.

Benson, Herbert. (1993). The relaxation response. In Daniel Goleman & Joel Gurin (Eds.), *Mind/body medicine: How to use your mind for better health.* Yonkers, NY: Consumer Reports Books.

Berk, Michael. (2007). Should we be targeting exercise as a routine mental health intervention? *Acta Neuropsychiatrica, 19*(3), 217–218.

Berkman, Lisa F. (1995). The role of social relations in health promotion. *Psychosomatic Medicine, 57,* 245, 254.

Berkman, Lisa F.; Leo-Summers, Linda; & Horowitz, Ralph I. (1992). Emotional support and survival after myocardial infarction. *Annals of Internal Medicine, 117,* 1003–1009.

Berkman, Lisa F., & Syme, S. Leonard. (1979). Social networks, host resistance, and mortality: A nine-year follow-up study of Alameda County residents. *American Journal of Epidemiology, 109,* 186–204.

Berry, John W. (1994). Acculturative stress. In Walter J. Lonner & Roy Malpass (Eds.), *Psychology and culture.* Boston: Allyn & Bacon.

Berry, John W. (2003). Conceptual approaches to acculturation. In Kevin M. Chun, Pamela Balls-Organista, & Gerardo Marin (Eds.), *Acculturation: Advances in theory, measurement and applied research.* Washington, DC: American Psychological Association.

Berry, John W. (2006). Acculturative stress. In P. T. P. Wong, C. J. Lilian (Eds.), *Handbook of multicultural perspectives on stress and coping* (pp. 287–298). Dallas, TX: Spring Publications.

Berry, John W., & Kim, Uichol. (1988). Acculturation and mental health. In Pierre R. Dasen, John W. Berry, & Norman Sartorius (Eds.), *Health and cross-cultural psychology: Toward applications* (Cross-cultural Research and Methodology Series, Vol. 10). Newbury Park, CA: Sage.

Bolger, Niall, & Schilling, Elizabeth A. (1991). Personality and problems of everyday life: The role of neuroticism in exposure and reactivity to stress. *Journal of Personality, 59,* 355–386.

Bolger, Niall, & Zuckerman, Adam. (1995). A framework for studying personality in the stress process. *Journal of Personality and Social Psychology, 69,* 890–902.

Bottos, Shauna, & Dewey, Deborah. (2004). Perfectionists; appraisal of daily hassles and chronic headache. *Headache: The Journal of Head and Face Pain, 44*(8), 772–779.

Brissette, Ian; Scheier, Michael F.; & Carver, Charles S. (2002). The role of optimism in social network development, coping, and psychological adjustment during a life transition. *Journal of Personality and Social Psychology, 82,* 102–111.

Burks, Nancy, & Martin, Barclay. (1985). Everyday problems and life change events: Ongoing versus acute sources of stress. *Journal of Human Stress, 11,* 27–35.

Burns, Melanie, & Seligman, Martin E. P. (1989). Explanatory style across the lifespan: Evidence for stability over 52 years. *Journal of Personality and Social Psychology, 56,* 471–477.

Burman, Bonnie, & Margolin, Gayla. (1992). Analysis of the association between marital relationships and health problems: An interactional perspective. *Psychological Bulletin, 112,* 39–63.

Burns, Victoria E.; Carroll, Douglas; Drayson, Mark; Whitham, Martin; & Ring, Christopher. (2003). Life events, perceived stress and antibody response to influenza vaccination in young, healthy adults. *Journal of Psychosomatic Research, 55,* 569–572.

Cannon, Walter B. (1932). *The wisdom of the body.* New York: Norton.

Carter, C. Sue, & DeVries, A. Courtney. (1999). Stress and soothing: An endocrine perspective. In Michael Lewis & Douglas Ramsay (Eds.), *Soothing and stress.* Mahwah, NJ: Erlbaum.

Cass, Hyla. (2006). Stress and the immune system. *Total Health, 27*(6), 24–25, 2p; (AN 20292514).

Castillo, Linda G.; Conoley, Collie W.; & Brossart, Daniel F. (2007). Construction and validation of the Intragroup marginalization inventory. *Cultural Diversity & Ethnic Minority Psychology, 13*(3), 232–240.

Cheng, Cecilia. (2003). Cognitive and motivational process underlying coping flexibility: A dual-process model. *Journal of Personality and Social Psychology, 84,* 425–438.

Chun, Kevin M.; Balls-Organista, Pamela; & Marin, Gerardo (Eds.). (2003). *Acculturation: Advances in theory, measurement and applied research.* Washington, DC: American Psychological Association.

Cohen, Sheldon; Alper, Cuneyt M.; & Doyle, William J. (2006). Positive emotional style predicts resistance to illness after experimental exposure to rhinovirus or influenza A virus. *Psychosomatic Medicine, 68*(6), 809–815.

Cohen, Sheldon; Frank, Ellen; Doyle, William J.; Skoner, David P.; Rabin, Bruce; & Gwaltney, Jack M., Jr. (1998). Types of stressors that increase susceptibility to the common cold in healthy adults. *Health Psychology, 17,* 214–223.

Cohen, Sheldon; Gottlieb, Benjamin H.; & Underwood, Lynn G. (2000). Social relationships and health. In Sheldon Cohen, Lynn Underwood, & Benjamin H. Gottlieb (Eds.), *Social support measurement and intervention: A guide for health and social scientists.* New York: Oxford University Press.

Cohen, Sheldon, & Herbert, Tracy B. (1996). Health psychology: Psychological factors and physical disease from the perspective of human psychoneuroimmunology. *Annual Review of Psychology, 47,* 113–142.

Cohen, Sheldon; Tyrrell, David A. J.; & Smith, Andrew P. (1991). Psychological stress and susceptibility to the common cold. *New England Journal of Medicine, 325,* 606–612.

Cohen, Sheldon; Tyrrell, David A. J.; & Smith, Andrew P. (1993). Negative life events, perceived stress, negative affect, and susceptibility to the common cold. *Journal of Personality and Social Psychology, 64,* 131–140.

Colten, Harvey R., & Altevogt, Bruce R. (Eds.). (2006). *Sleep disorders and sleep deprivation: An unmet public health problem.* Institute of Medicine of the National Academies. National Academies Press.

Contrada, Richard J.; Ashmore, Richard D.; Gary, Melvin L.; Coups, Elliot; Egerth, Jill D.; Sewell, Andrea; & others. (2000). Ethnicity-related sources of stress and their effects on well-being. *Current Directions of Psychological Science, 9,* 136–139.

Coyne, James C., & Downey, Geraldine. (1991). Social factors and psychopathology: Stress, social support, and coping processes. *Annual Review of Psychology, 42,* 401–425.

Coyne, James C.; Ellard, John H.; & Smith, David A. F. (1990). Social support, interdependence, and the dilemmas of helping. In Barbara R. Sarason, Irwin G. Sarason, & Gregory R. Pierce (Eds.), *Social support: An interactional view.* New York: Wiley.

Dasgupta, Manisha, & Sanyal, Nilanjana. (2007). Relationship between controllability awareness and cognitive emotion regulation in selected clinical samples: A psychosocial perspective. *Journal of Projective Psychology & Mental Health, 14*(1), 64–75.

DeLongis, Anita; Coyne, James C.; Dakof, C.; Folkman, Susan; & Lazarus, Richard S. (1982). Relationship of daily hassles, uplifts, and major life events to health status. *Health Psychology, 1,* 119–136.

DeLongis, Anita; Folkman, Susan; & Lazarus, Richard S. (1988). The impact of stress on health and mood: Psychological and social resources as mediators. *Journal of Personality and Social Psychology, 54,* 486–495.

Dickerson, Sally S., & Kemeny, Margaret E. (2004). Acute stressors and cortisol responses: A theoretical integration and synthesis of laboratory research. *Psychological Bulletin, 130,* 355–391.

Dohrenwend, Bruce P.; Raphael, Karen G.; Schwartz, Sharon; Stueve, Ann; & Skodol, Andrew. (1993). The structured event probe and narrative rating method for measuring stressful life events. In Leo Goldberger & Schlomo Brenitz (Eds.), *The function of dreaming.* Albany, NY: State University of New York Press.

Ekwall, Anna Kristensson, & Hallberg, Ingalill Rahm. (2007). The association between caregiving satisfaction, difficulties and coping among older family caregivers. *Journal of Clinical Nursing, 16*(5), 832–844.

Emmons, Robert, & King, Laura. (1988). Conflict among personal strivings. Immediate and long-term implications for psychological and physical well-being. *Journal of Personality and Social Psychology, 54,* 1040–1048.

Ensel, Walter M., & Lin, Nan. (2004). Physical fitness and the stress process. *Journal of Community Psychology, 32,* 81–101.

Fields, Howard L., & Levine, Jon D. (1984). Placebo analgesia: A role for endorphins. *Trends in Neuroscience, 7,* 271–273.

Finch, Brian Karl, & Vega, William A. (2003). Acculturation stress, social support, and self-rated health among Latinos in California. *Journal of Immigrant Health, 5,* 109–117.

Folkman, Susan, & Lazarus, Richard S. (1991). Coping and emotion. In Alan Monat & Richard S. Lazarus (Eds.), *Stress and coping: An anthology* (3rd ed.). New York: Columbia University Press.

Folkman, Susan, & Moskowitz, Judith Tedlie. (2007). Positive affect and meaning-focused coping during significant psychological stress. In Miles Hewstone, Henk A. W. Schut, John B. F. De Wit, Kees Van Den Bos, & Margaret S. Stroebe (Eds.), *The scope of social psychology: Theory and applications* (pp. 193–208). New York: Psychology Press.

Francis, Darlene; Diorio, Josie; Liu, Dong; & Meaney, Michael J. (1999). Nongenomic transmission across generations of maternal behavior and stress responses in the rat. *Science, 286,* 1155–1158.

Fredrickson, Barbara L.; Tugade, Michele M.; Waugh, Christian E.; & Larkin, Gregory R. (2003). How good are positive emotions in crises? A prospective study of resilience and emotions following the terrorist attacks on the United States on September 11, 2001. *Journal of Personality and Social Psychology, 84,* 365–376.

Friedman, Howard S., & Booth-Kewley, Stephanie. (1987). The "disease-prone personality": A meta-analytic view of the construct. *American Psychologist, 42,* 539–555.

Friedman, Howard S., & Booth-Kewley, Stephanie. (2003). The "disease-prone personality": A meta-analytic view of the construct. In Peter Salovey & Alexander J. Rothman (Eds.), *Social psychology of health* (pp. 305–324). New York: Psychology Press.

Friedman, Meyer, & Rosenman, Ray H. (1974). *Type A behavior and your heart.* New York: Knopf.

Fuente-Fernández, Raúl de la; Ruth, Thomas J.; Sossi, Vesna; & others. (2001). Expectation and dopamine release: Mechanism of the placebo effect in Parkinson's disease. *Science, 293,* 1164–1166.

Gallo, Linda C., & Matthews, Karen A. (2003). Understanding the association between socioeconomic status and physical health: Do negative emotions play a role? *Psychological Bulletin, 129,* 10–51.

Gilham, Jane E.; Shatte, Andrew J.; Reivich, Karen J.; & Seligman, Martin E. P. (2001). Optimism, pessimism, and explanatory style. In Edward C. Chang (Ed.), *Optimism and pessimism: Implications for theory, research, and practice.* Washington, DC: American Psychological Association.

Glaser, Ronald, & Kiecolt-Glaser, Janice K. (2005). Stress-induced immune dysfunction: Implications for health. *Nature Reviews Immunology, 5,* 243–250.

Glynn, Laura M.; Christenfeld, Nicholas; & Gerin, William. (1999). Gender, social support, and cardiovascular responses to stress. *Psychosomatic Medicine, 61,* 234–242.

Gross, James J. (2007). The cultural regulation of emotions. In J. J. Gross (Ed.), *Handbook of emotion regulation* (pp. 486–503). New York: Guilford Press.

Gunnar, Megan, & Quevedo, Karina. (2007). The neurobiology of stress and development. *Annual Review of Psychology, 58,* 145–173.

Hamilton, Nancy A.; Catley, Delwyn; & Karlson, Cynthia. (2007). Sleep and the affective response to stress and pain. *Health Psychology, 26*(3), 288–295.

Hammen, Constance. (2005). Stress and depression. *Annual Review of Clinical Psychology, 1,* 293–319.

Heinrichs, Markus; Baumgartner, Thomas; Kirschbaum, Clemens; & Ehlert, Ulrike. (2003). Social support and oxytocin interact to suppress cortisol and subjective responses to psychosocial stress. *Biological Psychiatry, 54,* 1389–1398.

Herbert, Tracy Bennett, & Cohen, Sheldon. (1993). Depression and immunity: A meta-analytic review. *Psychological Bulletin, 113,* 472–486.

Heth, Josephine Todrank, & Somer, Eli. (2002). Characterizing stress tolerance: "Controllability awareness" and its relationship to perceived stress and reported health. *Personality and Individual Differences, 33,* 883–895.

Hobfoll, Stevan E.; Lilly, Roy S.; & Jackson, Anita P. (1992). Conservation of social resources and the self. In Hans O. F. Veiel & Urs Baumann (Eds.), *The meaning and measurement of social support.* New York: Hemisphere.

Hobfoll, Stevan E., & Stephens, Mary Ann Parris. (1990). Social support during extreme stress: Consequences and intervention. In Barbara R. Sarason, Irwin G. Sarason, & Gregory R. Pierce (Eds.), *Social support: An interactional view.* New York: Wiley.

Hobfoll, Stevan E., & Vaux, Alex. (1993). Social support: Resources and context. In Leo Goldberger & Shlomo Breznitz (Eds.), *Handbook of stress: Theoretical and clinical aspects* (2nd ed.). New York: Free Press.

Hobson, Charles J., & Delunas, Linda. (2001). National norms and life-event frequencies for the revised Social Readjustment Rating Scale. *International Journal of Stress Management, 8,* 299–314.

Hock, Roger R. (2007). Racing against your heart. In Alan Monat, Richard S. Lazarus, & Gretchen Reevy (Eds.), *The Praeger handbook on stress and coping* (vol. 1, pp. 341–348). Westport, CT: Praeger Publishers/Greenwood.

Holmes, Thomas H., & Masuda, Minoru. (1974). Life change and illness susceptibility. In Barbara Snell Dohrenwend & Bruce P. Dohrenwend (Eds.), *Stressful life events: Their nature and effects.* New York: Wiley.

Holmes, Thomas H., & Rahe, Richard H. (1967). The Social Readjustment Rating Scale. *Journal of Psychosomatic Research, 11,* 213–218.

Irwin, Michael R., & Miller, Andrew H. (2007). Depressive disorders and immunity: 20 years of progress and discovery. *Brain, Behavior, and Immunity, 21*(4), 374–383.

Iwanaga, Makoto; Yokoyama, Hiroshi; & Seiwa, Hidetoshi. (2004). Coping availability and stress reduction for optimistic and pessimistic individuals. *Personality and Individual Differences, 36,* 11–22.

Jackson, Benita; Sellers, Robert M.; & Peterson, Christopher. (2002). Pessimistic explanatory style moderates the effect of stress on physical illness. *Personality and Individual Differences, 32,* 567–573.

Jamil, Hikmet; Nassar-McMillan, Sylvia C.; & Lambert, Richard G. (2007). Immigration and attendant psychological sequelae: A comparison of three waves of Iraqi immigrants. *American Journal of Orthopsychiatry, 77*(2), 199–205.

Janisse, Michel Pierre, & Dyck, Dennis G. (1988). The Type A behavior pattern and coronary heart disease: Physiological and psychological dimensions. In Michel Pierre Janisse (Ed.), *Individual differences, stress, and health psychology.* New York: Springer-Verlag.

Johnson, Katrina W.; Anderson, Norman B.; Bastida, Elena; Kramer, B. Josea; Williams, David; & Wong, Morrison. (1995). Panel II: Macrosocial and environmental influences on minority health. *Health Psychology, 14,* 601–612.

Johnson, Laura R., & Sandhu, Daya Singh. (2007). Isolation, adjustment, and acculturation issues of international students: Intervention strategies for counselors. In Hemla D. Singaravelu & Mark Pope (Eds.), *A handbook for counseling international students in the United States* (pp. 13–35). Alexandria, VA: American Counseling Association.

Kanner, Allen D.; Coyne, James C.; Schaefer, Catherine; & Lazarus, Richard S. (1981). Comparison of two modes of stress management: Daily hassles and uplifts versus major life events. *Journal of Behavioral Medicine, 4,* 1–39.

Kessler, Ronald C.; Price, Richard H.; & Wortman, Camille B. (1985). Social factors in psychopathology: Stress, social support, and coping processes. *Annual Review of Psychology, 36,* 531–572.

Kiecolt-Glaser, Janice K. (1999). Stress, personal relationships, and immune function: Health implications. *Brain, Behavior and Immunity, 13*(1), 61–72.

Kiecolt-Glaser, Janice K., & Glaser, Ronald. (1991). Stress and immune function in humans. In Robert Ader, David L. Felten, & Nicholas Cohen (Eds.), *Psychoneuroimmunology.* San Diego, CA: Academic Press.

Kiecolt-Glaser, Janice K., & Glaser, Ronald. (1993). Mind and immunity. In Daniel Goleman & Joel Gurin (Eds.), *Mind/body medicine: How to use your mind for better health.* Yonkers, NY: Consumer Reports Books.

Kiecolt-Glaser, Janice K.; McGuire, Lynanne; Robles, Theodore F.; & Glaser, Ronald. (2002). Emotions, morbidity, and mortality: New perspectives from psychoneuroimmunology. *Annual Review of Psychology, 53,* 83–107.

Kiecolt-Glaser, Janice K., & Newton, Tamara L. (2001). Marriage and health: His and hers. *Psychological Bulletin, 127,* 472–503.

Kimzey, Stephen L. (1975). The effects of extended spaceflight on hematologic and immunologic systems. *Journal of the American Medical Women's Association, 30,* 218–232.

Krantz, David S., & McCeney, Melissa K. (2002). Effects of psychological and social factors on organic disease: A critical assessment of research on coronary heart disease. *Annual Review of Psychology, 53,* 341–369.

LaFromboise, Teresa D.; Coleman, Hardin L. K.; & Gerton, Jennifer. (1993). Psychological impact of biculturalism: Evidence and theory. *Psychological Bulletin, 114,* 395–412.

LaFromboise, Teresa D.; Trimble, Joseph E.; & Mohatt, Gerald V. (1993). Counseling intervention and American Indian tradition: An integrative approach. In Donald R.

Atkinson, George Morten, & Derald Wing Sue (Eds.), *Counseling American minorities: A cross-cultural perspective* (4th ed.). Madison, WI: Brown & Benchmark.

Langer, Ellen, & Rodin, Judith. (1976). The effects of choice and enhanced personal responsibility for the aged: A field experiment in an institutional setting. *Journal of Personality and Social Psychology, 34,* 191–198.

Lazarus, Richard S. (1999). *Stress and emotion: A new synthesis.* New York: Springer.

Lazarus, Richard S. (2000). Toward better research on stress and coping. *American Psychologist, 55,* 665–673.

Lazarus, Richard S., & Folkman, Susan. (1984). *Stress, appraisal, and coping.* New York: Springer.

Leach, Carolyn S., & Rambaut, Paul C. (1974). Biochemical responses of the Skylab crewmen. *Proceedings of the Skylab Life Sciences Symposium, 2,* 427–454.

Lepore, Stephen J. (1993). Social conflict, social support, and psychological distress: Evidence of cross-domain buffering effects. *Journal of Personality and Social Psychology, 63,* 857–867.

Leuchter, Andrew F.; Cook, Ian A.; Witte, Elise A.; & others. (2002). Changes in brain function of depressed subjects during treatment with placebo. *American Journal of Psychiatry, 159,* 122–129.

Light, Kathleen C.; Smith, Tara E.; Johns, Josephine M.; Brownley, Kimberly A.; Hofheimer, Julie A.; & Amico, Janet. (2000). Oxytocin responsivity in mothers of infants: A preliminary study of relationships with blood pressure during laboratory stress and normal ambulatory activity. *Health Psychology, 19,* 560–567.

Liu, Dong; Diorio, Josie; Tannenbaum, Beth; Caldji, Christian; Francis, Darlene; Freedman, Alison; & others. (1997). Maternal care, hippocampal glucocorticoid receptors, and hypothalamic-pituitary-adrenal responses to stress. *Science, 277,* 1659–1662.

Liu, Ruth X., & Chen, Zeng-Yin. (2006). The effects of marital conflict and marital disruption on depressive affect: A comparison between women in and out of poverty. *Social Science Quarterly, 87*(2), 250–271.

Lovallo, William R.; al'Absi, Mustafa; Pincomb, Gwen A.; Everson, Susan A.; Sung, Bong Hee; Passey, Richard B.; & Wilson, Michael F. (1996). Caffeine and behavioral stress effects on blood pressure in borderline hypertensive Caucasian men. *Health Psychology, 15,* 11–17.

Lynch, Denis J.; McGrady, Angele; Alvarez, Elizabeth; & Forman, Justin. (2005). Recent life changes and medical utilization in an academic family practice. *Journal of Nervous and Mental Disease, 193,* 633–635.

Lyness, Scott A. (1993). Predictors of differences between Type A and B individuals in heart rate and blood pressure reactivity. *Psychological Bulletin, 114,* 266–295.

Maier, Steven F., & Watkins, Linda R. (2000). The neurobiology of stressor controllability. In Jane E. Gillham (Ed.), *The science of optimism and hope: Research essays in honor of Martin E. P. Seligman.* Philadelphia: Templeton Foundation Press.

Mandler, George. (1993). Thought, memory, and learning: Effects of emotional stress. In Leo Goldberger & Shlomo

Breznitz (Eds.), *Handbook of stress: Theoretical and clinical aspects* (2nd ed.). New York: Free Press.

Marco, Christine A., & Suls, Jerry. (1993). Daily stress and the trajectory of mood: Spillover, response assimilation, contrast, and chronic negative affectivity. *Journal of Personality and Social Psychology, 64,* 1053–1063.

Marsella, Anthony J., & Dash-Scheuer, Alice. (1988). Coping, culture, and healthy human development: A research and conceptual overview. In Pierre R. Dasen, John W. Berry, & Norman Sartorius (Eds.), *Health and cross-cultural psychology: Toward applications* (vol. 10, Cross-cultural Research and Methodology Series). Newbury Park, CA: Sage.

Marshall, Grant N.; Wortman, Camille B.; Kusulas, Jeffery W.; Hervig, Linda K.; & Vickers, Ross R., Jr. (1992). Distinguishing optimism from pessimism: Relations to fundamental dimension of mood and personality. *Journal of Personality and Social Psychology, 62,* 1067–1074.

Marucha, Phillip T.; Kiecolt-Glaser, Janice K.; & Favagehi, Meghrdad. (1998). Mucosal wound healing is impaired by examination stress. *Psychosomatic Medicine, 60,* 362–365.

Masters, Kevin S.; Stillman, Alexandra M.; & Spielmans, Glen I. (2007). Specificity of social support for back pain patients: Do patients care who provides what? *Journal of Behavioral Medicine, 30*(1), 11–20.

Maybery, D. J.; Neale, Jason; Arentz, Alex; & Jones-Ellis, Jenny. (2007). The Negative Even Scale: Measuring frequency and intensity of adult hassles. *Anxiety, Stress & Coping, 20*(2), 163–176.

McAndrew, Francis T.; Akande, Adebowale; Turner, Saskia; & Sharma, Yadika. (1998). A cross-cultural ranking of stressful life events in Germany, India, South Africa, and the United States. *Journal of Cross-Cultural Psychology, 29,* 717–727.

McCallie, Martha S.; Blum, Claire M.; & Hood, Charlaine J. (2006). Progressive muscle relaxation. *Journal of Human Behavior in the Social Environment, 13*(3), 51–66.

McKenry, Patrick C., & Price, Sharon J. (Eds.). (2005). *Families and change: Coping with stressful events and transitions.* Thousand Oaks, CA: Sage.

Mellers, Barbara A. (2000). Choice and the relative pleasure of consequences. *Psychological Bulletin, 126,* 910–924.

Miller, Gregory E.; Cohen, Sheldon; & Ritchey, A. Kim. (2002). Chronic psychological stress and the regulation of pro-inflammatory cytokines: A glucocorticoid-resistance model. *Health Psychology, 21,* 531–541.

Mohr, David; Vedantham, Kumar; Neylan, Thomas; Metzler, Thomas J.; Best, Suzanne; & Marmar, Charles R. (2003). The mediating effects of sleep in the relationship between traumatic stress and health symptoms in urban police officers. *Psychosomatic Medicine, 65,* 485–489.

Myrtek, Michael. (2007). Type A behavior and hostility as independent risk factors for coronary heart disease. In Jochen Jordan, Benjamin Bardé, & Andreas Michael Zeiher (Eds.), *Contributions toward evidence-based psychocardiology: A systematic review of the literature* (pp. 159–183). Washington, DC: American Psychological Associations.

National Sleep Foundation. (2004). *2004 "Sleep in America" poll: Final report.* Washington, DC: National Sleep Foundation. Retrieved from http://www.sleepfoundation.org/polls/2004SleepPollFinalReport.pdf.

Ng, Debbi M., & Jeffery, Robert W. (2003). Relationships between perceived stress and health behaviors in a sample of working adults. *Health Psychology, 22,* 638–642.

O'Connor, Daryl B., & Shimizu, Mikiko. (2002). Sense of personal control, stress and coping style: A cross-cultural study. *Stress and Health, 18,* 173–183.

Palmblad, J.; Petrini, B.; Wasserman, J.; & Akerstedt, T. (1979). Lymphocyte and granulocyte reactions during sleep deprivation. *Psychosomatic Medicine, 41,* 273–278.

Park, Crystal L.; Armeli, Stephen; & Tennen, Howard. (2004). Appraisal-coping goodness of fit: A daily Internet study. *Personality and Social Psychology Bulletin, 30,* 558–569.

Pawlow, L. A.; O'Neil, P. M.; & Malcolm, R. J. (2003). Night eating syndrome: Effects of brief relaxation training on stress, mood, hunger, and eating patterns. *International Journal of Obesity & Related Metabolic Disorders, 27,* 970–978.

Peirce, Robert S.; Frone, Michael R.; Russell, Marcia; & Cooper, M. Lynne. (1996). Financial stress, social support, and alcohol involvement: A longitudinal test of the buffering hypothesis in a general population study. *Health Psychology, 15,* 38–47.

Peterson, Christopher. (2000). Optimistic explanatory style and health. In Jane E. Gillham (Ed.), *The science of optimism and hope: Research essays in honor of Martin E. P. Seligman.* Philadelphia: Templeton Foundation Press.

Peterson, Christopher, & Bossio, Lisa M. (1993). Healthy attitudes: Optimism, hope, and control. In Daniel Goleman & Joel Gurin (Eds.), *Mind/body medicine: How to use your mind for better health.* Yonkers, NY: Consumer Reports Books.

Peterson, Christopher, & Bossio, Lisa M. (2001). Optimism and physical well-being. In Edward C. Chang (Ed.), *Optimism and pessimism: Implications for theory, research, and practice.* Washington, DC: American Psychological Association.

Peterson, Christopher; Seligman, Martin E. P.; & Vaillant, George E. (1988). Pessimistic explanatory style as a risk factor for physical illness: A thirty-five-year longitudinal study. *Journal of Personality and Social Psychology, 55,* 23–27.

Petrovic, Predrag; Kalso, Eija; Petersson, Karl Magnus; & Ingvar, Martin. (2002). Placebo and opioid analgesia—Imaging a shared neuronal network. *Science, 295,* 1737–1740.

Pillow, David R.; Zautra, Alex J.; & Sandler, Irwin. (1996). Major life events and minor stressors: Identifying meditational links in the stress process. *Journal of Personality and Social Psychology, 70,* 381–394.

Rahe, Richard H. (1972). Subjects' recent life changes and their near-future illness reports. *Annals of Clinical Research, 4,* 250–265.

Rejeski, W. Jack; Gregg, Edward; Thompson, Amy; & Berry, Michael. (1991). The effects of varying doses of acute aerobic exercise on psychophysiological stress responses in highly trained cyclists. *Journal of Sport and Exercise Psychology, 13,* 188–199.

Rejeski, W. Jack; Thompson, Amy; Brubaker, Peter H.; & Miller, Henry S. (1992). Acute exercise: Buffering psychosocial responses in women. *Health Psychology, 11*, 355–362.

Repetti, Rena L. (1989). Effects of daily workload on subsequent behavior during marital interaction: The roles of withdrawal and spouse support. *Journal of Personality and Social Psychology, 57*, 651–659.

Repetti, Rena L. (1993). Short-term effects of occupational stressors on daily mood and health complaints. *Health Psychology, 12*, 125–131.

Repetti, Rena L., & Wood, Jenifer. (1997). The effects of daily stress at work on mothers' interactions with preschoolers. *Journal of Family Psychology, 11*, 90–108.

Richman, Laura Smart; Kubzansky, Laura; Masello, Joanna; Kawachi, Ichiro; Choo, Peter; & Bauer, Mark. (2005). Positive emotion and health: Going beyond the negative. *Health Psychology, 24*, 422–429.

Robbins, Ann S.; Spence, Janet T.; & Clark, Heather. (1991). Psychological determinants of health and performance: The tangled web of desirable and undesirable characteristics. *Journal of Personality and Social Psychology, 61*, 755–765.

Robles, Theodore K.; Glaser, Ronald; & Kiecolt-Glaser, Janice K. (2005). Out of balance: A new look at chronic stress, depression, and immunity. *Psychological Science, 14*, 111–115.

Rodin, Judith. (1986). Aging and health: Effects of the sense of control. *Science, 233*, 1271–1275.

Rodin, Judith, & Langer, Ellen. (1977). Long-term effects of a control-relevant intervention with the institutionalized aged. *Journal of Personality and Social Psychology, 35*, 897–902.

Rook, Karen S. (1992). Deterimental aspects of social relationships: Taking stock of an emerging literature. In Hans O. F. Veiel & Urs Baumann (Eds.), *The meaning and measurement of social support.* New York: Hemisphere.

Rosekind, Mark. (2003). Quoted in National Sleep Foundation press release, "Sleep is important when stress and anxiety increase, says the National Sleep Foundation." Washington, DC. Retrieved from http://www.sleepfoundation.org /PressArchives/stress.cfm.

Rosenman, Ray H., & Chesney, Margaret A. (1982). Stress, Type A behavior, and coronary disease. In Leo Goldberger & Shlomo Breznitz (Eds.), *Handbook of stress: Theoretical and clinical aspects.* New York: Free Press.

Russek, Linda G., & Schwartz, Gary E. (1997). Perceptions of parental caring predict health status in midlife: A 35-year follow-up to the Harvard Mastery of Stress Study. *Psychosomatic Medicine, 59*, 144–149.

Schneiderman, Neil; Ironson, Gail; & Siegel, Scott D. (2005). Stress and health: Psychological, behavioral, and biological determinants. *Annual Review of Clinical Psychology, 1*, 607–628.

Schulz, Marc S.; Cowan, Philip A.; Cowan, Carolyn Pape; & Brennan, Robert T. (2004). Coming home upset: Gender, marital satisfaction, and the daily spillover of workday experience into couple interactions. *Journal of Family Psychology, 18*, 250–263.

Scully, Judith A.; Tosi, Henry; & Banning, Kevin. (2000). Life event checklists: Revisiting the Social Readjustment Rating Scale after 30 years. *Educational and Psychological Measurement, 60*, 864–876.

Segerstrom, Suzanne C.; Castañeda, Jay O.; & Spencer, Theresa E. (2003). Optimism effects on cellular immunity: Testing the affective and persistence models. *Personality and Individual Differences, 3*, 1615–1624.

Segerstrom, Suzanne C., & Miller, Gregory E. (2004). Psychological stress and the human immune system: A meta-analytic study of 30 years of inquiry. *Psychological Bulletin, 130*, 601–630.

Segerstrom, Suzanne C.; Taylor, Shelley E.; Kemey, Margaret E.; & Fahey, John L. (1998). Optimism is associated with mood, coping, and immune change in response to stress. *Journal of Personality and Social Psychology, 74*, 1646–1655.

Seligman, Martin E. P. (1990). *Learned optimism.* New York: Knopf.

Seligman, Martin E. P. (1992). *Helplessness: On development, depression, and death.* New York: Freeman.

Selye, Hans. (1956). *The stress of life.* New York: McGraw-Hill.

Selye, Hans. (1976). *The stress of life* (Rev. ed.). New York: McGraw-Hill.

Shumaker, Sally A., & Hill, D. Robin (1991). Gender differences in social support and physical health. *Health Psychology, 10*, 102–111.

Shuval, Judith T. (1993). Migration and stress. In Leo Goldberger & Shlomo Breznitz (Eds.), *Handbook of stress: Theoretical and clinical aspects* (2nd ed.). New York: Free Press.

Siegel, Daniel J. (2007). *The mindful brain: Reflection and attunement in the cultivation of well-being.* New York: Norton.

Siegel, Judith M. (1990). Stressful life events and use of physician services among the elderly. *Journal of Personality and Social Psychology, 58*, 1081–1086.

Smith, Barry D.; Cranford, David; & Green, Lee. (2001). Hostility and caffeine: Cardiovascular effects during stress and recovery. *Personality & Individual Differences, 30*, 1125–1137.

Smith, Timothy W. (1992). Hostility and health: Current status of a psychosomatic hypothesis. *Health Psychology, 11*, 139–150.

Southwick, Steven M.; Vythilingam, Meena; & Charney, Dennis S. (2005). The psychobiology of depression and resilience to stress: Implications for prevention and treatment. *Annual Review of Clinical Psychology, 1*, 255–291.

Spiegel, David. (1993). Social support: How friends, family, and groups can help. In Daniel Goleman & Joel Gurin (Eds.), *Mind/body medicine: How to use your mind for better health.* Yonkers, NY: Consumer Reports Books.

Spiegel, David; Bloom, J. R.; Kraemer, H. C.; & Gottheil, E. (1989). Effect of psychosocial treatment on survival of patients with metastatic breast cancer. *Lancet, 2*, 888–891.

Stanton, Annette L., & Snider, Pamela R. (1993). Coping with a breast cancer diagnosis: A prospective study. *Health Psychology, 12*, 16–23.

Steig, Philip E. (2004). Quoted in Jamie Talan, "Christopher Reeve dies at 52." *Newsday*. Retrieved from http://www.newsday.com/other/education/ny-news101304.story.

Stone, Arthur A.; Cox, Donald S.; Valdimarsdottir, Heiddis; Jandorf, Lina; & Neale, John M. (1987). Evidence that secretory IgA antibody is associated with daily mood. *Journal of Personality and Social Psychology, 52,* 988–993.

Stone, Arthur A.; Neale, John M.; Cox, Donald S.; Napoli, Anthony; Valdimarsdottir, Heiddis; & Kennedy-Moore, Eileen. (1994). Daily events are associated with a secretory immune response to an oral antigen in men. *Health Psychology, 13,* 440–446.

Storch, Maja; Gaab, Jens; & Küttel, Yvonne. (2007). Psychoneuroendocrine effects of resource-activating stress management training. *Health Psychology, 26*(4), 456–463.

Suls, Jerry, & Bunde, James. (2005). Anger, anxiety, and depression as risk factors for cardiovascular disease: The problems and implications of overlapping affective dispositions. *Psychological Bulletin, 131,* 260–300.

Swickert, Rhonda J.; Rosentreter, Christina J.; Hittner, James B.; & Mushrush, Jane E. (2002). Extraversion, social support processes, and stress. *Personality and Individual Differences, 32,* 877–891.

Taylor, Shelley, E., & Aspinwall, Lisa G. (1993). Coping with chronic illness. In Leo Goldberger & Shlomo Breznitz (Eds.), *Handbook of stress: Theoretical and clinical aspects* (2nd ed.). New York: Free Press.

Taylor, Shelley E.; Kemeny, Margaret E.; Bower, Julienne E.; Gruenewald, Tara L.; & Reed, Geoffrey M. (2000). Psychological resources, positive illusions, and health. *American Psychologist, 55,* 99–109.

Taylor, Shelley E.; Klein, Laura Cousino; Lewis, Brian P.; Gruenewald, Tara L.; Gurung, Regan A. R.; & Updegraff, John A. (2000). Biobehavioral responses to stress in females: Tend-and-befriend, not fight-or-flight. *Psychological Review, 107,* 411–429.

Taylor, Shelley E.; Lewis, Brian P.; Gruenewald, Tara L.; Gurung, Regan A. R.; Updegraff, John A.; & Klein, Laura Cousino. (2002). Sex differences in biobehavioral response to threat: Reply to Geary and Flinn (2002). *Psychological Review, 109,* 751–753.

Thompson, Suzanne C.; Nanni, Christopher; & Levine, Alexandra. (1994). Primary versus secondary and central versus consequence-related control in HIV-positive men. *Journal of Personality and Social Psychology, 67,* 540–547.

Thompson, Suzanne C., & Spacapan, Shirlynn. (1991). Perceptions of control in vulnerable populations. *Journal of Social Issues, 47,* 1–21.

Todd, Michael. (2004). Daily processes in stress and smoking: Effects of negative events, nicotine dependence, and gender. *Psychology of Addictive Behaviors, 18,* 31–39.

Tomaka, Joe; Blascovich, Jim; Kelsey, Robert M.; & Leitten, Christopher L. (1993). Subjective, physiological, and behavioral effects of threat and challenge appraisal. *Journal of Personality and Social Psychology, 65,* 248–260.

Townes, Glenn. (2007). Report shows link between discrimination and health. *Amsterdam News, 98*(30), 31.

Tversky, Amos, & Shafir, Eldar. (1992). Choice under conflict: The dynamics of deferred decision. *Psychological Science, 3,* 358–361.

Uchino, Bert N.; Cacioppo, John T.; & Kiecolt-Glaser, Janice K. (1996). The relationship between social support and physiological processes: A review with emphasis on underlying mechanisms and implications for health. *Psychological Bulletin, 119,* 488–531.

Vlahov, David; Galea, Sandro; Resnick, Heidi; Shern, Jennifer; Boscarino, Joseph A.; Bucuvalas, Michael; & others. (2002). Increased use of cigarettes, alcohol, and marijuana among Manhattan, New York, residents after the September 11 terrorist attacks. *American Journal of Epidemiology, 155,* 988–996.

Vollman, Michael W.; LaMontagne, Lynda L.; & Hepworth, Joseph T. (2007). Coping with depressive symptoms in adults living with heart failure. *Journal of Cardiovascular Nursing, 22*(2), 125–130.

Waelde, Lynn C.; Thompson, Larry; & Gallagher-Thompson, Dolores. (2004). A pilot study of a yoga and meditation intervention for dementia caregiver stress. *Journal of Clinical Psychology, 60,* 677–687.

Walton, Kenneth G.; Schneider, Robert H.; Nidich, Sanford I.; Salerno, John W.; Nordstrom, Cheryl K.; & Merz, C. Noel Bairey. (2002). Psychosocial stress and cardiovascular disease, part 2: Effectiveness of the Transcendental Meditation program in treatment and prevention. *Behavioral Medicine, 28,* 106–123.

Ward, Colleen, & Rana-Deuba, Arzu. (1999). Acculturation and adaptation revisited. *Journal of Cross-Cultural Psychology, 30*(4), 422–442.

West, Michael A. (1987). Traditional and psychological perspectives on meditation. In Michael A. West (Ed.), *The psychology of meditation.* New York: Oxford University Press.

Wethington, Elaine; McLeod, Jane D.; & Kessler, Ronald C. (1987). The importance of life events for explaining sex differences in psychological distress. In Rosalind C. Barnett, Lois Biener, & Grace K. Baruch (Eds.), *Gender and stress.* New York: Free Press.

Wijndaele, Katrien; Matton, Lynn; & Duvigneaud, Nathalie. (2007). Associations between leisure time physical activity and stress, social support and coping: A cluster-analytical approach. *Psychology of Sport and Exercise, 8*(4), 425–440.

Wise, Deborah, & Rosqvist, Johan. (2006). Explanatory style and well-being. In Jay C. Thomas, Daniel L. Segal, & Michel Hersen (Eds.), *Comprehensive handbook of personality and psychopathology: Vol. 1: Personality and everyday functioning.* Hoboken, NJ: John Wiley & Sons.

Wong, Paul T. P., & Wong, Lilian C. J. (Eds.). (2006). *Handbook of multicultural perspectives on stress and coping.* New York, NY: Springer.

Zubieta, Jon-Kar; Bueller, Joshua A.; Jackson, Lisa R.; Scott, David J.; Xu, Yanjun; Koeppe, Robert A.; Nichols, Thomas E.; & Stohler, Christian S. (2005). Placebo effects mediated by endogenous opioid activity on u-opioid receptors. *Journal of Neuroscience, 25,* 7754–7762.

Practicing Your Textbook Reading Skills

1. Examine the "Chapter Outline" on page 539 to determine which of the following is not a *major* topic of the chapter.

   a. "Physical Effects of Stress: The Mind-Body Connection"

   b. "The Mysterious Placebo Effect"

   c. "Individual Factors That Influence the Response to Stress"

   d. "Coping: How People Deal with Stress"

2. The chapter prologue ("Katie's Story") on pages 539–40

   a. provides a historical overview of the study of stress.

   b. summarizes the chapter's main points.

   c. outlines the chapter's organization.

   d. introduces an example that is used throughout the chapter to explain stress.

3. What is the meaning of the word *bizarre* as it is used in the seventh paragraph of the chapter prologue ("Katie's Story")?

   a. a Middle Eastern market

   b. eerily unfamiliar

   c. mildly amusing

   d. chaotic

4. Which sentence summarizes the main idea of the first section of the chapter ("What Is Stress?")?

   a. "When events are perceived as exceeding your ability to cope with them, you experience an unpleasant emotional and physical state—called stress."

   b. "What is health psychology, and what is the biopsychosocial model?"

   c. "How do life events, daily hassles, and conflict contribute to stress?"

   d. "What are some social and cultural sources of stress?"

5. According to Table 13.1, on page 542, which of the following events is the most stressful?

   a. death of a close friend

   b. marriage

   c. change in work responsibilities

   d. minor violations of the law

6. The subtitle of the "Critical Thinking" box on page 557 asks, "do personality factors cause disease?" How do the authors answer the question?

   a. Yes.

   b. No.

   c. Maybe.

   d. It's impossible to tell.

7. What kind of conflict is illustrated by the *Cathy* cartoon on page 546?

   a. approach-approach

   b. avoidance-avoidance

   c. approach-avoidance

   d. none of the above

8. Of the following psychologists, who is identified in this chapter as a key person?

   a. Amos Tyversky

   b. Sigmund Freud

   c. Janice Kiecolt-Glaser

   d. Lisa F. Berkman

9. The specialized meaning of *distancing* for psychology is

   a. separating yourself physically from something.

   b. acknowledging a stressor but attempting to minimize or eliminate its emotional impact.

   c. measuring the length between two points.

   d. recording a period of time.

10. The boxed feature "Application: Minimizing the Effects of Stress" on pages 566–67

   a. suggests how you might use the information in the chapter in your real life.

   b. describes an influential study.

   c. offers information on jobs in health psychology.

   d. includes statistics on psychological studies.

Testing Your Understanding

Identify the following statements as *true* or *false*.

1. Two people may respond very differently to the same potentially stressful event.

   T _____   F _____

2. The Social Readjustment Rating Scale accurately predicts how stressors will affect people's health.

   T _____   F _____

3. A person who has a sense of control over a potentially stressful situation will be less stressed by it than a person who does not feel a sense of control.

   T _____   F _____

4. Pessimistic people tend to be healthier than optimistic people.

   T _____   F _____

5. Research shows that loneliness can harm your health as much as smoking, having high cholesterol, being overweight, or not exercising.

   T _____   F _____

Select the best answer to each of the following questions.

6. According to the *biopsychosocial model*, health and illness are determined by

   a. our cognitive appraisal of an event and the resources we have to deal with it.

   b. the complex interaction of biological factors, psychological and behavioral factors, and social conditions.

   c. everyday occurrences that annoy and upset people.

   d. how people characteristically explain their failures and defeats.

7. Daily hassles strongly affect stress levels because they are

   a. annoying.

   b. unpredictable.

   c. cumulative.

   d. minor.

8. All of the following are types of conflict except

   a. approach-approach.

   b. avoidance-avoidance.

   c. approach-avoidance.

   d. vacillation.

9. Whose research in the 1970s revolutionized psychologists' understanding of the relationship between the mind and the immune system?

   a. Robert Ader and Nicholas Cohen

   b. Ron Glaser and Janice Kiecolt-Glaser

     c. Walter B. Cannon

     d. Hans Selye

10. Which of the following might explain why chronically negative people are more likely to suffer serious health problems than positive people are?

     a. Positive people are more likely to be affected by daily hassles.

     b. Positive people react more intensely to stressors.

     c. Negative people suffer from learned helplessness.

     d. Negative people experience more stress than positive people do.

11. All of the following are characteristics of Type A behavior except

     a. extreme confidence.

     b. exaggerated sense of time urgency.

     c. general sense of hostility.

     d. intense ambition and competitiveness.

12. Having friends can benefit your health because

     a. knowing that they support you can make a situation seem less threatening.

     b. their presence decreases the intensity of physical reactions to a stressor.

     c. loneliness increases levels of stress hormones and weakens the immune system.

     d. all of the above

13. Which of the following is an example of an adaptive coping strategy?

     a. smoking

     b. maintaining self-esteem

     c. drinking

     d. hostile confrontation

14. Which of the following is more likely than the others to worsen the physical effects of stress?

     a. watching television

     b. exercising regularly

     c. avoiding stimulants

     d. practicing a relaxation technique

15. All of the following are examples of emotion-focused coping except

    a. escape-avoidance.

    b. seeking social support.

    c. planful problem solving.

    d. denial.

Using your own words, define the following terms as they are used in the chapter.

16. *conflict*

    _____

    _____

17. *acculturative stress*

    _____

    _____

18. *fight-or-flight response*

    _____

    _____

19. *corticosteroids*

    _____

    _____

20. *coping*

    _____

    _____

Answer each of the following questions using the space provided.

21. Identify two strategies for resolving an approach-avoidance conflict.

    _____

    _____

    _____

22. What physical symptoms might occur when a person faces immediate danger?

    _____

_____

_____

23. Outline and briefly describe the three stages of general adaptation syndrome.

_____

_____

_____

_____

24. Describe the differences in how men and women experience and cope with stress.

_____

_____

_____

_____

_____

_____

25. Provide two examples of how Americans' and Asians' coping strategies differ.

_____

_____

_____

_____

Making Thematic Connections

The history chapter reprinted in Unit 4 of this reader describes working conditions in late-nineteenth-century America and how different people and organizations responded to them. For example, as laborers found they had less control over their work, cheap forms of entertainment—such as arcades, amusement parks, and dance halls—became increasingly popular. (See page 528 of that chapter for more information.) How would you categorize that development as a coping strategy? Is spending time on amusements an emotion-focused or a problem-focused coping strategy? Is it adaptive or maladaptive? Explain your answer. (Note that _adaptive_ behavior helps people get everyday tasks done, while _maladaptive_ behavior interferes with people's ability to perform such tasks.)

Environmental Science

"Land: Public and Private"

Introduction

Environmental science studies environmental systems and the impact that human beings have on our planet. Building on contributions from biology, chemistry, economics, and many other disciplines, environmental scientists attempt to understand complex interactions in the natural world and to find solutions to environmental problems. Like other sciences, environmental science focuses on things that can be observed and tested. Scientists ask questions and look for answers to them by conducting laboratory and field research. They also consider what others before them have learned. Sometimes they add to the scientific body of knowledge; sometimes they learn things that change what they and their colleagues believed: these findings in turn lead to new questions. In other words, environmental scientists observe details, make connections, make inferences, and draw conclusions. They think critically about what they do and what they know. As a student of environmental science and as a critical reader, you must do the same.

Environmental Science: Foundations and Applications, by Andrew Friedland, Rick Relyea, and David Courard-Hauri, introduces students to the study of environmental systems and aims to provide a grounding in the basics of the field. Because environmental scientists are concerned with practical issues and the trade-offs among choices, the book emphasizes the relevance of environmental science to everyday activities and decisions. In the chapter "Land: Public and Private," the authors discuss the challenges that arise when individuals, businesses, and governments compete for a limited resource.

As you read the chapter you'll see that a variety of elements are provided to help you understand its content:

- The case study that opens the chapter focuses on a compelling story to show how the ideas in the chapter play out in real life.

- A list of key ideas following the case study previews the main points of the discussion.

- Annotated figures, graphs, and photographs put scientific concepts into a visual format, reinforcing the textual discussion and making complex information easier to comprehend.

- Important terms, which you can find defined in the glossary, are printed in boldface.

- A highlighted feature, "Working Toward Sustainability," explains how a particular group of people has worked to protect the environment.

- A chapter summary and multiple-choice questions review the main points and help you prepare for quizzes and tests.

- Three additional exercises on the last page encourage you to apply the information in the chapter to your own life.

Environmental science is one of the fastest-growing fields of employment in the United States and around the world. As concerns about the planet's

---

This unit's textbook reading comes from *Environmental Science: Foundations and Applications*, by Andrew Friedland, Rick Relyea, and David Courard-Hauri, W. H. Freeman and Company, 2012, Chapter 10, pages 260–81.

health continue to rise, many companies are looking for ways to reduce their environmental impact without sacrificing profits. The chapter you're about to read provides explanations of land-use issues and summaries of research findings that will give you an idea of the kinds of work environmental scientists do. Such issues and efforts arise in many disciplines and fields of work. The chapter on public relations in Unit 3, for instance, describes railroad executives' strategies for acquiring government land as well as a corporate response to an environmental disaster, and the history chapter in Unit 4 discusses several land-use issues at the end of the nineteenth century, from farming to migration to the growth of cities. Understanding how and why the government regulates development today will give you an important insight into the challenges and opportunities facing contemporary businesses and workers.

Preparing to Read the Textbook Chapter

1. Environmental regulations are often controversial. Some groups argue that attempts to protect wildlife and natural resources cost people their jobs; others insist that allowing companies to do whatever they want comes at a cost to the planet. What is your opinion? Should businesses be required to find ways to limit the impact they have on the environment? Why or why not?

2. Skim through the chapter, focusing your attention on the headings, the photographs and figures, and the terms in bold print. Without reading anything closely, what are the main ideas of the chapter?

3. Where do you expect to live and work after you've finished school? Do you want to be in the city, in the country, or do you hope to end up in the suburbs? Why? What are the advantages and disadvantages of each option?

CHAPTER

10

Land: Public and Private

Who Owns a Tree? Julia Butterfly Hill versus Maxxam

For most of its history, northern California's Pacific Lumber Company was a leader in environmental stewardship. It pioneered the practice of selectively cutting some trees on its land while leaving nearby trees intact. Unlike the usual practice of clear-cutting—clearing all the trees from an area of land—selective cutting allows the roots of the remaining trees to

The ultimate goal of a tree sit is to remain in a tree long enough to save it from logging. However, many such actions merely delay the inevitable. Still, activists support tree sits because they gain time for further legal proceedings and increase media awareness. But Julia Butterfly Hill proved indomitable. In her most famous tree sit, she occupied Luna, a 55-meter (180-foot) redwood tree that was nearly a thousand

> Julia Butterfly Hill proved indomitable. In her most famous tree sit, she occupied Luna, a 55-meter (180-foot) redwood tree that was nearly a thousand years old.

retain water and hold soil in place. In addition, the surviving trees allow forest regrowth that more closely mimics natural succession after a disturbance. Pacific Lumber developed a 100-year sustainable logging plan that ensured relatively healthy forests as well as job security for the loggers and their families.

In 1986, however, Pacific Lumber was purchased by new owners and renamed Maxxam. To increase revenue from the company's land holdings, the new management clear-cut hundreds of thousands of acres of redwood forests. Because the new harvesting method removed vegetation and tree roots, Maxxam's practices left the forests susceptible to soil erosion and landslides. On December 31, 1996, an immense landslide began on a steeply sloped Maxxam site above the town of Stafford, California. The landslide destroyed a number of homes and drastically altered the natural environment.

The adjacent uncut land, owned by Maxxam, was home to the largest remaining intact forest of ancient redwood trees and to a number of endangered species. Environmental activist Julia Butterfly Hill was appalled by Maxxam's forest management practices. In response, she joined a "tree sit" on Maxxam's land organized by the direct action group Earth First!

years old, and resolved to remain there until Maxxam agreed to spare the tree. She spent 2 years in the tree without coming down once. She stayed through gale-force winds, two winters, intimidation tactics, the death of another activist, and the cutting of most of the trees in the stand that she occupied. Julia's efforts were rewarded when Maxxam agreed to protect Luna, and a 61-meter (200-foot) buffer around it, in perpetuity. In a separate, complex deal that included many stipulations about logging practices, Maxxam and another company also agreed to sell the U.S. government 3,035 hectares (7,500 acres) of ancient forest for $480 million. That property has now become the Headwaters Forest Reserve.

Hill's actions cost Maxxam millions of dollars in delays and lost revenue and brought unsustainable logging practices to the attention of many people. Because of its large debt load, Maxxam filed for bankruptcy protection in January 2007, and its depleted assets were reorganized and transferred to a new company in 2008. Although ▶

Julia Butterfly Hill sitting in Luna.

◀ Headwaters Forest Reserve.

261

Maxxam's logging practices appeared to have placed profit before sustainability, the new company has stated that it will return to more sustainable practices with the trees that remain on its holdings.

The conflict over logging practices raises many questions. Do citizens of the United States have the right to influence what activities occur on private lands? What if the land is public? Was Julia Butterfly Hill a hero or a villain? Some see

her as having made a personal sacrifice to save an ancient tree and to bring the issue of unsustainable logging practices to the public's attention. Others see her as a lawbreaker who trespassed on private property in an effort to prevent a legal activity. ■

Sources: J. B. Hill, *The Legacy of Luna: The Story of a Tree, a Woman, and the Struggle to Save the Redwoods* (HarperCollins, 2000); H. Sims, The scion, *North Coast Journal*, July 20, 2006.

UNDERSTAND THE KEY IDEAS

The issues involved in land use are not simple, and there are no easy solutions to many of the conflicts that arise. In this chapter we will begin to explore how our use of land affects the environment and what we can do to minimize its negative impacts. We will look at land use and management in both the public and private sectors, and we will explore the topic of sustainable land use practices. We will also look at how land use has changed with shifting and growing populations.

After reading this chapter you should be able to

- describe the concepts of the tragedy of the commons and maximum sustainable yield, and explain how they pertain to land use.
- describe the function, operation, and efficacy of the four major public land management agencies in the United States.
- understand the causes and consequences of urban sprawl.
- describe approaches and policies that promote sustainable land use.

Human land use affects the environment in many ways

Agriculture, housing, recreation, industry, mining, and waste disposal are all uses of land that have benefits to humans. But, as we have seen in previous chapters, some of these activities also have negative consequences. Extensive logging may lead to mudslides. Deforestation of large areas contributes to climate change and many other environmental problems. Changes to the landscape are the single largest cause of species extinctions today. Paving over land surfaces reroutes water runoff. The paved surfaces also absorb heat from the sun and reradiate it, creating urban "heat islands." Overuse of farmland can lead to soil degradation and water pollution (FIGURE 10.1).

Humans value land for what it can provide: food, shelter, and natural resources. In addition, many people recognize that land has intrinsic value apart from its instrumental, or monetary, value. Every human use of land alters it in some way. Furthermore, individual activities on any parcel of land can have wide-ranging effects on other lands. For this reason, communities around the world use laws, regulations, and other methods to influence or regulate private and public land use.

As we saw in this chapter's opening story, people do not always agree on land use and management priorities. Do we save a beautiful, ancient stand of trees, or do we

harvest the trees in order to gain benefits in the form of jobs, profit, structures made of wood, and economic development? Such conflicts can arise from both public and private land uses.

Let's begin with three concepts that are essential for understanding land use: the *tragedy of the commons, externalities,* and *maximum sustainable yield*.

The Tragedy of the Commons

In certain societies, land was viewed as a common resource: anyone could use land for foraging, growing crops, felling trees, hunting, or mining. As populations increased, such common lands tended to become degraded—overgrazed, overharvested, and deforested. In 1968, ecologist Garrett Hardin brought the issue of overuse of common resources to the attention of the broader scientific community when he described the **tragedy of the commons:** the tendency of a shared, limited resource to become depleted because people act from self-interest for short-term gain. Hardin observed that when many individuals share a common resource without agreement on or regulation of its use, it is likely to become overused very quickly.

For example, imagine a communal pasture on which many farmers graze their sheep. At first, no single farmer appears to have too many sheep. But because an individual farmer gains from raising as many sheep as possible, each farmer may be tempted to continue adding sheep to the pasture. However, if the total number of sheep

(a)

(b)

(c)

(d)

FIGURE 10.1 **Some negative consequences of land use by humans.** (a) A mudslide caused by logging and poor land management. (b) Habitat conversion and land degradation due to shifting agriculture. (c) Logging and other habitat alteration can adversely affect many species, including this spotted owl. (d) Extensive paving of land due to the growth of cities reduces the amount of land available for vegetation and water infiltration.

owned by all the farmers continues to grow, it will soon exceed the carrying capacity of the land. The sheep will overgraze the common pasture to the point at which plants will not have a chance to recover. The common land will be degraded, and the sheep will no longer have an adequate source of nourishment, as FIGURE 10.2

Use of the commons is below the carrying capacity of the land. All users benefit.

If one or more users increase the use of the commons beyond its carrying capacity, the commons becomes degraded. The cost of the degradation is incurred by all users.

Unless environmental costs are accounted for and addressed in land use practices, eventually the land will be unable to support the activity.

FIGURE 10.2 **The tragedy of the commons.** If the use of common land is not regulated in some way—by the users or by a government agency—that land can easily be degraded to the point at which it can no longer support that use.

shows. Over a longer period, the entire community will suffer. When the farmers make decisions that benefit only their own short-term gain and do not consider the common good, everybody loses.

The tragedy of the commons applies not only to agriculture, but to any publicly available resource that is not regulated, including land, air, and water. For example, the use of many global fisheries as commons has led to the overexploitation and rapid decline of many commercially harvested fish species, and has upset the balance of entire marine ecosystems.

Externalities

The tragedy of the commons is the result of an economic phenomenon called a *negative externality*. More generally, an **externality** is a cost or benefit of a good or service that is not included in the purchase price of that good or service. For example, if a bakery moves into the building next to you and you wake up every morning to the delicious smell of freshly baked bread, you are benefiting from a positive externality. On the other hand, if the bakers arrive at three in the morning and make so much noise that they interrupt your sleep, and you are not as productive at your job the next day, you are suffering from a negative externality.

In environmental science, we are especially concerned with negative externalities because they so often lead to serious environmental damage for which no one is held legally or financially responsible. For example, if one farmer grazes too many sheep in a common pasture, his action will ultimately result in more total harm than total benefit. But, as long as the land continues to support grazing, the individual farmer will not have to pay for the harm he is causing—ultimately, this cost is *externalized* to the other farmers. If the farmer responsible for the extra sheep had to bear the cost of his overuse of the land, he would not graze the extra sheep on the commons; the cost of doing so would exceed the benefit. From this example, we can see that in order to calculate the true cost of using a resource, we must always include the externalized cost. In other words, we must account for any potential harm that comes from the use of that resource.

Some economists maintain that private ownership can prevent the tragedy of the commons. After all, a landowner is much less likely to overgraze his own land than common land. Regulation is another approach. For example, a local government could prevent overuse of a common pasture by passing an ordinance that permits only a certain number of sheep to graze there.

Challenging the idea that government regulation is necessary, Professor Elinor Ostrom of Indiana University showed that many commonly held resources can be managed effectively at the community level or by user institutions. Ostrom's work, for which she was awarded the 2009 Nobel Prize in Economics, has shown that

self-regulation by resource users can prevent the tragedy of the commons.

Maximum Sustainable Yield

When we want to obtain the maximum amount of a resource, we need to know how much of a given plant or animal population can be harvested without harming the resource as a whole.

Imagine a situation in which deer hunting in a public forest is unregulated. Each hunter is free to harvest as many deer as possible. As a result of unlimited hunting, the deer population could be depleted to the point of endangerment. This, in turn, would disrupt the functioning of the forest ecosystem. On the other hand, if hunting were prohibited entirely, the deer herd might grow so large that there would not be enough food in the forests and fields to support it. In extreme cases, such as that of the reindeer of St. Paul Island (summarized graphically in Figure 6.8), the population could grow unchecked until it crashed due to starvation.

Some intermediate amount of hunting will leave enough adult deer to reproduce at a rate that will maintain the population, but not so many that there is too much competition for food. This intermediate harvest is called the *maximum sustainable yield*. Specifically, the **maximum sustainable yield (MSY)** of a renewable resource is the maximum amount that can be harvested without compromising the future availability of that resource. In other words, it is the maximum harvest that will be adequately replaced by population growth.

MSY varies case by case, but a reasonable starting point is to assume that population growth is the fastest at about one-half the carrying capacity of the environment, as shown on the S-shaped curve in FIGURE 10.3. (You may wish to review the logistic growth model

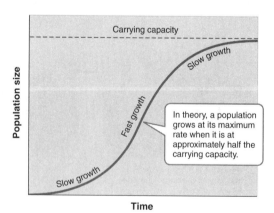

FIGURE 10.3 **Maximum sustainable yield.** Every population has a point at which a maximum number of individuals can be harvested sustainably. That point is often reached when the population size is about one-half the carrying capacity.

described in Chapter 6.) Looking at the graph, we can see that at a small population size, the growth curve is shallow and growth is relatively slow. As the population increases in size, the slope of the curve is steeper, indicating a faster growth rate. As the population size approaches the carrying capacity, the growth rate slows. The MSY is the amount of harvest that keeps the resource population at about one-half the carrying capacity of the environment.

Forest trees, like animal populations, have a maximum sustainable yield. Loggers may remove a particular fraction of the trees at a site in order to allow a certain amount of light to penetrate to the forest floor and reach younger trees. If they cut too many trees, an excess of sunlight will penetrate and dry the forest soil. This drying may create conditions inhospitable to tree germination and growth, thus inhibiting adequate regeneration of the forest.

In theory, harvesting the maximum sustainable yield will permit an indefinite use without depletion of the resource. In reality, it is very difficult to calculate MSY with certainty because in a natural ecosystem, it is difficult to obtain necessary information such as birth rates, death rates, and the carrying capacity of the system. Once an MSY calculation is made, we still cannot know if a yield is truly sustainable until months or years later, when we can evaluate the effect of the harvest on reproduction. By that time, if the harvest rate

has been too great, it is too late to prevent harm to the population.

GAUGE YOUR PROGRESS

✓ Why do humans value land?

✓ What is the tragedy of the commons? What is an externality?

✓ What is maximum sustainable yield?

Public lands are classified according to their use

All countries have public lands, which they manage for a variety of purposes, including environmental protection. The 2003 United Nations List of Protected Areas—the most recent global study of protected areas—includes almost 1.7 billion hectares (4.2 billion acres) of land in a variety of categories. Given that Earth's total land area is about 15 billion hectares (37 billion acres), this means that approximately 11 percent, or one-ninth, of Earth's land area is protected in one way or another. These areas, as well as protected marine areas, are shown on the map in FIGURE 10.4. Let's look at both international and national categories of land protection.

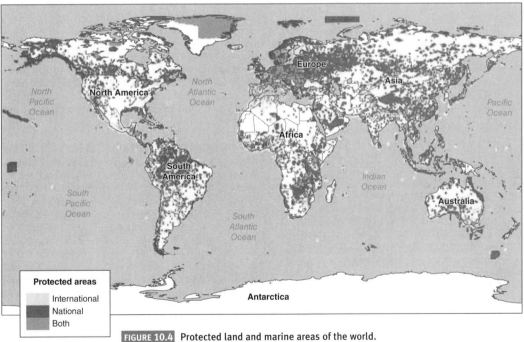

Protected areas
- International
- National
- Both

FIGURE 10.4 Protected land and marine areas of the world.
[From http://www.wdpa.org/wdpamapflex.aspx.]

International Categories of Public Lands

The 2003 United Nations List of Protected Areas classifies protected public lands into six categories according to how they are used:

- *National Parks.* There are roughly 3,400 national parks in the world, covering more than 400 million hectares (1 billion acres). This means that national parks make up about 2.7 percent of Earth's land area. National parks are managed for scientific, educational, and recreational use, and sometimes for their beauty or unique landforms. In most cases, they are not used for the extraction of resources such as timber or ore. Some of the most famous national parks in the world are found in Africa. These parks include Amboseli National Park in Kenya and Kruger National Park in South Africa. Parks like these generally exist to protect animal species such as elephants, rhinoceroses, and lions, as well as areas of great natural beauty. They also generate tourism, which can be a large source of income. On the negative side, in order to create and maintain national parks, governments have sometimes evicted and excluded indigenous human populations from the land. For example, in the winter of 2009, a new round of evictions from the Mau Forest in the Rift Valley of Kenya led to the displacement of 20,000 families. Such programs continue to generate controversy in Kenya and other countries.

- *Managed Resource Protected Areas.* This classification allows for the sustained use of biological, mineral, and recreational resources. In most countries, these areas are managed for multiple uses. There are approximately 4,100 such sites in the world, encompassing more than 440 million hectares (1.1 billion acres). In the United States, national forests are one example of this kind of area.

- *Habitat/Species Management Areas.* These areas are actively managed to maintain biological communities, for example with fire prevention or predator control. There are approximately 27,600 of these sites, covering more than 300 million hectares (740 million acres). Karelia, a part of Russia bordering Finland, has one of the highest proportions of protected areas in Europe: 5 percent of its total area. Of this total, more than one-half consists of habitat or species management areas that are actively managed for hunting and conservation.

- *Strict Nature Reserves and Wilderness Areas.* These areas are established to protect species and ecosystems. There are approximately 6,000 such sites worldwide, covering more than 200 million hectares (490 million acres). The Chang Tang Reserve, on the Tibetan Plateau in China, was set aside to protect a number of species—including the declining population of wild yak—from hunting, habitat destruction, and hybridization with domesticated animals.

- *Protected Landscapes and Seascapes.* These areas combine the nondestructive use of natural resources with opportunities for tourism and recreation. Orchards, villages, beaches, and other such areas make up the 6,500 such sites worldwide, which cover more than 100 million hectares (250 million acres). Among these protected areas is the Batanes Protected Landscape and Seascape in the northernmost islands of the Philippines, home to several endemic plant and animal species as well as important marine habitats.

- *National Monuments.* These areas are set aside to protect unique sites of special natural or cultural interest. There are almost 20,000 national monuments and landmarks in the world, covering nearly 28 million hectares (69 million acres). Most of these are established to protect historical landmarks, such as the Arc de Triomphe in Paris, France.

Public Lands in the United States

In the United States, publicly held land may be owned by federal, state, or local governments. Of the nation's land area, 42 percent is publicly held—a larger percentage than in any other nation. The federal government is by far the largest single landowner in the United States: it owns 240 million hectares (600 million acres), or roughly 25 percent of the country (FIGURE 10.5). Most of this land—55 percent—is in the 11 western continental states, and an additional 37 percent is in Alaska. Less than 10 percent of federal land is located in the Midwest and on the East Coast.

PUBLIC LAND CLASSIFICATIONS Public lands in the United States include rangelands, national forests, national parks, national wildlife refuges, and wilderness areas. Since the founding of the nation, many different individuals and groups have expressed interest in using these public lands. However, most environmental policies, laws, and management plans have been based, at least partially, on the *resource conservation ethic,* which calls for policy makers to consider the instrumental value of nature (recall our discussion of ecosystem services and instrumental value in Chapter 3). The **resource conservation ethic** states that people should maximize resource use based on the greatest good for everyone. In conservation and land use terms, it has meant that areas are preserved and managed for economic, scientific, recreational, and aesthetic purposes.

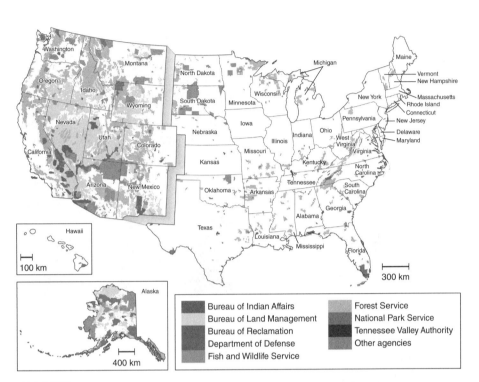

FIGURE 10.5 **Federal lands in the United States.** Approximately 42 percent of the land in the United States is publicly owned, and 25 percent of the nation's land is owned by the federal government. [After http://nationalatlas.gov.]

Of course, many of these purposes conflict. In order to manage competing interests, the U.S. government has, for decades, adopted the principle of *multiple use* in managing its public resources. Some public lands are in fact classified as **multiple-use lands,** and may be used for recreation, grazing, timber harvesting, and mineral extraction. Others are designated as protected lands in order to maintain a watershed, preserve wildlife and fish populations, or maintain sites of scenic, scientific, and historical value.

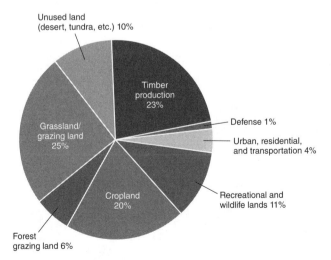

LAND USE AND FEDERAL AGENCIES As shown in **FIGURE 10.6**, land in the United States, both public and private, is used for many purposes. These uses can be divided into a number of categories. The probable use of public land determines how it is classified and which federal agency will manage it. More than 95 percent of all federal lands are managed by four federal agencies (see Figure 10.5): the Bureau of Land Management (BLM), the United States Forest Service (USFS), the National Park Service

FIGURE 10.6 **Land use in the United States.** Public and private land in the United States is used for many purposes. [After R. N. Lubowski et al., Major land uses in the United States, Economic Research Service, USDA, 2002.]

(NPS), and the Fish and Wildlife Service (FWS). BLM, USFS, and NPS lands are typically classified as multiple-use lands because most, and sometimes all, public uses are allowed on them.

Although individual tracts may differ, the following are typical divisions of public land uses:

- BLM lands: grazing, mining, timber harvesting, and recreation

- USFS lands: timber harvesting, grazing, and recreation

- NPS lands: recreation and conservation

- FWS lands: wildlife conservation, hunting, and recreation

GAUGE YOUR PROGRESS

✓ What are the main uses of public lands in the United States?

✓ How do human land use decisions influence categories of public land classification?

Land management practices vary according to land use

Now that we have a basic picture of how public land is classified and of the relationship between public land use and management agencies in the United States, let's turn to some of the specific issues involved in managing different types of public lands. Note that many of the management issues we discuss here apply to private lands as well.

Rangelands

Rangelands are dry, open grasslands. They are used primarily for cattle grazing, which is the most common use of land in the United States. Rangelands are semiarid ecosystems and are therefore particularly susceptible to fires and other environmental disturbances. If humans overuse rangelands, they can easily lose biodiversity.

Like most human activities, livestock grazing has mixed environmental effects. One environmental benefit of grazing is that ungulates—hoofed animals such as cattle and sheep—can be raised on lands that are too dry to farm. In addition, grazing these animals uses less fossil fuel energy than raising them in feedlots. However, improperly managed livestock can damage stream banks and pollute surface waters. Grazing too many animals can quickly denude a region of vegetation (FIGURE 10.7). Loss of vegetation leaves the land exposed to wind erosion and makes it difficult for soils to absorb and retain water when it rains.

FIGURE 10.7 **Overgrazed rangeland.** Overgrazing can rapidly strip an area of vegetation.

Many environmental scientists argue that rangeland ecosystems are too fragile for multiple uses. Certain environmental organizations have suggested that as much as 55 percent of U.S. rangeland soils are in poor or very poor condition, due in large part to overgrazing. However, the BLM, which manages most public rangelands in the United States, has maintained that the percentage is not nearly that high. Reconciling this difference is a challenge because of the many factors that influence how soil condition is determined.

The Taylor Grazing Act of 1934 was passed to halt overgrazing. It converted federal rangelands from a commons to a permit-based grazing system. The goal of a permit-based system is to limit the number of animals grazing in a particular area and thereby avoid a tragedy of the commons situation. However, critics maintain that the low cost of the permits continues to encourage overgrazing. In 2006, the federal government spent seven times more money managing its rangelands than it received in permit fees. Thus, in effect, grazing is subsidized with federal funds.

The BLM focuses on mitigating the damage caused by grazing. The agency considers "rangeland health" when it sets guidelines for grazing. For example, state and regional rangeland managers are required to ensure healthy watersheds, maintain ecological processes such as nutrient cycles and energy flow, preserve water quality, maintain or restore habitats, and protect endangered species. However, these managers are not given detailed guidance, and the BLM regulations do not require the involvement of environmental scientists. This omission gives the managers wide latitude to set their own guidelines and standards. As a result, BLM regulations are not consistently successful in preserving vulnerable rangeland ecosystems.

Forests

Forests are dominated by trees and other woody vegetation. Approximately 73 percent of the forests used for commercial timber operations in the United States are privately owned. Commercial logging companies are allowed to use U.S. national forests, usually in exchange for a *royalty*—a percentage of their revenues. Many national forests were originally established to ensure a steady and reliable source of timber. As with grazing, the federal government typically spends more money managing the timber program and building and maintaining logging roads than it receives from these royalties.

TIMBER HARVEST PRACTICES The two most common ways in which trees are harvested for timber production, both of which are illustrated in FIGURE 10.8, are *clear-cutting* and *selective cutting*. **Clear-cutting** involves removing all, or almost all, the trees within an area (Figure 10.8a). It is the easiest harvesting method and, in most cases, the most economical. When a *stand*, or cluster, of trees has been clear-cut, foresters often replant or reseed the area. Often the entire area will be replanted at the same time, so all the resulting trees will be the same age. Because they are exposed to full sunlight, clear-cut tracts of land are ideal for fast-growing tree species that achieve their maximum growth rates with large amounts of direct sunlight. Other species may not be so successful, which can lead to a reduction in overall biodiversity. However, if a commercially valuable tree species constitutes only a small fraction of a stand of trees, it may not be economically efficient to clear-cut the entire stand. This is particularly true in many tropical forests, where valuable species constitute only a small percentage of the trees and are mixed in with many other species.

Clear-cutting, especially on slopes, increases wind and water erosion, which causes the loss of soil and nutrients (FIGURE 10.9). Erosion also adds silt and sediment to nearby streams, harming aquatic populations. In addition, the denuded slopes are prone to dangerous mudslides like the Stafford, California, mudslide described in this chapter's opening story. Clear-cutting also increases the amount of sunlight that reaches rivers and streams. The increased sunlight raises water temperatures, which can adversely affect certain aquatic species. Even the replanting process can have negative environmental consequences. Timber companies often use fire or herbicides to remove bushy vegetation before a clear-cut is replanted. These practices reduce soil quality, and herbicides may contaminate water that runs off into streams and rivers. Many environmental scientists

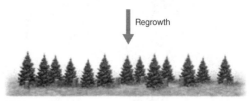

(a) Clear-cutting

(b) Selective cutting

FIGURE 10.8 **Timber harvest practices.** (a) Clear-cutting removes most, if not all, trees from an area and is often coupled with replanting. The resulting trees are all the same age. (b) In selective cutting, single trees or small numbers of trees are harvested. The resulting forest consists of trees of varying ages.

identify clear-cutting as a cause of habitat alteration and destruction and forest fragmentation. These effects, in turn, lead to decreased biodiversity and sometimes to a lower aesthetic value for the affected forest.

Selective cutting (Figure 10.8b) removes single trees or relatively small numbers of trees from among many in a forest. This method creates many small

FIGURE 10.9 **Clear-cut forest near Eureka, California.** A clear-cut on a steep slope increases the likelihood of erosion and delayed regeneration of vegetation.

openings in a stand where trees can reseed or young trees can be planted, so the regenerated stand contains trees of different ages. Because seedlings and young trees must grow next to larger, older trees, selective cutting produces optimum growth only among shade-tolerant tree species.

The environmental impact of selective cutting is less extensive than that of clear-cutting. However, many of the negative environmental impacts associated with logging remain the same. For example, whether a company uses clear-cutting or selective cutting, it will need to construct logging roads to carry equipment and workers into the area to be harvested. These roads fragment the forest habitat, leading to species diversity changes, and compact the soil, leading to nutrient loss and reductions in water infiltration.

A third approach to logging removes trees from the forest in ways that do not unduly affect the viability of other, noncommercial tree species. Known as **ecologically sustainable forestry,** this approach has a goal of

maintaining all species—both plants and animals—in as close to a natural state as possible (FIGURE 10.10). Some loggers have even returned to using animals such as horses to pull logs in order to reduce soil compaction, although the costs of such methods make it difficult to compete economically with mechanized logging practices.

LOGGING, DEFORESTATION, AND REFORESTATION

Approximately 30 percent of all commercial timber in the world is produced in the United States and Canada. Compared with South America and Africa, forest losses in these two major timber-producing countries have been relatively small over the last several decades. Still, timber production presents important ecological challenges in these countries.

Throughout this chapter we have seen examples of the conflicts over land use created by competing interests and values. Perhaps nowhere is this conflict so clear as in the case of logging. For example, timber

FIGURE 10.10 **Sustainable forestry.** Logging without the use of fossil fuels, as is done in this forest in Oregon, further enhances the sustainability of a forestry project.

production has always been a part of the mission of the USFS. Yet maintaining biodiversity is an equally important goal. It would seem that we can't have both.

All logging disrupts habitat and usually has an effect, either negative or positive, on plant and animal species. One such species is the marbled murrelet (*Brachyramphus marmoratus*). This bird spends most of its life along the coastal waters of the Pacific Northwest, but it nests in coastal redwood forests. With the intensive logging of these forests, the marbled murrelet has become endangered. The tree sit described in this chapter's opening story brought this species, among others, to the public's attention.

Logging often replaces complex forest ecosystems with **tree plantations:** large areas typically planted with a single rapidly growing tree species. These same-aged stands can be easily clear-cut for commercial purposes, such as pulp and wood, and then replanted. Because of this cycle of planting and harvesting, tree plantations never develop into mature, ecologically diverse forests. If too many planting and harvesting cycles occur, the soil may become depleted of important nutrients such as calcium.

Since 1982, federal regulations have required the USFS to provide appropriate habitat for plant and animal communities while also meeting multiple-use goals. However, these regulations fail to specify how biodiversity protection should be achieved or how the results should be quantified, leaving the USFS to choose its own approach to biodiversity management. Critics charge that the USFS is not adequately protecting biodiversity and forest ecosystems. The USFS maintains that it is doing the best it can at meeting many different objectives.

FIRE MANAGEMENT In many ecosystems, fire is a natural process that is important for nutrient cycling and regeneration. As discussed briefly in Chapter 3, when fires periodically move through an ecosystem, they liberate nutrients tied up in dead biomass. In addition, areas where vegetation is killed by the fire provide openings for early-successional species.

Humans have followed a variety of management policies with respect to fire. For many years, managers of forest ecosystems, including the USFS, did everything they could to suppress fires. This strategy led to the accumulation of large quantities of dead biomass on the forest floor. Eventually, this fuel built up until a large fire became inevitable. One method for reducing the accumulation of dead biomass is a **prescribed burn,** in which a fire is deliberately set under controlled conditions. Prescribed burns help reduce the risk of uncontrolled natural fires and provide some of the other benefits of fire as well. More recently, forest managers have allowed certain natural fires to burn. This policy appears to have been accepted in many parts of the United States, as long as human life and property are not threatened.

Probably the best-known forest fires in the United States are those that occurred in Yellowstone National Park in the summer of 1988, the driest year on record at the park. A combination of human activity and lightning set off multiple fires (FIGURE 10.11). Over 25,000 people participated in fighting the fires. While this effort saved human lives and property, the firefighters had little impact on the fires. When the fires were over, more than one-third of Yellowstone National Park had burned. Initially, many people were outraged that the NPS and others had "allowed" the park to burn. However, within

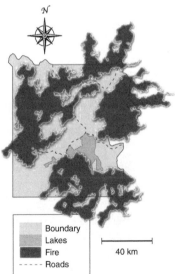

FIGURE 10.11 **Yellowstone fires of 1988.** As can be seen from the map, extensive areas of the park were burned in this exceptionally hot and dry year.

Boundary
Lakes
Fire
Roads

40 km

a few years, it became clear that the fires had created new, nutrient-rich habitat for early-successional plant species, which attracted elk and other herbivores. Ultimately, researchers and forest managers concluded that the Yellowstone fires of 1988 provided many benefits to the Yellowstone ecosystem. Today, a typical visitor viewing a portion of the park that burned in 1988 probably wouldn't even know that there had been a major fire so recently.

National Parks

As we have already noted, many national parks were established to preserve scenic views and unusual landforms. Today, national parks are managed for scientific, educational, aesthetic, and recreational use. Since Yellowstone National Park was founded in 1872, 58 national parks have been established in the United States. The NPS manages a total of 391 national parks and other areas, such as historical parks and national monuments, and the list continues to grow.

THE GOALS OF NATIONAL PARK MANAGEMENT Management of national parks, like that of national forests, is based on the multiple-use principle. Unlike the national forests, the U.S. national parks were set aside specifically to protect ecosystems. In establishing Yellowstone National Park, Congress mandated the Interior Department to regulate the park in a manner consistent with the preservation of timber resources, mineral resources, and "natural curiosities." However, it did not require a management process based on ecological principles.

It was not until the 1960s that ecology became a focus of national park management. In 1963, an advisory board on wildlife management presented the Leopold Report to Secretary of the Interior Stewart Udall. This report established the guiding principles of national park management today. It proposed that the primary purpose of NPS should be to maintain the parks in the same biotic condition in which they were first found by European settlers. To this end, the authors believed that NPS should focus its efforts on conservation and on protection of wildlife species and their habitats. The report claimed that human activity had severely affected normal ecological processes in the parks and that active intervention was required to achieve the goal of a return to a more "natural" state.

Today, NPS applies environmental science to maintain biodiversity and ecosystem function in all national parks. As we saw in the example of the Yellowstone fires, its policies continue to be controversial. Each national park adapts U.S. policy to its specific needs. In parks with high levels of endemic biodiversity, for example, management focuses on conserving endemic species. For instance, the Channel Islands National Park off the coast of southern California is an important breeding ground for many seabirds, including a pelican species that is rare elsewhere in the western United States.

FIGURE 10.12 **ATV-caused damage near Olympic National Park in Washington State.** Although today many national parks limit ATV use, the conflict between those who want to use the parks for this form of recreation and those who wish to protect biodiversity remains.

Because of this special feature, the park is managed primarily to conserve its biodiversity. Other national parks balance biodiversity protection with recreational use.

NATIONAL PARKS AND HUMAN ACTIVITIES Reducing the impact of human activities both outside and inside the park borders is the primary challenge of most national parks throughout the world. Air and water pollution from distant sources can reduce biodiversity as well as recreational value and economic opportunities. Ongoing development adjacent to park boundaries can be particularly problematic. In many locations, national parks have become islands of biodiversity amid increasing human development, but even their protected status cannot defend them completely from invasive species and other problems, such as pollution. These external threats require large-scale evaluation, planning, and management that extend beyond park borders.

National parks are also victims of their popularity. Although the park system was established in part to make areas of great beauty accessible to people, human overuse can harm the very environment that people visit to enjoy. For example, all-terrain vehicles (ATVs) are a major cause of air and noise pollution in national parks, as well as a direct cause of habitat destruction (FIGURE 10.12). Today, many parks strictly limit or even ban the use of ATVs. Still, park managers grapple with how to determine appropriate limits on human activity. In many cases, the trade-off between short-term recreational uses and long-term protection of biodiversity does not permit an easy answer.

Wildlife Refuges and Wilderness Areas

National wildlife refuges are the only federal public lands managed for the primary purpose of protecting wildlife. The Fish and Wildlife Service manages more than 450 national wildlife refuges and 28 waterfowl production areas on 34.4 million hectares (85 million acres) of publicly owned land.

National wilderness areas are set aside with the intent of preserving large tracts of intact ecosystems or landscapes. Sometimes only a portion of an ecosystem is included. Wilderness areas are created from other public lands, usually national forests or rangelands, and are managed by the same federal agency that managed them prior to their designation as wilderness.

National wilderness areas allow only limited human use and are designated as roadless. Although logging, road building, and mining are banned in national wilderness areas, roads that existed before the designation sometimes remain in use, and activities, such as mining, that were previously permitted on the land are allowed to continue. More than 38.5 million hectares (95 million acres) of federal land, 60 percent of which is in Alaska, are classified as wilderness.

Federal Regulation of Land Use

Government regulation can influence the use of private as well as public lands. The 1969 **National Environmental Policy Act (NEPA)** mandates an environmental assessment of all projects involving federal money or federal permits. Along with other major laws of the 1960s and 1970s, such as the Clean Air Act, the Clean Water Act, and the *Endangered Species Act,* NEPA creates an environmental regulatory process designed to ensure protection of the nation's resources.

Before a project can begin, NEPA rules require the project's developers to file an **environmental impact statement (EIS).** An EIS typically outlines the scope and purpose of the project, describes the environmental context, suggests alternative approaches to the project, and analyzes the environmental impact of each alternative. NEPA does not require that developers proceed in the way that will have the least environmental impact. However, in some situations, NEPA rules may stipulate that building permits or government funds be withheld until the developer submits an **environmental mitigation plan** stating how it will address the project's environmental impact. In addition, preparation of the EIS sometimes uncovers the presence of endangered species in the area under consideration. When this occurs, the protection measures of the **Endangered Species Act,** a 1973 law designed to protect species from extinction, are applied.

Members of the public are entitled to give input into the environmental assessment, and decision makers are required to respond. And, although developers are not obligated to act in accordance with public wishes, in practice, public concern often improves the project's outcome. For this reason, attending information sessions and providing input is a good way for concerned citizens to learn more about local land use decisions and to help reduce the environmental impact of land development.

GAUGE YOUR PROGRESS

✓ What are the ways in which timber is harvested in U.S. forests, and how do they compare in terms of their environmental impact?

✓ What is the significance of the National Wilderness Area designation for parts of federally owned lands?

✓ What is NEPA, and what is an environmental impact statement (EIS)?

Residential land use is expanding

While many public lands are located in relatively rural areas, there is a very different kind of land use pressure in locations close to cities. In the last 50 years, the greatest percentage of population growth in the United States has occurred in two classes of communities: *suburban* and *exurban.* **Suburban** areas surround metropolitan centers and have low population densities compared with those urban areas. **Exurban** areas are similar to suburban areas, but are unconnected to any central city or densely populated area. Since 1950, more than 90 percent of the population growth in metropolitan areas has occurred in suburbs, and two out of three people now live in suburban or exurban communities.

FIGURE 10.13 shows U.S. population trends since 1950. The population of cities has grown somewhat in absolute terms, but has declined as a percentage of the U.S. population. The rural population has been declining since 1900, and a century later it made up less than

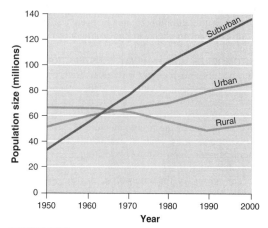

FIGURE 10.13 Distribution of suburban, urban, and rural populations in the United States between 1950 and 2000. The shift in population from rural to suburban areas can be clearly seen in this graph. [After http://www.sdi.gov/curtis/Pop_Trends.html (Figure 1.4).]

a fifth of the total U.S. population. These population shifts have brought with them a new set of environmental problems, including *urban sprawl* and *urban blight*. Attempts to find creative solutions to these problems have been increasingly successful.

Urban Sprawl

If you have ever been to a strip mall, you are familiar with the phenomenon known as urban sprawl, which occurs when populations shift away from rural and urban areas and into suburban and exurban areas. **Urban sprawl** is the creation of urbanized areas that spread into rural areas and remove clear boundaries between the two. The landscape in these areas is characterized by clusters of housing, retail shops, and office parks, which are separated by miles of road. Large feeder roads and parking lots that separate "big box" retail stores from the road discourage pedestrian traffic.

Urban sprawl has had a dramatic environmental impact. Dependence on the automobile has led to suburban residents driving more than twice as much as people who live in cities. Between 1950 and 2000, the number of vehicle miles traveled per person in U.S. suburban areas tripled. Because suburban house lots tend to be significantly larger than urban parcels, suburban communities also use more than twice as much land per person as urban communities. Urban sprawl tends to occur at the edge of a city, often replacing farmland and increasing the distance between farms and consumers. In its most recent survey, the U.S. Department of Agriculture estimated that between 1992 and 1997, U.S. farmland was being converted to residential uses at a rate of 500,000 hectares (1.2 million acres) per year.

Causes and Effects of Sprawl

There are four main causes of urban sprawl in the United States: automobiles and highway construction, living costs, urban blight, and government policies.

AUTOMOBILES AND HIGHWAY CONSTRUCTION Before automobiles and highway systems existed, transportation into and out of cities was difficult: horses were slow, roads were bad, and trolley services rarely went far beyond the city limits. In those days, if you wanted to take advantage of the many amenities of city life, such as job opportunities, cultural institutions, shopping, and social activities, you had to live within a few miles of the city center.

The advent of the automobile, and the subsequent development of the interstate highway system in the 1950s and 1960s, changed everything. Today we think nothing of working in the city during the day and commuting home to the suburbs at night. And if you live in the suburbs but want to get into the city on a Saturday night for dinner, a concert, or a movie, that's no problem either. With rapid, comfortable transportation between urban and suburban areas, it became possible to work or play in the city and return to a large home in a quiet neighborhood. For the first time in history, people could enjoy the best of both worlds.

LIVING COSTS Many people find suburban living more desirable than city living because they can obtain more land and a larger house for the same amount of money. Because land is readily available in the suburbs, it is relatively inexpensive compared with land in the city. For the cost of a tiny one-bedroom condominium in a desirable section of a city, you may be able to purchase a five-bedroom house with a big yard in the suburbs. In addition, because suburban governments usually provide fewer public services than cities do, tax rates in the suburbs are likely to be lower. For these reasons, moving to the suburbs allows some people to enjoy a higher standard of living than they could afford with the same income in the city.

On the other hand, those with lower incomes may not be able to afford these benefits. Although single-family homes in the suburbs are likely to be less expensive than desirable housing in the city, they are still out of reach for many people. Most suburban communities have little, if any, low-income or "affordable" housing. Because single-family homes are usually the only housing option available in the suburbs, those with lower incomes are excluded. Furthermore, in many suburban locations, it is difficult to commute to the city without a car, which compounds the difficulties for lower-income individuals. Even when public transportation is available, commuting costs can be high.

URBAN BLIGHT As population shifts to the suburbs, the city's revenue from sources such as property, sales, and service taxes begins to shrink. At the same time, the cost of maintaining urban services, including public transportation, police and fire protection, and social services, remains stable. Faced with declining tax receipts, cities are forced to reduce services, raise tax rates, or both. As services decline, crime rates may increase, either because police resources are stretched thin or because conditions for lower-income residents decline even further. Infrastructure also deteriorates, leading to a decline in the quality of the built environment. These problems, combined with higher taxes, make cities less attractive places to live, and those who can afford to move away are more likely to do so.

In addition, as the population shifts to the suburbs, jobs and services follow. Suburbanization has spawned suburban office parks, which have led to an increase in suburb-to-suburb commuting. Commuting patterns develop around cities rather than into and out of them. These new traffic patterns make it more difficult to provide public transportation to the spreading region. As wealthy and middle-income people leave cities, urban retail stores lose customers. As stores close, people have

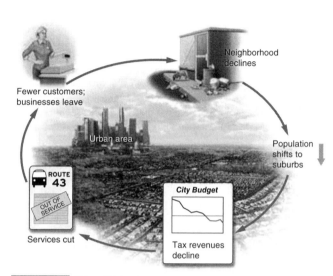

FIGURE 10.14 **Urban blight.** As people move away from a city to suburbs and exurbs, the city often deteriorates, causing yet more people to leave. This cycle is an example of a positive feedback system. The green arrow indicates the starting point of the cycle.

fewer reasons to go to the city to shop, further decreasing the customer base for the remaining stores. This cascade of effects leads to the positive feedback loop shown in FIGURE 10.14. This loop creates **urban blight:** the degradation of the built and social environments of the city that often accompanies and accelerates migration to the suburbs.

Historically, urban blight has contributed to racial segregation. In the 1950s and 1960s, when migration to the suburbs began in earnest, those leaving the cities for the suburbs were predominantly middle- or upper-income Caucasians. This so-called "white flight" resulted in highly concentrated minority populations in city centers and almost entirely white populations in the suburbs. Over time, the disparity of opportunity increased because higher property tax revenues in suburban communities often allowed for better schools. Very recently, some of this segregation has begun to decline as Caucasians return to the cities and more minorities, after having accumulated wealth, move out to the suburbs. Nevertheless, large racial disparities remain.

GOVERNMENT POLICIES Urban sprawl has also been influenced by federal and local laws and policies, including the Highway Trust Fund, zoning laws, and subsidized mortgages.

The **Highway Trust Fund,** begun by the Highway Revenue Act of 1956 and funded by a federal gasoline tax, pays for the construction and maintenance of roads and highways. We have already seen that highways allow people to live farther from where they work. FIGURE 10.15 shows the resulting positive feedback loop. More highways mean more driving and more gasoline purchases, which lead to more gasoline tax receipts, and so on. As people move farther away from their jobs, traffic congestion increases, and roads are expanded. But the new, even larger roads encourage even more people to live farther away from work. This cycle exemplifies a phenomenon known as **induced demand,** in which an increase in the supply of a good causes demand to grow.

Governments may use *zoning* to address issues of traffic congestion, urban sprawl, and urban blight. **Zoning** is a planning tool developed in the 1920s to separate industry and business from residential neighborhoods and create quieter, safer communities. Governments that use zoning can classify land areas into "zones" in which certain land uses are restricted. For instance, zoning ordinances might prohibit developers from building a factory or a strip mall in a residential area or a multi-dwelling apartment building in a single-home neighborhood. Nearly all metropolitan governments across the United States have adopted zoning.

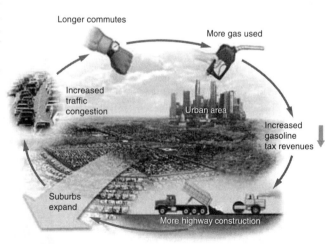

FIGURE 10.15 **Induced demand as a cause of traffic congestion and urban sprawl.** The use of gasoline tax money to build highways leads to development of suburbs and traffic congestion, at which point yet more money is spent on highways to alleviate the congestion. The green arrow indicates the starting point of the cycle.

Zoning often regulates much more than land use. The number of parking spaces a building must have, how far from the street a building must be placed, or even the size and location of a home's driveway are among the development features that zoning may stipulate. Zoning laws have been helpful in addressing issues of safety and sometimes in minimizing environmental damage caused by new construction. One negative aspect of zoning, however, is that it generally prohibits suburban neighborhoods from developing a traditional "Main Street" with shops, apartments, houses, and businesses clustered together. Many communities are now attempting to incorporate *multi-use zoning* into their municipal plans. **Multi-use zoning** allows retail and high-density residential development to coexist in the same area. However, most zoning in the United States continues to promote automobile-dependent development.

The federal government has also played a large part in encouraging the growth of suburbs through the Federal Housing Administration (FHA). Congress established the FHA during the Great Depression of the 1930s, in part to jump-start the economy by creating more demand for new housing. Through the FHA, people could apply for federally subsidized mortgages that offered low interest rates. This program allowed many people who otherwise could not afford a house to purchase one. However, the FHA financed mortgages only for homes in financially "low risk" areas. Inevitably, these areas were almost always the newly built, low-density suburbs. When, at the end of World War II, the GI Bill extended generous credit terms to war veterans, the suburban housing boom continued. The greater availability of cars as well as mass-produced housing, which allowed developers to sell newly convenient suburban homes at a steep discount, made the suburbs even more attractive.

Smart Growth

People are beginning to recognize and address the problems of urban sprawl. One way they are doing so is through the principles of *smart growth*. **Smart growth** focuses on strategies that encourage the development of sustainable, healthy communities. The Environmental Protection Agency lists 10 basic principles of smart growth:

1. *Mixed land uses.* Smart growth mixes residential, retail, education, recreation, and business land uses. Mixed-use development allows people to walk or bicycle to various destinations and encourages pedestrians to be in a neighborhood at all times of the day, increasing safety and interpersonal interactions.

2. *Create a range of housing opportunities and choices.* By providing housing for people of all income levels, smart growth counters the concentration of poverty in failing urban neighborhoods. Mixed housing also allows more people to find jobs near where they live, improves schools, and generates strong support for neighborhood transit stops, commercial centers, and other services.

3. *Create walkable neighborhoods.* Walkable neighborhoods are created by mixing land uses, reducing the speed of traffic, encouraging businesses to build stores directly up to the sidewalk, and placing parking lots behind buildings. In neighborhoods that encourage walking, people use their cars less, which both reduces fossil fuel use and traffic congestion and provides health benefits. Communities with more pedestrians tend to see more interaction among neighbors because people stop to talk with each other. This, in turn, creates opportunities for civic engagement. When people interact, the environment usually benefits.

4. *Encourage community and stakeholder collaboration in development decisions.* There is no single "right" way to build a neighborhood; residents and **stakeholders**—people with an interest in a particular place or issue—need to work together to determine how their neighborhoods will appear and be structured.

5. *Take advantage of compact building design.* Smart growth incorporates multistory buildings and parking garages—as opposed to sprawling lots—to reduce a neighborhood's environmental footprint and protect more open space. Ideally, shops, cafés, and small businesses should be easily accessible to pedestrian traffic on the ground floor near

FIGURE 10.16 **The French Quarter of New Orleans.** One principle of smart growth is to foster communities with a strong sense of place. The French Quarter of New Orleans, Louisiana, is known for its architecture, food, and, especially, music.

sidewalks, with two or three stories of apartments and offices above.

6. *Foster distinctive, attractive communities with a strong sense of place.* A **sense of place** is the feeling that an area has a distinct and meaningful character. Many cities have such unique neighborhoods. For example, the French Quarter of New Orleans (FIGURE 10.16) has a sense of place that adds to the quality of life for people living there. Smart growth attempts to foster this sense of place through development that fits into the neighborhood.

7. *Preserve open space, farmland, natural beauty, and critical environmental areas.* Working farmland is a source of fresh local produce and other goods. Open space provides opportunities for recreation and enjoyment. Land protected from development through restricted growth also provides habitats for a variety of species.

8. *Provide a variety of transportation choices.* **Transit-oriented development (TOD)** attempts to focus dense residential and retail development around stops for public transportation, giving people convenient alternatives to driving. Bicycle racks and safe roads, pleasant sidewalks for walking, frequent bus service, and light rail can all aid in this goal (FIGURE 10.17). Car-sharing networks such as Zipcar can provide easy access to a fleet of rental automobiles. This increasingly popular service reduces the need for private car ownership where public transportation is not available.

9. *Strengthen and direct development toward existing communities.* Development that fills in vacant lots within existing communities, rather than expanding into new land outside the city, is known as **infill.** This type of development can help to reinvigorate urban neighborhoods that are caught in a vicious cycle of depopulation and blight and can protect rural lands from sprawl. Some cities, such as Portland, Oregon, have had success with **urban growth boundaries,** which place restrictions on development outside a designated area.

10. *Make development decisions predictable, fair, and cost-effective.* One reason why suburban developments in all regions of the country often look the same is that standardized designs allow developers to move rapidly through the permitting process. A streamlined approval process that encourages smart growth could increase the number of individualized plans rather than promoting cookie-cutter development.

Of course, no individual new development or neighborhood plan is likely to incorporate all of these ideals, but as a guide to thinking about how to build

FIGURE 10.17 **Light rail system.** Light rail is one option in transit-oriented development (TOD), which strives to develop communities with a denser mix of retail and residential components around a convenient public transportation system.

communities, the smart growth concept has been quite successful.

Smart growth can have important environmental benefits. Compact development reduces the amount of impervious surface, reducing runoff and flooding downstream. A 2000 study found that smart growth in New Jersey would reduce water pollution by 40 percent compared with the more common, dispersed growth pattern. By mixing uses and providing transportation options, smart growth also reduces fossil fuel consumption. A 1999 EPA study found that infill development can reduce miles driven by as much as 58 percent. A 2005 study in Seattle found that residents of neighborhoods incorporating just a few of the techniques to make nonauto travel more convenient traveled 26 percent fewer vehicle miles than residents of more dispersed, less-connected neighborhoods.

GAUGE YOUR PROGRESS

✓ What are urban sprawl and smart growth?

✓ How can zoning help reduce urban sprawl?

WORKING TOWARD SUSTAINABILITY

The Dudley Street area of Roxbury and North Dorchester, in Boston, was once a prime example of urban blight. In the 1980s, years of urban decay and the loss of large numbers of primarily Caucasian families to the suburbs had left 21 percent of the Dudley Street neighborhood vacant—amounting to 1,300 abandoned parcels. Almost 30 percent of the neighborhood's residents had an income below the federal poverty level, making the neighborhood one of the poorest in Boston. Fires were a particular problem; in some cases, arsonists attempted to gain insurance money on homes that could not be sold. The residents felt that they were being ignored by City Hall. Some suggested that this was because 96 percent of the neighborhood's residents were members of ethnic minority groups.

In 1984, residents banded together to turn their neighborhood around. They formed the Dudley Street Neighborhood Initiative (DSNI), designed to allow the residents to move toward a common vision for a sustainable neighborhood. Participants chose a large Board of Directors—34 members—so that they would hear a diversity of perspectives and, in coming to consensus, ensure that decisions had broad support. The DSNI also obtained something no other neighborhood organization has: the power of *eminent domain*. **Eminent domain** allows a government to acquire property at fair market value even if the owner does not wish to sell it. It is frequently used to acquire land for highway projects, but also has been used recently, and controversially, in urban redevelopment.

By 1987, DSNI had worked with community members to develop a comprehensive revitalization plan,

The Dudley Street Neighborhood

which has been periodically updated since then. The main goals of the DSNI plan are

- to rehabilitate existing housing
- to construct homes that are affordable according to criteria set by residents
- to assemble parcels of vacant land for redevelopment, using the power of eminent domain if necessary
- to plan environmentally sound, affordable development that is physically attractive
- to convert some vacant properties into safe play areas, gardens, and facilities that the entire community can enjoy
- to run a full summer camp program for area children
- to develop strong public and private partnerships to ensure the economic vitality of the neighborhood
- to increase both the economic and political power of residents

DSNI has had many successes. Its first major action was to force the city to remove trash, appliances, and abandoned cars that littered the streets and vacant lots. The city also cleaned up two illegal dumps in the area. Residents planted community gardens to grow produce and flowers. DSNI successfully reduced drug dealing in the neighborhood park, although that remains a constant struggle. And, perhaps most significantly, its work led to the construction of 300 new homes on formerly vacant lots. New residents help to add vitality to the neighborhood, reversing the cycle of depopulation and business closure.

It is evident that the individuals involved in DSNI have taken many of the principles of smart growth to heart. The community mixes residential with retail development, and residents live within walking distance of a grocery store, ethnic markets, and other amenities (FIGURE 10.18). Moreover, since the founding of DSNI, two small manufacturing businesses—a furniture maker and an electronics company—have moved into the neighborhood, providing additional jobs within walking distance for residents.

The Dudley Street neighborhood still has a relatively low per capita income, and its development choices have not been without controversy. However, it serves as an example of one of hundreds of neighborhoods that have begun to turn the positive feedback loop of urban decay into one of urban renewal and hope.

FIGURE 10.18 **The Dudley Street neighborhood.** This neighborhood in Boston, Massachusetts, was once a symbol of urban decay. Today it is a thriving urban community that has adopted many of the principles of smart growth.

References

Benfield, F. K., J. Terris, and N. Vorsanger. 2001. *Solving Sprawl: Models of Smart Growth in Communities Across America*. Island Press.

Dudley Street Neighborhood Initiative. http://www.dsni.org.

REVISIT THE KEY IDEAS

■ **Describe the concepts of the tragedy of the commons and maximum sustainable yield and explain how they pertain to land use issues.**

Individuals have no incentive to conserve common resources when they do not bear the cost of using those resources. A cost or benefit not included in the price of a good is an externality. The lack of incentive to conserve common resources leads to overuse of these resources, which may be degraded if their use is not regulated. The maximum sustainable yield is the largest amount of a renewable resource that can be harvested indefinitely. Harvesting at the MSY keeps the resource population at about one-half the carrying capacity of the environment. However, uncertainty about population dynamics can lead to a miscalculation of the MSY and overharvesting.

■ **Describe the function, operation, and efficacy of the four major public land management agencies in the United States.**

In the United States, public land is managed for multiple uses, including grazing, timber harvesting, recreation, and wildlife conservation. The Bureau of Land Management manages rangeland, which is used for grazing. Grazing is subsidized with federal funds, and some lands are overgrazed. The United States Forest Service manages national forests, which are used for timber harvesting, recreation, and other uses. Timber can be harvested by clear-cutting or selective cutting, both of which have environmental impacts, or by ecologically sustainable forestry methods. National parks, managed by the National Park Service, were created primarily for preservation of their scenery and unique landforms, although scientific, educational, and recreational uses have become more important over time. The Fish and Wildlife Service manages national wildlife refuges, which are designed to protect wildlife.

■ **Understand the causes and consequences of urban sprawl.**

Causes of urban sprawl include the development of the automobile, construction of highways, less expensive land at the urban fringe, and urban blight. Government institutions and policies, such as the federal Highway Trust Fund, zoning, and subsidized mortgages also contribute to the problem. The result of urban sprawl is automobile dependence, traffic congestion, and social isolation including less involvement in community affairs.

■ **Describe approaches and policies that promote sustainable use of land.**

Smart growth is one possible response to urban sprawl. It advocates more compact, mixed-use development that encourages people to walk, bicycle, or use public transportation. Smart growth not only consumes less land than more typical, dispersed development, but has numerous other environmental benefits.

CHECK YOUR UNDERSTANDING

1. Which of the following is *not* an example of the tragedy of the commons?
   (a) Overgrazing by sheep on community-owned pastures
   (b) Depletion of fish stocks in international waters
   (c) Automobile congestion in Yellowstone National Park
   (d) Depletion of soil minerals by farmers on private land
   (e) Tropical deforestation due to clearing land for agriculture and then moving on to another location

2. In the accompanying graph of the population growth of the common pheasant, one of the world's most hunted birds, X represents
   (a) carrying capacity.   (d) endangered species designation.
   (b) maximum sustainable yield. (e) population overshoot.
   (c) resource depletion.

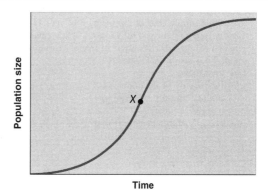

3. Under the provisions of the National Environmental Policy Act (NEPA), which of the following would require the preparation of an environmental impact statement (EIS)?
   (a) The construction of a house on privately owned land
   (b) The paving of a parking lot for a local business
   (c) The expansion of an interstate highway
   (d) The planting of trees in front of City Hall
   (e) The revision of local zoning ordinances

4. Federally owned land in the United States can *best* be described as
   (a) 25 percent of all land, with the majority of it in the west.
   (b) 42 percent of all land, with the majority of it in the east.
   (c) 28 percent of all land, with most of it in Texas.
   (d) 20 percent of all land, with 10 percent of it in the west.
   (e) 35 percent of all land, with the majority of it in the east.

5. The four major public land management agencies in the United States operate under the principle of multiple use. Which of the following uses is common to all four agencies' lands?
   (a) Hunting
   (b) Mining
   (c) Grazing
   (d) Timber harvesting
   (e) Recreation

6. For many years, forest fires were suppressed to protect lives and property. This policy has led to
   (a) a buildup of dead biomass that can fuel larger fires.
   (b) many forest species being able to live without having their habitats destroyed.
   (c) increased solar radiation in most ecosystems.
   (d) soil erosion on steep slopes.
   (e) economic instability.

7. When we purchase an item, we are charged for the labor and supply costs of producing that item. However, we are not charged for the costs of any environmental damage that occurred in manufacturing that item. Those costs are known as
   (a) externalities.
   (b) the tragedy of the commons.
   (c) the maximum sustainable yield.
   (d) marginal costs.
   (e) economic cost-benefit analysis.

8. Which of the following is *not* an environmental consequence of clear-cutting?
   (a) Increased soil erosion and sedimentation in nearby streams
   (b) Decreased biodiversity due to habitat fragmentation
   (c) Increased fish populations due to the influx of nutrients into streams
   (d) Decreased tree species diversity due to the loss of shade-tolerant species
   (e) Stands of same-aged trees

9. Which of the following are environmental impacts of urban sprawl?
   I   Greater reliance on the automobile and increased fossil fuel consumption
   II Increased consumption of land for housing and highway construction
   III Loss of valuable farmlands
   (a) I only
   (b) II only
   (c) I and II only
   (d) II and III only
   (e) I, II, and III

10. Which of the following was a significant cause of urban sprawl over the past 50 years?
    (a) Migration of people from rural areas to large central cities
    (b) Increased availability of public transportation
    (c) Lower property taxes in urban areas
    (d) Use of the federal gasoline tax to construct and maintain highways
    (e) Improved infrastructure and reduced crime rates in urban areas

11. Which of the following is *not* an environmental benefit of smart growth?
    (a) Reduced flooding
    (b) Increased impervious surfaces
    (c) Reduced fossil fuel consumption
    (d) Increased open space
    (e) Decreased water pollution

APPLY THE CONCEPTS

1. The property pictured below is the Farm Barn at Shelburne Farms, a National Historic Landmark, non-profit environmental education center, and 1,400-acre working farm on the shores of Lake Champlain. However, for the sake of this exercise, let's assume that the property pictured below belongs to the federal government.

   (a) Identify and explain which of the four public land management agencies would be involved in managing this public land.
   (b) Applying any three of the basic principles of smart growth, explain how the private land surrounding this federally owned property might be developed to minimize environmental impacts.
   (c) Define *environmental impact statement* and describe one condition under which an EIS might be required for the use of either the privately owned or federally owned lands associated with this tract.

2. The town of Fremont met recently to discuss the pros and cons of protecting prairie dogs. Prairie dogs are burrowing rodents the size of rabbits that live in colonies underground in grasslands and prairies. Their numbers have been greatly reduced over the last few decades. Dr. Masser, a local biologist, pointed out that prairie dogs are an important part of the prairie food web, as they are prey for many birds and mammals. Without federal protection from both the Bureau of Land Management and the U.S. Fish and Wildlife Service, they could become extinct in a few years. Dr. Masser also explained that 2 of the 5 species of prairie dogs are already listed as either threatened or endangered. Local ranchers disagreed. Mr. Smith stated that he will continue to poison or shoot the prairie dogs on his land because they destroy the grasses that are needed by his livestock, and he encouraged the BLM to do the same on public lands.
   (a) Explain the tragedy of the commons in general terms. Then, using the information you just read about the prairie dog and any other relevant information, incorporate the town of Fremont's discussion into your explanation.
   (b) Identify and discuss *one* argument in favor of preserving western grasslands as habitat for prairie dogs and *one* argument in favor of maintaining those grasslands for the grazing of livestock.
   (c) Identify *one* action that the Bureau of Land Management and *one* action that the U.S. Fish and Wildlife Service could take to resolve this land use conflict.

MEASURE YOUR IMPACT

The Costs of Commuting Imagine that you are one of 1,000 people who used to live in a downtown area and walked or took public transportation to work. Now you and the others have moved to the suburbs and drive 20 km per day each way.
   (a) How many additional kilometers are being driven each day by those 1,000 people?
   (b) How many additional kilometers are being driven each week by those 1,000 people? (Assume that each person works 5 days a week.)
   (c) How many additional kilometers are being driven each year by those 1,000 people?
   (d) If the average car gets 10 km per liter, how many liters of gasoline will be used by those 1,000 people each year?
   (e) Assuming that you are not going to move back to an urban area or change your job, what measures could you take to lessen your impact on the environment?

ENGAGE YOUR ENVIRONMENT

Do you live in a smart growth community? Evaluate the transportation options and open space in your community.

See Engage Your Environment Activity 10 at the end of this book.

Practicing Your Textbook Reading Skills

1. What is the purpose of the chapter-opening story about Julia Butterfly Hill and Maxxam?

   a. It outlines the main points of the chapter.

   b. It provides an example of the chapter's topic.

   c. It identifies the chapter's learning objectives.

   d. none of the above

2. What are the key ideas covered in the chapter?

   a. land use, land management, urban sprawl, and sustainable practices

   b. economics, government, and individual responsibility

   c. farming and forestry

   d. externalities, resource conservation ethics, ecologically sustainable forestry, and environmental mitigation plans

3. Evaluate the chapter's headings to identify which of the following is a subtopic of "Land management practices vary according to land use."

   a. The Tragedy of the Commons

   b. Public Lands in the United States

   c. Forests

   d. Residential land use is expanding.

4. Of the following statements, what is the textbook's definition of *zoning*?

   a. "Governments may use *zoning* to address issues of traffic congestion, urban sprawl, and urban blight."

   b. "*Zoning* is a planning tool developed in the 1920s to separate industry and business from residential neighborhoods and create quieter, safer communities."

   c. "Governments that use zoning can classify land areas into 'zones' in which certain land uses are restricted."

   d. "For instance, zoning ordinances might prohibit developers from building a factory or a strip mall in a residential area or a multi-dwelling apartment building in a single-home neighborhood."

5. According to Figure 10.6, on page 267, what category of use takes up the most land in the United States?

   a. timber production

   b. cropland

   c. urban, residential, and transportation

   d. grassland/grazing land

6. How does Figure 10.8 (on page 269) explain the differences between clear-cutting and selective cutting in logging?

   a. The pictures show that clear-cutting is bad and selective cutting is good.

   b. The pictures show that clear-cutting can cause erosion and that selective cutting can cause reduced ecodiversity.

   c. The pictures show that clear-cutting removes all of the trees in an area at once, resulting in a forest where all the trees are the same age; selective cutting removes only some trees, resulting in a forest with trees of different ages.

   d. none of the above

7. What concept is illustrated by Figures 10.14 and 10.15 on page 275?

   a. automobiles and highway construction

   b. living costs

   c. urban blight

   d. government policies

8. Which of the following statements presents the main idea of the section titled "Federal Regulation of Land Use" (page 273)?

   a. "The 1969 **National Environmental Policy Act (NEPA)** mandates an environmental assessment of all projects involving federal money or federal permits."

   b. "Along with other major laws of the 1960s and 1970s, such as the Clean Air Act, the Clean Water Act, and the *Endangered Species Act*, NEPA creates an environmental regulatory process designed to ensure protection of the nation's resources."

   c. "NEPA does not require that developers proceed in the way that will have the least environmental impact."

   d. "For this reason, attending information sessions and providing input is a good way for concerned citizens to learn more about local land use decisions and help reduce the environmental impact of land development."

9. Why is the section titled "Working Toward Sustainability" on page 278 bordered by lines at the top and bottom of the page?

   a. It is unimportant and reading it is optional.

   b. It summarizes the chapter and is highlighted so that readers will be able to find it easily.

   c. It is an extended example of a concept discussed in the main text; although you don't have to read it to understand the discussion, the example applies the concept to real life.

   d. It presents an idea that conflicts with the information provided in the main text.

10. Judging by what's discussed in the chapter summary on page 279, what topics from the chapter are important to understand?

    a. the tragedy of the commons and maximum sustainable yield

    b. public land management

    c. urban sprawl

    d. all of the above

Testing Your Understanding

Identify the following statements as *true* or *false*.

1. The federal government owns about 25 percent of the land in the United States.

    T _____   F _____

2. Forest fires are always destructive.

    T _____   F _____

3. Since the mid-twentieth century, suburbs have grown at a faster rate than cities.

    T _____   F _____

4. All-terrain vehicles are banned from some national parks.

    T _____   F _____

5. The residents of the Dudley Street neighborhood in Boston are mostly upper-middle class.

    T _____   F _____

Select the best answer to each of the following questions.

6. Which of the following terms is *not* an international category of public lands?

    a. Managed Resource Protected Areas

    b. Federal Lands

    c. National Monuments

    d. National Parks

7. According to Professor Elinor Ostrom of Indiana University, what will happen if governments do not regulate land use?

    a. Self-regulation by communities and institutions will effectively prevent overuse of resources.

    b. Self-interested behavior by communities and institutions will result in overuse of resources.

    c. Farmers will graze their sheep on public lands until there is not enough grass to support wild animal populations.

    d. Private land owners will overgraze their own properties.

8. Which federal agency manages hunting?

    a. The Bureau of Land Management

    b. The United States Forest Service

    c. The National Park Service

    d. The Fish and Wildlife Service

9. In environmental terms, what is *maximum sustainable yield*?

    a. environmental costs and benefits that are not reflected in the purchase price of goods or services

    b. regulations limiting the number of deer that hunters may take in any given season

    c. the highest quantity of a renewable resource that can be used before such use reduces that resource's renewability

    d. a rate of harvest that reduces future availability of a renewable resource

10. Which of the following examples illustrates the concept of *urban sprawl*?

    a. office parks

    b. strip malls

    c. feeder roads

    d. all of the above

11. Why has the marbled murrelet become an endangered species?

    a. The birds nest in redwood forests that have been heavily harvested for timber; the loss of habitat has made it difficult for them to reproduce.

    b. The birds live in coastal waters that have been polluted, and the pollution has poisoned them in large numbers.

    c. Forest fires have destroyed the birds' natural habitat, forcing them to relocate to suburban areas, where there is not enough food to sustain them.

    d. Environmental scientists do not know why the marbled murrelet has become endangered.

12. Which of the following might be required of a developer who receives federal funding or applies for a federal permit?

    a. an environmental impact statement

    b. an environmental mitigation plan

    c. responses to public concerns

    d. all of the above

13. Which of the following is *not* a principle of smart growth?

    a. walkable neighborhoods

    b. sense of place

    c. highway expansion

    d. transit-oriented development

14. What is the goal of ecologically sustainable forestry?

    a. keeping the populations of forest species as close as possible to their natural state

    b. harvesting as much timber as possible

    c. preventing logging companies from going out of business

    d. bringing back the practice of using animals to haul cut timber out of forests

15. What was the environmental consequence of the fires that burned more than one-third of Yellowstone National Park in 1988?

    a. More than 25,000 acres of land were destroyed.

    b. The National Park Service was criticized for inaction and forced to change its policies.

    c. The fires cleared the way for new plants to grow, attracting new animal species and improving the park's ecosystems.

    d. The park became a breeding ground for elk and other herbivores.

Using your own words, define the following terms as they are used in the chapter.

16. *tragedy of the commons*

_____

_____

17. *externalities*

_____

_____

18. *resource conservation ethic*

_____

_____

19. *urban sprawl*

_____

_____

20. *infill*

_____

_____

Answer each of the following questions using the space provided.

21. Why do environmental scientists find it difficult to calculate maximum sustainable yield accurately?

_____

_____

_____

22. Explain why some critics believe that not enough is being done to preserve rangelands.

_____

_____

_____

_____

23. Describe clear-cutting and selective cutting and discuss the costs and benefits of each practice.

_____

_____

_____

24. Briefly explain why the popularity of national parks threatens to undermine their purpose.

_____

_____

_____

_____

_____

25. In your own words, describe the cycle that causes urban blight.

_____

_____

_____

_____

Making Thematic Connections

The migration to the suburbs and exurbs described at the end of this chapter reverses the trend of urbanization discussed in the history chapter reprinted in Unit 4. What do you think has changed in the last century to so drastically affect where people choose to live and work? In what ways, if any, might current environmental and economic concerns encourage people to return to city living?

Glossary of Terms

acculturative stress   The stress that results from the pressure of adapting to a new culture. [Unit 5]

astroturf lobbying   Phony grassroots public affairs campaigns engineered by public relations firms; coined by U.S. Senator Lloyd Bentsen of Texas (named after AstroTurf, the artificial grass athletic field surface). [Unit 3]

biopsychosocial model   The belief that physical health and illness are determined by the complex interaction of biological, psychological, and social factors. [Unit 5]

catecholamines   Hormones secreted by the adrenal medulla that cause rapid physiological arousal; include adrenaline and noradrenaline. [Unit 5]

clear-cutting   A method of harvesting trees that involves removing all or almost all of the trees within an area. [Unit 6]

conflict   A situation in which a person feels pulled between two or more opposing desires, motives, or goals. [Unit 5]

coping   Behavioral and cognitive responses used to deal with stressors; involves our efforts to change circumstances, or our interpretation of circumstances, to make them more favorable and less threatening. [Unit 5]

corticosteroids   Hormones released by the adrenal cortex that play a key role in the body's response to long-term stressors. [Unit 5]

daily hassles   Everyday minor events that annoy and upset people. [Unit 5]

ecologically sustainable forestry   An approach to removing trees from forests in ways that do not unduly affect the viability of other trees. [Unit 6]

eminent domain   A principle that grants government the power to acquire a property at fair market value even if the owner does not wish to sell it. [Unit 6]

Note: The definitions are derived from the units of this book and referenced accordingly. The units are as follows: Unit 1, College Success: "Majors & Career Choices"; Unit 2, Composition: "Document Design"; Unit 3, Mass Communication: "Public Relations and Framing the Message"; Unit 4, History: "The Growth of America's Cities, 1870–1900"; Unit 5, Psychology: "Stress, Health, and Coping"; and Unit 6, Environmental Science: "Land: Public and Private."

emotion-focused coping   Coping efforts primarily aimed at relieving or regulating the emotional impact of a stressful situation. [Unit 5]

Endangered Species Act   A 1973 U.S. law designed to protect species from extinction. [Unit 6]

environmental impact statement (EIS)   A document outlining the scope and purpose of a development project, describing the environmental context, suggesting alternative approaches to the project, and analyzing the environmental impact of each alternative. [Unit 6]

environmental mitigation plan   A plan that outlines how a developer will address concerns raised by a project's impact on the environment. [Unit 6]

externality   The cost or benefit of a good or service that is not included in the purchase price of that good or service. [Unit 6]

exurban   Describes an area similar to a suburb, but unconnected to any central city or densely populated area. [Unit 6]

fight-or-flight response   A rapidly occurring chain of internal physical reactions that prepare people either to fight or take flight from an immediate threat. [Unit 5]

forest   Land dominated by trees and other woody vegetation and sometimes used for commercial logging. [Unit 6]

general adaptation syndrome   Hans Selye's term for the three-stage progression of physical changes that occur when an organism is exposed to intense and prolonged stress. The three stages are alarm, resistance, and exhaustion. [Unit 5]

health psychology   The branch of psychology that studies how biological, behavioral, and social factors influence health, illness, medical treatment, and health-related behaviors. [Unit 5]

Highway Trust Fund   A U.S. federal fund that pays for the construction and maintenance of roads and highways. [Unit 6]

immune system   Body system that produces specialized white blood cells that protect the body from viruses, bacteria, and tumor cells. [Unit 5]

induced demand   The phenomenon in which increase in the supply of a good causes demand to grow. [Unit 6]

infill   Development that fills in vacant lots within existing communities. [Unit 6]

lobbying   In government public relations, the process of attempting to influence the voting of lawmakers to support a client's or an organization's best interests. [Unit 3]

lymphocytes   Specialized white blood cells that are responsible for immune defenses. [Unit 5]

maximum sustainable yield (MSY)   The maximum amount of a renewable resource that can be harvested without compromising the future availability of that resource. [Unit 6]

multiple-use lands   A U.S. classification used to designate lands that may be used for recreation, grazing, timber harvesting, and mineral extraction. [Unit 6]

multi-use zoning   A zoning classification that allows retail and high-density residential development to coexist in the same area. [Unit 6]

National Environmental Policy Act (NEPA)   A 1969 U.S. federal act that mandates an environmental assessment of all projects involving federal money or federal permits. [Unit 6]

national wilderness area   An area set aside with the intent of preserving a large tract of intact ecosystem or a landscape. [Unit 6]

national wildlife refuge   A federal public land managed for the primary purpose of protecting wildlife. [Unit 6]

optimistic explanatory style   Accounting for negative events or situations with external, unstable, and specific explanations. [Unit 5]

pessimistic explanatory style   Accounting for negative events or situations with internal, stable, and global explanations. [Unit 5]

prescribed burn   A fire deliberately set under controlled conditions in order to reduce the accumulation of dead biomass on a forest floor. [Unit 6]

press agent   The earliest type of public relations practitioner, who sought to advance a client's image through media exposure. [Unit 3]

press releases   In public relations, announcements—written in the style of a news report—that give new information about an individual, a company, or an organization and that pitch a story idea to the news media. [Unit 3]

problem-focused coping   Coping efforts primarily aimed at directly changing or managing a threatening or harmful stressor. [Unit 5]

propaganda   In advertising and public relations, a communication strategy that tries to manipulate public opinion to gain support for a special issue, program, or policy, such as a nation's war effort. [Unit 3]

pseudo-events   In public relations, any circumstance or event created solely for the purpose of obtaining coverage in the media. [Unit 3]

psychoneuroimmunology   An interdisciplinary field that studies the interconnections among psychological processes, nervous and endocrine system functions, and the immune system. [Unit 5]

public relations   The total communication strategy conducted by a person, a government, or an organization attempting to reach and persuade its audiences to adopt a point of view. [Unit 3]

public service announcements (PSAs)   Reports or announcements, carried free by radio and TV stations, that promote government programs, educational projects, voluntary agencies, or social reform. [Unit 3]

publicity   In public relations, the positive and negative messages that spread controlled and uncontrolled information about a person, a corporation, an issue, or a policy in various media. [Unit 3]

rangeland A dry, open grassland. [Unit 6]

resource conservation ethic The belief that people should maximize use of resources, based on the greatest good for everyone. [Unit 6]

selective cutting The method of harvesting trees that involves the removal of single trees or a relatively small number of trees from among many in a forest. [Unit 6]

sense of place The feeling that an area has distinct and meaningful character. [Unit 6]

smart growth A set of principles for community planning that focuses on strategies to encourage the development of sustainable, healthy communities. [Unit 6]

social support The resources provided by other people in times of need. [Unit 5]

stakeholder A person or organization with an interest in a particular place or issue. [Unit 6]

stress A negative emotional state occurring in response to events that are perceived as taxing or exceeding a person's resources or ability to cope. [Unit 5]

stressors Events or situations that are perceived as harmful, threatening, or challenging. [Unit 5]

suburban Describes an area surrounding a metropolitan center, with a comparatively low population density. [Unit 6]

tragedy of the commons The tendency of a shared, limited resource to become depleted because people act from self-interest for short-term gain. [Unit 6]

transit-oriented development (TOD) Development that attempts to focus dense residential and retail development around stops for public transportation; a component of smart growth. [Unit 6]

tree plantation A large area typically planted with a single rapidly growing tree species. [Unit 6]

Type A behavior pattern A behavioral and emotional style characterized by a sense of time urgency, hostility, and competitiveness. [Unit 5]

urban blight The degradation of the built and social environments of the city that often accompanies and accelerates migration to the suburbs. [Unit 6]

urban growth boundary A restriction on development outside a designated area. [Unit 6]

urban sprawl Urbanized areas that spread into rural areas, removing clear boundaries between the two. [Unit 6]

video news release (VNR) In public relations, the visual counterpart to a press release; it pitches a story idea to the TV news media by mimicking the style of a broadcast news report. [Unit 3]

zoning A planning tool used to separate industry and business from residential neighborhoods. [Unit 6]

Answer Key

1. College Success: "Majors & Career Choices"

Preparing to Read the Textbook Chapter

Answers will vary.

Practicing Your Textbook Reading Skills

1. d (p. 154)	6. a (p. 155)
2. c (p. 153)	7. d (p. 147)
3. b (pp. 152–53)	8. a (p. 154)
4. b (p. 151)	9. c (p. 156)
5. c (p. 148)	10. d (p. 157)

Testing Your Understanding

1. F (pp. 150–51)	9. b (p. 156)
2. F (pp. 154–55)	10. c (p. 152)
3. T (p. 148)	11. a (p. 155)
4. T (p. 155)	12. c (p. 153)
5. F (p. 151)	13. d (p. 154)
6. a (pp. 148–49)	14. d (p. 150)
7. c (p. 151)	15. a (p. 151)
8. d (p. 149)	

Answers to questions 16–25 will vary.

16. Textbook's definition: A situation in which industries have become multinational, not only moving into overseas markets but also seeking cheaper labor, capital, and resources abroad (p. 148).
17. Textbook's definition: A workplace policy that cuts product and service delivery time to a minimum (p. 149).
18. Textbook's definition: The ability to work cooperatively and collaboratively with different people while maintaining autonomous control over some assignments (p. 149).
19. Textbook's definition: College and university programs in which students spend some terms in class and other terms in temporary job settings in their fields (p. 155).
20. Textbook's definition: A form of academic advising that helps students see beyond individual classes and works to help them initiate a career search (p. 157).
21. Possible answer: According to Holland's model, personality types fall into six general categories: (1) realistic people tend to be practical and physical, (2) investigative people like to solve problems, (3) artistic people are interested in creative expression, (4) social types are people-oriented helpers, (5) enterprising people are ambitious and competitive, and (6) conventional people value organization and appearance (p. 152).
22. Possible answer: Jobs in one's preferred field aren't always available: It might take years to settle into the career a person wants. At the same time, the job market is unstable and unpredictable. Even if someone does his or her job well, the employer might decide to outsource the position, to restructure the organization, or to lay off staff members (p. 151).
23. Possible answer: Why? Who? How? What? Where? When? (p. 150)
24. Possible answer: Internships provide relevant, real-world experience in jobs that might interest a student. Interns gain insight into particular career fields as well as the organizations within them; they also get a feel for what it's like to work for a potential employer and gain valuable

contacts for future networking. Finally, college internships strengthen students' résumés (p. 155).

25. Possible answers: Career centers offer free career counseling and job information; academic advising; skills, personality, and aptitude assessments; practice interviews and résumé help; and listings for on-campus jobs, off-campus jobs, and internships. Many also have libraries that specialize in career information (p. 157).

Making Thematic Connections

Answers will vary.

2. Composition: "Document Design"

Preparing to Read the Textbook Chapter

Answers will vary.

Practicing Your Textbook Reading Skills

1. b (p. 727)
2. a (p. 728)
3. a (pp. 728–46)
4. d (p. 733)
5. c (p. 739)
6. d (p. 730)
7. b (p. 735)
8. c (p. 737)
9. c (p. 734)
10. a (pp. 744–46)

Testing Your Understanding

1. F (p. 729)
2. T (p. 730)
3. F (pp. 733, 735)
4. F (p. 734)
5. T (p. 742)
6. a (p. 730)
7. b (p. 730)
8. d (p. 731)
9. c (p. 733)
10. b (p. 734)
11. a (p. 734)
12. c (p. 738)
13. d (p. 741)
14. b (p. 744)
15. d (p. 746)

Answers to questions 16–25 will vary.

16. Textbook's definition: Design is how you format a document for a printed page or for a computer screen (p. 728).
17. Textbook's definition: Pie charts compare a part or parts to the whole. Segments of the pie represent percentages of the whole (and always total 100 percent) (p. 736).
18. Textbook's definition: Scannable résumés might be submitted on paper, by e-mail, or through an online employment service. The résumés are scanned and searched electronically, and a database matches keywords in the job description with keywords in the résumés (p. 744).
19. Textbook's definition: Usually brief and to the point, a memo reports information, makes a request, or recommends an action (p. 744).
20. Textbook's definition: Full Block Style is a format for business letters: Paragraphs are not indented and are typed single-spaced, with double-spacing between them (p. 738).
21. Possible answer: The purpose of document design—formatting, layout, font choices, visuals, and so forth—is to promote readability (p. 728).
22. Possible answer: Academic papers should be double-spaced and left-aligned, with one- or one-and-a-half-inch margins. Writers should choose a standard font, such as Times New Roman or Courier, and font styles such as boldface or all-capital letters should be used sparingly (pp. 728–30, 738–39).
23. Possible answers: Typical categories include an objective, education, experience, activities, portfolio, and references (p. 743).
24. Possible answer: Double-spacing and generous margins leave room for editing and comments on a draft; in a final document, the extra white space creates a visual frame and makes the material easier to read. Business writing is the exception: memos and letters are single-spaced with extra space between paragraphs both to save paper and to make it easier to skim them for information (p. 729).
25. Possible answer: Business documents should be brief and to the point to show respect for other people's time. Workers in an office environment are busy: They don't have the time to sort through long passages of prose or to figure out what's being asked of them. Keeping messages short and direct improves the chances that they will be read and that you'll accomplish your purpose in writing (pp. 738, 742, 744–46).

Making Thematic Connections

Answers will vary.

3. Mass Communication: "Public Relations and Framing the Message"

Preparing to Read the Textbook Chapter

Answers will vary.

Practicing Your Textbook Reading Skills

1. d (pp. 313–14)
2. c (pp. 316–17)
3. b (p. 319)
4. b (pp. 317–18)
5. a (p. 329)
6. c (p. 321)
7. b (pp. 324–25)
8. b (p. 327)
9. a (pp. 334–36)
10. c (p. 337)

Testing Your Understanding

1. F (p. 314)
2. T (p. 316)
3. T (p. 320)
4. T (pp. 322–23)
5. T (pp. 332–33)
6. b (p. 314)
7. d (pp. 316–17)
8. c (p. 318)
9. c (p. 314)
10. a (p. 326)
11. b (p. 322)
12. d (pp. 322–23)
13. a (pp. 328–29)
14. b (pp. 327–28)
15. b (p. 324)

Answers to questions 16–25 will vary.

16. Textbook's definition: Publicity is a type of PR communication that uses various media messages to spread information and interest (or "buzz") about a person, a corporation, an issue, or a policy (p. 316).

17. Textbook's definition: Any circumstance created for the purpose of gaining coverage in the media (p. 327).

18. Textbook's definition: Communication that is presented as advertising or publicity and that is intended to gain public support for a special issue, program, or policy—such as a nation's war effort (p. 322).

19. Textbook's definition: The process of trying to influence lawmakers to support legislation that would serve an organization's or industry's best interests (p. 328).

20. Textbook's definition: Phony grassroots public-affairs campaigns engineered by unscrupulous public relations firms (pp. 328–29).

21. Possible answer: They pioneered some public relations strategies to convince both the public and the government to help pay their expenses. Some railroads bribed reporters to write stories in their favor; others gave out free passes to the press to encourage them to use the rail service and write positive reviews. Once they succeeded in obtaining government funds, the railroads further lobbied for government regulation of rates and fares, which drove many smaller lines out of business (p. 317).

22. Possible answers: vote buying, hiring writers to publish supportive articles, planting favorable histories in textbooks (pp. 317–18).

23. Possible answer: Because local news is usually broadcast live during that time slot, politicians like to create these kinds of pseudo-events in the hope that the networks will air their views as part of the evening news programs (p. 327).

24. Possible answer: *Agencies* are companies whose entire purpose is to provide public relations services to their clients. *In-house services* are departments within a company or organization that handle that company's own public relations needs (pp. 320–21).

25. Possible answers: Journalism depends on public relations as a source of story ideas and news leads, but many journalists resent the interference of PR workers when they try to reach interviewees. Some journalists also believe that public relations routinely distorts the truth in the service of clients. Understaffing in journalism forces writers to rely on PR workers for information, but a primary function of public relations is to limit or control reporters' access to sensitive or damaging information about a client. Many journalists resent how public relations people allow corporations and individuals to get free publicity through the news media, reducing the credibility of news writers.

These journalists believe that such publicity should be purchased through ads (pp. 329–31).

Making Thematic Connections

Answers will vary.

4. History: "The Growth of America's Cities, 1870–1900"

Preparing to Read the Textbook Chapter

Answers will vary.

Practicing Your Textbook Reading Skills

1. b (p. 510)	6. c (p. 519)
2. c (p. 512)	7. c (p. 520)
3. b (p. 525)	8. b (p. 531)
4. a (pp. 514–15)	9. d (pp. 510–33)
5. a (p. 514)	10. c (pp. 509, 533)

Testing Your Understanding

1. T (p. 529)	9. c (p. 516)
2. F (pp. 518–19)	10. b (p. 528)
3. T (p. 523)	11. b (pp. 522–24)
4. F (p. 519)	12. c (p. 524)
5. F (p. 528)	13. b (p. 525)
6. c (pp. 510–11)	14. c (pp. 530–31)
7. a (pp. 517–18)	15. d (p. 530)
8. d (p. 530)	

Answers to questions 16–25 will vary.

16. Possible answer: Immigrants, mostly European men, who came to the United States to work for a short period of time, then returned to their home countries with their earnings, often more than once (p. 513).

17. Possible answer: A phrase used to describe the sentimentalized view of the home as a feminine sanctuary or escape from the masculine working world. This new ideology stressed that woman's place was in the home, and led to an increase in the use of live-in hired help, ironically giving middle-class women new opportunities to participate in public activities (pp. 527–28).

18. Possible answer: The predominant form of urban government in the mid- to late-nineteenth century. Typically led by "bosses" who didn't hold elected office, machines gained power through bribery and graft. Although they were corrupt, machines were popular with cities' working-class and immigrant residents because they provided money and services unavailable from other sources (pp. 530–31).

19. Possible answer: A system of laws that segregated black and white institutions in the American South after the Civil War and Reconstruction. The laws encouraged intimidation and persecution, leading many blacks to relocate to northern cities, especially New York, Philadelphia, and Chicago (p. 514).

20. Possible answer: A trend, in the second half of the nineteenth century, toward replacing skilled workers with machines, such as weavers, sewing machines, typewriters, and cash registers. As machines became more common, jobs were broken down into repetitive tasks that could be done by unskilled laborers, driving down wages (pp. 517–18).

21. Possible answer: Factors responsible for the late-nineteenth-century rise in urbanization include the availability of wage labor for unskilled workers; immigration, fueled by inexpensive transportation and a shift in agricultural practices (as well as political and economic turmoil in Eastern Europe and Russia); and a tendency for newcomers to stay in cities once they arrived (pp. 510–16).

22. Possible answer: The industrial workforce was diverse. Immigrants, ethnic minorities, women, and children constituted a large percentage of workers in factories, mills, offices, and department stores. Many (if not most) workers moved to industrial centers from rural agricultural areas both in the United States and around the world. Pay was low and work was unreliable, so most industrial workers were very poor (pp. 517–21).

23. Possible answer: The Knights of Labor advocated broad-ranging reforms, such as income tax and equal pay for women, to benefit working-class people; although this organization did not officially condone

strikes, many of its achievements were the result of an 1885 strike against railroads. The American Federation of Labor emphasized the power of unions and strikes to gain specific benefits and improvements in the workplace (pp. 524–26).

24. Possible answer: The 1886 Haymarket "riot" started as a rally to protest the treatment of strikers at Chicago's McCormick works. The turnout was relatively small, but an unexpected bomb thrown at the police resulted in a bout of violence that left seven policemen and an unknown number of civilians dead. Although there was no evidence of who was responsible for the bomb, the Illinois state attorney decided to use the incident to make an example, and a number of radicals and labor organizers were jailed or executed. The attack on the labor movement that this event started essentially worked to frighten workers from involvement with unions (pp. 525–26).

25. Possible answers: The exhibition fairgrounds exemplify both the positive and negative aspects of urbanization. Chicago's White City, as it was known, was a showcase for achievements in architecture, urban planning, and recreation. At the same time, it also revealed a stark contrast between ideals and reality, and between rich and poor. When the fair closed, many of Chicago's homeless and unemployed residents moved into the abandoned buildings and grounds and made them their own, making well-off neighbors nervous. Within a year, the once-gleaming showcase was destroyed during a violent conflict between management and labor, highlighting another major trend of the period (p. 532).

Making Thematic Connections

Answers will vary.

5. Psychology: "Stress, Health, and Coping"

Preparing to Read the Textbook Chapter

Answers will vary.

Practicing Your Textbook Reading Skills

1. b (p. 539)
2. d (pp. 539–40)
3. b (p. 539)
4. a (p. 541)
5. b (p. 542)
6. c (p. 557)
7. c (p. 546)
8. c (pp. 550, 569)
9. b (p. 563)
10. a (pp. 566–67)

Testing Your Understanding

1. T (p. 541)
2. F (pp. 542–43)
3. T (p. 553)
4. F (pp. 554–55)
5. T (p. 559)
6. b (p. 542)
7. c (p. 543)
8. d (p. 544)
9. a (p. 549)
10. d (p. 555)
11. a (pp. 556–57)
12. d (p. 559)
13. b (p. 562)
14. a (pp. 566–67)
15. c (pp. 563–64)

Answers to questions 16–25 will vary.

16. Textbook's definition: A situation in which a person feels pulled between two or more opposing desires, motives, or goals (p. 544).

17. Textbook's definition: The stress that results from the pressure of adapting to a new culture (p. 545).

18. Textbook's definition: A rapidly occurring chain of internal physical reactions that prepare people either to fight or take flight from an immediate threat (p. 547).

19. Textbook's definition: Hormones released by the adrenal cortex that play a key role in the body's response to long-term stressors (p. 549).

20. Textbook's definition: Behavioral and cognitive responses used to deal with stressors; involves efforts to change circumstances, or your interpretation of circumstances, to make them more favorable and less threatening (p. 561).

21. Possible answers: (1) Accept that not all decisions are easy; (2) try to use a *partial approach strategy* in which you consider a decision or commitment but leave yourself the option of changing your mind; (3) research your options thoroughly; (4) seek advice (pp. 544, 546).

22. Possible answers: fast breathing, rapid heart rate, elevated blood pressure, increased blood flow to muscles, poor digestion, enlarged pupils (pp. 547–48).

23. Possible answer: The *alarm stage* occurs as an immediate response to a stressor; it is characterized by intense arousal. The next stage is *resistance*, in which the body fights or tries to adjust to the stressor. The final stage, *exhaustion*, occurs if the stress continues for a long period of time, and can result in illness and even death (pp. 548–49).

24. Possible answer: In terms of *social support*, women tend to be caregivers more than men, so they carry the added stress of supporting others. Also, because women tend to have larger and more intimate social networks, they are affected negatively by the stresses of others more than men are. Because men tend to have smaller social networks, they are more prone to isolation. In terms of *coping*, women generally reach out to others for support, whereas men under stress tend to withdraw (p. 564).

25. Possible answers: Americans are less likely to seek social support than Asians are; Americans tend to favor problem-solving strategies whereas Asians tend to prefer emotion-focused coping strategies (p. 565).

Making Thematic Connections

Answers will vary.

6. Environmental Science: "Land: Public and Private"

Preparing to Read the Textbook Chapter

Answers will vary.

Practicing Your Textbook Reading Skills

1. b (pp. 261–62)
2. a (p. 262)
3. c (p. 269)
4. b (p. 275)
5. d (p. 267)
6. c (p. 269)
7. d (p. 275)
8. b (p. 273)
9. c (p. 278)
10. d (p. 279)

Testing Your Understanding

1. T (p. 266)
2. F (pp. 271–72)
3. T (p. 273)
4. T (p. 272)
5. F (p. 278)
6. b (p. 266)
7. a (p. 264)
8. d (pp. 267–68)
9. c (pp. 264–65)
10. d (p. 274)
11. a (p. 271)
12. d (p. 273)
13. c (pp. 276–77)
14. a (p. 270)
15. c (pp. 271–72)

Answers to questions 16–25 will vary.

16. Textbook's definition: The tendency of a shared, limited resource to become depleted because people act from self-interest for short-term gain (p. 262).

17. Textbook's definition: A cost or benefit of a good or service that is not included in the purchase price of that good or service (p. 264).

18. Textbook's definition: The principle that people should maximize resource use based on the greatest good for everyone (p. 266).

19. Textbook's definition: The creation of urbanized areas that spread into rural areas and remove clear boundaries between the two (p. 274).

20. Textbook's definition: Development that fills in vacant lots within existing communities, rather than expanding into land outside the city (p. 277).

21. Possible answer: Maximum sustainable yield (MSY) cannot be determined with precision because the information necessary to calculate it—such as actual birth and death rates—is difficult to obtain; furthermore, once the MSY of a resource is estimated, scientists need a long time to confirm its accuracy, at which point excessive yields will have already depleted renewability (pp. 264–65).

22. Possible answer: Rangelands are heavily used and yet especially susceptible to environmental damage. Some organizations maintain that the soil in more than half of U.S. rangelands is in bad condition because of overgrazing, a charge the Bureau of Land Management disputes. Ranchers need permits to graze their animals on federal lands, but the fees are not high enough to discourage overuse or to cover the cost of managing the land. At the same time, rules governing the use of rangelands are not consistent or strict; consequently, those rules have not always succeeded in protecting rangeland ecosystems (pp. 268–69).

23. Possible answer: Clear-cutting is the practice of removing all or most of the trees in an area, sometimes followed by replanting or reseeding. Selective cutting is the practice of removing only a few of the trees from an area. Clear-cutting is easier and more profitable in most cases, but it tends to cause erosion, to raise the temperature in local bodies of water, to reduce biodiversity, and to contaminate soil and water. Selective cutting, which is usually more expensive, allows for more biodiversity in tree regrowth, although it limits the new growth to shade-tolerant tree species. Both practices require logging roads, which themselves affect habitat, species diversity, and irrigation (pp. 269–70).

24. Possible answer: National parks are often multiple-use lands intended both for environmental preservation and popular recreation. When people visit the parks, however, their activities tend to cause environmental damage (p. 272).

25. Possible answer: When urban residents move to the suburbs for a better quality of life, the quality of life in the city tends to decline, which in turn causes more people to leave the city, creating a cycle that repeats itself indefinitely. With each exodus, the city collects less in taxes, forcing government to cut services; lack of services leads to higher crime and pushes customers and businesses away, making the city an even less desirable place to be (pp. 274–75).

Making Thematic Connections

Answers will vary.

Acknowledgments (continued)

Text

UNIT 1

Holland, John. "The Holland Model: Personality Characteristics," Reproduced by special permission of the publisher, Psychological Assessment Resource, Inc., 16204 North Florida Ave., Lutz, FL 33549. Adapted from *The Self Directed Search: Professional User's Guide,* by John L. Holland, Ph.D. Copyright 1985, 1987, 1994, 1997. Further reproduction is prohibited without permission from PAR, Inc.

Illustrations

UNIT 1

Pages 146–47, 151 Jonathan Stark   **153** Reproduced by special permission of the Publisher, Psychological Assessment Resources, Inc., 16204 North Florida Ave., Lutz, FL 33549. Adapted from *Making Vocational Choices*, Third Edition. Copyright 1973, 1985, 1992, 1997 by Psychological Assessment Resources, Inc. All rights reserved   **154** Jonathan Stark

UNIT 2

Page 735 National Sleep Foundation (2002)   **736** (*top*) Kaiser Foundation; (*middle*) US Census Bureau; (*bottom*) UNAIDS   **737** (*1*) Photo "Tornado Touch" by Fred Zwicky. Copyright © 2004 by Fred Zwicky. Reprinted by permission of the author; (*2*) NIAMS; (*3*) Arizona Board of Regents; (*4*) Lynn Hunt et al.

UNIT 3

Page 312 Columbia Pictures/Photofest   **316** Library of Congress   **318** (*left*) © Bettmann/Corbis; (*right*) Courtesy of the Rockefeller Archive Center   **319** (*left*) © Bettmann/Corbis; (*right*) NYPL-PC   **322** Library of Congress   **323** Office of National Drug Control Policy/Partnership for a Drug-Free America   **323** AP Photo   **326** Courtesy of R. Eliot-Fagley   **327** Jeff Zelevansky/Getty Images   **328** Photo courtesy of Rainforest Action Network   **330** "Trust Us, We're Experts!" by Sheldon Rampton and John Stauber © 2002   **333** Scott J. Ferrell/Congressional Quarterly/Getty Images

UNIT 4

Page 508 Picture Research Consultants & Archives **509** National Park Service Collection, gift of Angelo Forgione/Picture Research Consultants & Archives **510** Keystone-Mast Collection, UCR/ California Museum of Photography, University of California, Riverside **516** (*left*) Museum of the City of New York; (*right*) Collection of the New York Historical Society **517** George Eastman House **518** Division of Work & Industry, National Museum of American History, Smithsonian Institution **519** Alice Austin photo, Staten Island Historical Society **521** Brown Brothers **522** Carnegie Library of Pittsburgh **525** Chicago Historical Society **526–27** Library of Congress **528** Smithsonian Institution Collections, National Museum of American History, Behring Center **529** Culver Pictures; (*inset*) Picture Research Consultants & Archives **531** Collection of Janice L. and David J. Frent **533** (*top*) Picture Research Consultants & Archives; (*bottom*) National Park Service Collection, gift of Angelo Forgione/Picture Research Consultants & Archives **535** (*top left*) Keystone-Mast Collection, UCR/California Museum of Photography, University of California, Riverside; (*top right*) George Eastman House; (*bottom left*) Culver Pictures; (*bottom right*) Library of Congress

UNIT 5

Page 538 Josee Masse **540** (*top*) AP Photo/Steve C. Wilson; (*bottom left*) AP Photo/Paul Hawthorne; (*bottom right*) AP Photo/ Ed Bailey **541** Corbis **543** (*top*) Redlink Production/Corbis; (*bottom*) Courtesy of Richard S. Lazarus/University of California, Berkeley **544** AP Photo/Bebeto Matthews **545** Joe Raedle/Getty Images **546** 7/20/97 © 1997 Cathy Guisewithe. Permission of Universal Press Syndicate **547** (*top left*) National Sleep Foundation (2002); (*top right*) AP Photo/Tina Fineberg; (*bottom*) Edgar Fahs Smith Collection, University of Pennsylvania Libraries **548** (*top*) Custom Medical Stock Photo/Alamy; (*bottom*) © 1974 John Olson/People Weekly **549** (*top*) Omikron/Science Source/Photo Researchers; (*bottom left*) Courtesy of Robert Ader, photo by James Montanus, University of Rochester; (*bottom right*) Courtesy of Nicholas Cohen, University of Rochester **550** (*top*) RubberBall/ Alamy; (*bottom*) Courtesy of Janice Kiecolt-Glaser, Ohio State University College of Medicine **551** *Science*, 295, 1737–1740. Petrovic, Predrag; Kalso, Eija; Petersson, Karl M.; and Ingvar, Martin. "Placebo and opioid analgesia — Imaging a shared neuronal network" **553** REUTERS/John Gress **554** © The New Yorker Collection 1990 Roz Chast from Cartoonbank.com. All rights reserved **555** (*top*) David Lassman/Syracuse Newspapers/The Image Works; (*bottom*) 5/11 by Bill Watterson © 1993 Watterson. Dist by Universal Press Syndicate **556** (*top*) istockphoto **557** © The New